Cambridge Monographs in African Archaeology
88
Series Editors: Laurence Smith, Brian Stewart and Stephanie Wynne-Jone

Paleoethnobotanical Study of Ancient Food Crops and the Environmental Context in North-East Africa, 6000 BC–AD 200/300

Alemseged Beldados

BAR International Series 2706
2015

Published in 2016 by
BAR Publishing, Oxford

BAR International Series 2706

Cambridge Monographs in African Archaeology 88
Paleoethnobotanical Study of Ancient Food Crops and the Environmental Context in North-East Africa, 6000 BC–AD 200/300

ISBN 978 1 4073 1357 3

BAR Publishing is the trading name of British Archaeological Reports (Oxford) Ltd.
British Archaeological Reports was first incorporated in 1974 to publish the BAR
Series, International and British. In 1992 Hadrian Books Ltd became part of the BAR
group. This volume was originally published by Archaeopress in conjunction with
British Archaeological Reports (Oxford) Ltd / Hadrian Books Ltd, the Series principal
publisher, in 2015. This present volume is published by BAR Publishing, 2016.

Printed in England

BAR
PUBLISHING

BAR titles are available from:

BAR Publishing
122 Banbury Rd, Oxford, OX2 7BP, UK
EMAIL info@barpublishing.com
PHONE +44 (0)1865 310431
FAX +44 (0)1865 316916
www.barpublishing.com

Table of Contents

Acknowledgements

First I thank *Weizero* Semhar Daniel from Shire Adminstrative Zone, who traveled with me tirelessly, as a translator from *Tigrigna* to *Amharic*, up the shire Plateau and down the low-lying, hot areas of Adrar and Kushet Adrar abandoning her 3 years old baby with his grandmother. After days of work and long distance walking, I remember the day and time you told me that your right leg is broken due to a car accident and you were able to walk by an artificial support. Your sincere desire to help has precluded your pain and for me it remains to be a permanent source of inspiration for commitment and hard work. You were a very good translator.

I am most grateful to my major supervisor Prof. Rodolfo Fattovich. I benefited a lot from the academic assets and experience of Rodolfo two times in my life. First when I was M.A student in archaeology at the Department of History and Heritage Management, Archaeology Unit, Addis Ababa University as my thesis Co-supervisor. Secondly, as my tutor and major Supervisor while doing this research work between 2008 and 2011. Rodolfo has an important part in my professional upbringing in the field of archaeology.

My highest academic debt goes to my co-supervisor Prof. Lorenzo Costantini since the original dissertation would not have been complete without his help. As one of the archaeobotanists who are highly influenced by the Vavilovian school of thought and the subsequent debates, every one of his lectures started by telling me the importance of understanding the Center and non-center theory. His students of him are always reminded to keep their lab space clean, to care for and document the traditional agricultural systems and genetic variety of the world as a daily routine. Discipline and intensive analysis of the data are among the most important qualities I learned from him. Basic botanical knowledge, appreciating the indigenous knowledge of traditional farmers, the techniques of identifying plant impressions, documenting the data from pencil plotting to using microscopes and camera are some among many that I benefited from Lorenzo.

My thanks and gratitude also extends to Dr. Andrea Manzo who has been providing a continuous help from the very beginning to the very end of my stay in Italy. The help I acquired from him ranges from solving my immediate academic inquiries in terms of discussions and accessing and giving me access to the relevant literature, to the most complex administrative problems. He has very kindly, incorporated me as a member of the Italian Archaeological Mission in Eastern Sudan and allowed me to excavate at Mahal Teglinos and bring samples for analysis back to Rome, as a result of which the research result of the dissertation gained depth and direction.

Prof. Yacob Beyene has made my stay in Italy easy and friendly. With him it was possible to adopt the culture and the education system readily. As a fatherly figure, he used to remind me to work hard and check progress on my research from time to time.

As a co-ordinator of PhD programme in African Studies and out of his personal interest for African historical and prehistoric past, Prof. Alexandro Truilzi has helped me a lot for a timely accomplishment of my dissertation. The office which he was running has kindly funded my travels from Naples to the Bio-archaeological Research Center, Rome, for over two years and half.

I thank Prof. Katherina Neumann, Prof. Catherine D'Andrea, Dr. Dorian Fuller and Dr. Elisabeth Hildebrand for generously sharing their research results, published and in press, which helped me to grasp the state of art in the field of archaeobotany.

I am grateful to staff members of the Ethiopian National Herbareum, Department of Biology at Addis Ababa University for politely providing data on botanical resources of Ethiopia and Eritrea.

Habab and Sara tried their best to translate the ethnographic interviews at Kassala from Arabic into English, for whom I owe too much. I thank also Mr. Fabrizio Pica, Bio-archaeological reaserch center of Oriental Art Museum, Rome, for beautiful SEM images. The following colleagues deserve special thanks for helping me in both my social and academic life during my study; Dr. Kassaye Begashaw, Dr. Luisa Sernicola, Dr. Antonella Brita, Ato Nega Gebresilassie, Vincenzo Zoppi and Marco Barbarino.

My father, Beldados Aleho, who passed away in the middle of my PhD training, had rather waited long my academic accomplishments. I can acknowledge now that I have inherited your patience, the habit of reading and above all endurance for challenges.

The strength and consistent behavior of my wife, Rahel Yitbarek in times of good and bad and the continuous unconscious tolerance of my son Jossy (Yosef Alemseged) while I am away for long were alarm clocks for me day in and day out. Through your affection tasks that look impossible became possible. I love you both.

Abstract

Archaeobotanical investigation was conducted on a total of thirty two thousand (n=32,000) pot fragments, baked clay and fired clay collected from different sites belonging to five Cultural Groups in Eastern Sudan. The Cultural Groups include Amm Adam, Butana, Gash, Jebel Mokram, and Hagiz. Soil samples (6 kilos) were also analyzed from various excavation spots at Mahal Teglinos, a major site that rendered data on Butana, Gash, Jebel Mokram and Hagiz Groups. The objective of the study was to reconstruct ancient food systems of the pre-historic inhabitants of a region of Northeast Africa and its environmental milieu. The result of the study demonstrated the subsistence bases of the inhabitants from ca. 6,000 B.C. to 200/300 A.D. Crops like the small seeded millets (*Setaria sp., Eleusine sp., Paspalum sp., Echinochloa sp., Pennisetum sp.*), *Sorghum verticilliflorum, Sorghum bicolor bicolor, Hordeum sp., Triticum monococcum/dicoccum*, and seeds and fruit stones *(Vigna unguiculata, Grewia bicolor Juss., Ziziphus sp.* (mainly *Ziziphus spina christi*) and *Celtis integrifolia)* were cultivated for consumption during this period. The study has also shed new light on the domestication history of Sorghum bicolor. The wild Sorghum, *Sorghum bicolor verticilliflorum* and its cultivated variety, *Sorghum bicolor* were simultaneously exploited by the Jebel Mokram Group people between 2,000 B.C. and 1,000 B.C. One of the oldest domesticated morphotype of *Sorghum bicolor,* i.e. an intermediary phase between the wild progenitor and its domesticated variety was revealed by the same investigation. Morphological change that has occurred while the species was evolving from wild to cultivated is measured using a Leica Qwin software.

List of Illustrations

List of Tables

Glossary

Dorsal surface (as applied to seeds): derived from the Latin word *dorsum* meaning 'back'. Regarding the usage of the term for seeds, it means the rear side of the seed. The opposite side of the ventral surface.

Ventral surface (as applied to seeds): derived from the Latin word *venter* meaning 'belly'. Regarding the usage of the term for seeds, it means the frontal part of the seed. The opposite side of the dorsal surface.

Chaff: the dry scaly protective cover of the seeds of cereals.

Glume: a basal, membranous, sterile husk of in the flowers of grasses (Poaceae).

Spikelet: a part of a grass inflorescence most of the time consisting of two bracts.

Chapter I
INTRODUCTION

1.1 THEORETICAL FRAMEWORK ON THE ORIGIN OF PLANT CULTIVATION AND DOMESTICATION IN NORTHEAST AFRICA

The Swiss botanist de Candolle (1985) had indicated that the geographic location of the origin of edible plants is not uniform in the world. He came up to this conclusion based on multidisciplinary approach of acquiring data from botany, history, archaeology, paleontology and philology. According to him, places like China and India supplied in great amount for our understanding of the origin of plants while others provided little (Abbo *et al.* 2010:319). Following de Candolle, the most dominant concept for area of origin for agriculture happens to be the eight centers approach as suggested by the Russian geneticist Vavilov (1951).

The Ethiopian highlands were taken as one of the eight centers for the origin of agriculture by Vavilov. This assumption was based on the idea that the presence of crop diversity in an area could indicate place of origin for agriculture. He emphasized that the chosen eight centers have a high degree of genetic diversity for the crop complexes they posses. This arguement was in the forefront for almost four decades. The same approach was followed by the Italian agronomist Raffaele Ciferri who published a series of articles documenting almost all of the indigenous plants of 'abyssinia' and other genetic resources (Ciferri 1939, 1942a, 1942b, 1942c, 1942d, 1942e, and 1943). Contesting the Vavilovian model which equates area of origin for agriculture with crop diversity, Harlan (1971) categorized the same highlands as non-centers or secondary centers. He argued against Vavilov by mentioning Ethiopian tetraploid wheat varieties where its domestication could not be traced in the highlands due to absence of wild progenitor. In line with the same concept, Harlan (1971) proposed temperate centers and tropical non-centers (Abbo *et al.* 2010:319).

Studies have shown that the Ethiopian center is home for variety of plants which pass through independent process of cultivation and domestication like as *Eragrostis tef, Guizotia abyssinica, Eleusine coracana, Ensete ventricosum, Catha edulis, Pisum abyssinicum and Coccinia abyssinica* (Simoons 1965, Ehret 1979, Brandt 1984, Marshal and Hildebrand 2002, Hildebrand 2003, Butler 2003, Lyons and D'Andraia 2003, Hildebrand *et al.* 2010a).

In contrast to the highlands, the adjacent lowlands of the Ethio-Eritreo-Sudanese borders are one of the poorly documented areas in terms of crop distribution and the study of the origin of agriculture. However, there are theories which try to elucidate the important role of the lowlying territories for the beginning of crop agriculture and animal husbandry. For researchers like Mudrock (1959), Clark (1977) and Haaland (1992), the Neolithic Revolution that marks the biggest jump for humanity from a total dependence on nature to adding the value of culture was achieved by the pre-historic inhabitants of the Nile Valley of Egypt and the Sudan far before their counter-parts in the Horn of Africa. Therefore, the knowledge of plant exploitation and animal husbandry reached the highlands of the Horn through the lowlands.

Murdock (1959) asserted that cultivation of sorghum and animal husbandry were introduced into the Horn of Africa from Eastern Sudan by ca. 5000 B.P. Clark on his part gave the credit for the C-Group immigrants from Nubia who moved Southeast during the mid-Holocene climatic aridity. For Haaland (1992), the knowledge of specialized pastoralism reached the Horn of Africa through the Medjay of the Pan-Grave culture.

The Ethio-Eritrean and Sudanese lowlands, are worth investigation as the proposed immediate influencing area for the beginning of food production in the Ethiopian and Eritrean plateau. The result of this specific research could play a clarifying role on the model of the origin of food production in the region through a critical investigation of the type of plants utilized in the highlands and the adjacent lowlands.

1.2 BAKING BREAD FROM PALEOETHNOBOTANY: WHAT IS PALEOETHNOBOTANY?
Paleoethnobotany / archaeobotany / botanical archaeology / phytoarchaeology / palaeocarpology

Depending on the methodological orientation of the researcher and the language used, the above five terminologies could refer to the same discipline. However, the most commonly used synonym for paleoethnobotany is archaeobotany. Paleoethnobotany is a branch of environmental archaeology that deals with botanical remains recovered from archaeological contexts with the intention of studying human-plant interaction and the environment in which it took place. Coneptually, the study is expected to incorporate vegetation distribution and indigenous knowledge of the locality under consideration. Paleobotanical remains can be microscopic like pollen and phytoliths and macro remains like larger seeds/grains, stones of fruit, leaves, charcoal and wood. Both of these remains can be accumulated into an archaeological spot due to natural and cultural processes. The botanical remains "are preserved by carbonization, water logging, desiccation and mineralization, as stomach contents and residues, e.g. coprolites, and as impressions in ceramics. They are identified (on the basis of their external morphology) by comparing them with reference collection manuals, and by sorting types, size, measurements, shape and surface texture" (Magid 2004:2 see also Magid 1989:64).

The primary focus of this discipline is on the reconstruction and understanding of cultural changes of past populations, subsistence being most imperative. Understanding of past subsistence will include the type of food that human beings ate, the way they acquired their food, the technologies they employ to process, collect and store their food. Despite its shallow history, this field of study has contributed a lot for our increasing knowledge in the evolution, utilization, early agriculture and domestication of a number of edible plants. In addition; Paleoethnobotanists also try to appreciate past environment, rituals, trade and construction materials (Renfrew 1973:1, Magid 1989:459).

Some argue that paleoethnobotany and archaeobotany/botanical archaeology could not be synonyms since paleoethnobotany is a study of archaeobotanical remains to acquire data on the interaction of human beings with plants. Whereas by definition archaeobotany excludes the human element and concentrates on the non-cultural aspects of the data without questioning the data on past human-plant interaction. Critics of this argument see it as splitting a hair and states that it is not rational to make an essential division between paleoethnobotany and archaeobotany (Buurman 1994:1).

Archaeobotany as a discipline started to emerge at the end of the 19th and at the beginning of the 20th centuries, a period in which archaeological study itself was basically descriptive by approach. Artefacts and any other findings were compiled without systematic sampling methods. At the time archaeobotany was not practiced by professional archaeologists rather by professional botanists who occasionally extend their methodological reaches for academic purposes. It was during this early stage that a forseeble argument was put forward by Hans Helbaek who proposed a need for change in the interpretation of a pre-domestication phase particularily in the study of wheat and barley in Near Eastern and European Neolithic (Fuller 2009:16).

In the late 1960s and 1970s archaeologists began to explore more information by a systematic manipulation of the data. Interest in a comprehensive sampling and analysis grew. Attempts to acquire answer for more complex inquiries from the data show progress. In Europe and America, this period coincides with the onset of the 'New Archaeology', a departure in the theory and practice of cultural processes. Some manifestations of changes in the field of archaeology during this period include more need for explanation instead of description, deductive reasoning by formulating hypothesis, producing models and observing their results, designing research projects targeting specific problems and using quantitative data for sampling (Renfrew and Bahn 1996:37). The desire to see methodological progress in the science of archaeology was accompanied by the adoption of new techniques: sieving and flotation. Recovering plant remains by flotation and animal bones by sieving have became standards for the study of the beginning of food production (Fuller 2009:17).

In the study of the beginning of agriculture, archaeobotany is recently obtaining an important place. Its methods are enabling us to appreciate the biological transformations that came along with agricultural revolution, which in turn, gear us to enable us to visualise better the social changes. The discipline can explain in better terms the borders between environment, anthropogenic impact and plant morphology (ibid. 16).

Every discipline is judged by the contribution it provides for the growth of science and in its capacity in addressing societal problems and needs. Magid (2004:12), put forward the possibilities in which paleoethnobotany could be tapped in giving service to human needs. Some of the potentials are presented as follow:

1- Rapidly vanishing indigenous knowledge on botanical resources could be conserved by the methodological assets of paleoethnobotany,

2- The discipline can contribute to the rehabilitation of dislocated populations because of natural and anthropogenic catastrophes,

3- It can also furnish pharmaceutical research on medicine, diet, cosmetics, etc. by providing knowledge on botanical data.

1.3 THE STUDY OF PLANT KINGDOM IN THE BIOSPHERE

Until recently there were two taxonomic kingdoms in the biosphere: animals and plants. Fungi and algae were included under plants and bacteria being between the two kingdoms. Nowadays, the two kingdom taxonomy is changed to five. These are Monera, Protista, Fungi, Plantae and Animalia. Each kingdom is further divided into different phyla or divisions. The Monera encompasses unicellular and colonial bacteria and blue-green algae, and within Protista there are unicellular protozoans and multicellular algae. The Fungi kingdom incorporates all the fungi. Trees, shrubs, flowers, mosses, ferns, and all species with diploid life cycles are within the Plantae. Under the umbrella of Kingdom Animalia there are multicellular animals without photosynthetic pigments and without cell walls. With progress in the science of microbiology such five kingdoms taxonomic classifications will be refined even more (Dincauze 2000:329).

Plants can grow almost everywhere in the geosphere and hydrosphere. It, thus, means systematic documentation of plant remains is very essential for reconstructing past environments. While reconstructing past environment it is necessary to consider the local and regional variants since different species on different environments could provide data in different magnitudes. For example, pollen from lake sediments renders data on regional plants history. On the other hand pollen from soils often provides us data on restricted environment. Plants as producers are found at the base of the food web. The study of plants in time and space can give us information about the local animals, human life, types of soil and the climate of the area. Plants could react directly to fluctuations in climate. Due to changes in climate, vegetation composition also shifts in latitude and altitude and this will have an impact on human life (Evans 1978:13-15).

In archaeological researches the study of the flora is often neglected due to emphasis on faunal analysis and because bones can quickly be identified in excavations. In reality, in most cases, in archaeological sites the availability of plants is by far greater than that of bones. In the last few decades, however, with the development of techniques of recovering macro and micro botanical remains in archaeological sites and with increasing benefits from botanical sciences, the study of plants has come to the forefront (Renfrew and Bahn 1996:224).

The science of study about plants in particular can be categorized under botany, plant science or phytology (Dincauze, 2000:330). Micro and macro plant remains can be systematically studied to reconstruct past environment and human plant interaction. The analysis of microscopic plant bodies such as pollen, Phytoliths, diatoms are good sources of information. For understanding past environment palynology (the science of pollen grains and spores) happen to be the foremost field of study since the early decades of the twentieth century after the Swedish botanist, Lennart von Post, developed a means to correlate remains deposited in lacustrial and terrestrial sediments. Palynology has also become an important field for the study of past climate change particularly through the analysis of glacial and interglacial deposits during the Pleistocene epoch. In addition, pollen analysis was exploited more commonly for establishing dates until the coming of isotopic chronological methods like as radiocarbon dating (Evans 1978: 18-21).

The study of pollens of course cannot give us detail and complete information about the past environment but can fill an important gap in the reconstruction of past vegetation. For example, until the result of the pollen analysis by the French scientist Raymonde Bonnefille, the Hadar area and the Omo valley in Ethiopia were considered to be dry between 3 to 5 million years ago as is the case presently. The result, however, demonstrated that the areas were greener with dense forests along lakes and river valleys. When the environment was changing to a drier condition by about 2.5 million years B.P. the tropical vegetation changed into grasslands (Renfrew and Bahn 1996:228).

In many parts of the world, today, the changes in vegetation history have been documented based on the study of pollen grains and due to this any separate analysis could be viewed in line with the already eastablished sequences. In Europe, for instance, the post glacial period has been classified into sequences of pollen zones reflecting phases of climatic fluctuations. With analogies to current ecological set up, it is possible to relate the nature of the climate of the past and its change in time. One strong limitation for this kind of relative dating system is that a single zone as represented by tree pollen spectrum may cover a thousand years or more (Dimbelby 1969: 167).

Archaeology as a discipline can benefit from the study of pollen grains in the following summarized but interrelated areas; first, for eastablishing chronology; secondly, by gathering data for understanding the past vegetation and relating this to current environmental conditions and thirdly, reconstructing human impact on the environment. It does not mean, however, that every scientific investigation will simultaneously entertain the above mentioned three advantages (ibid.)

The study of phytoliths is currently gaining momentum and its methodology is also progressing from time to time. Phytoliths, less commonly known as plant opal, are very tiny sections of silica which are developed from the cells of plants. These microscopic particles can survive for a long period after the death or decomposition of the plant. Phytoliths can be found in pottery, stone tools and teeth of animals that feed on plants. They are also available in fire places and in sediments. In similar condition with pollen grains, phytoliths are produced abundantly. They are easily diagnosable since they have a distinctive morphology. However, genus or species level identification is often difficult (Evans 1978: 26-27).

The other approach for the study of paleoenvironment using microscopic plant remains is the analysis of diatoms. Diatoms are single-celled algae that have cell walls of silica not cellulose as is common in other plants. The silica cell walls remain intact far after the death of the algae. As water bodies are the preferred habitat for the growth of algae, diatoms can be tapped in great quantity at the bottom of lakes, seas, rivers and oceans and within shore sediments of these water bodies. The methodology of identification and classification is very similar to that of pollen analysis. The morphology of diatoms is highly distinctive and species level identification is possible. For the study of aquatic environments in particular, diatom analysis is recommended because it is possible to decipher the salinity, alkalinity of the water body as well as the lives that can be supported in the same locale. In broader terms, the degree of freshness and salinity of the aquatic environment can be interpreted to recognize the time of break up between lakes and seas in tectonically active places, transgression and regression of water bodies and the level of pollusion in local hydrology (Evans 1978: 27-28, http://www-marine.stanford.edu/profiles/diatoms.htm).

Macroscopic plant remains include large plant bodies like tree trunks, stumps and branches to smaller seeds. Macrobotanical remains are bigger in size and their recovery is relatively easier. It, however, requires abundant reference collection of different plants and a good knowledge of botany. Sieving and flotation techniques are widely used to retrieve such vegetal remains from sediments. Other than sediments, sources of macrobotanical remains include the stomach of animals, the coprolite of humans and other small and big game fauna and on the teeth of big animals. They can also be identified from artefacts such as pottery and stone tools. Plant bodies that can be identified as macrobotanical remains are grains, fruits, and woods. They basically render data on the characterstics of local environments (Evans 1978: 22-23).

Grains and fruit stones can be preserved for a long period through carbonization, water logging, desiccation and mineralization and could be identifiable upto the species level even after undergoing processes like carbonization (see chapter VIII of this volume). Sometimes, the whole grain or fruit stone could be fragmented and vanished and leave behind its imprint as on pottery. Imprints of leaves and grains also appear on tufa, plaster, leather and corroded bronze (see Helbaek 1996: 206-209). The techniques for detailed analysis and presentation of grains and fruit stones are presented in chapter IV and chapter VI respectively.

Most of the time plant remains survive in an archaeological site in the form of wood and charcoal. Under normal conditions plant bodies decay in the soil by bacterial action and can only survive when fully carbonized. When the environment is dry or water logged

vegetal parts may also survive. Charcoal is formed when wood is burned in an area with sufficient oxidization. Charcoal cannot decay in the soil since it possesses carbon. In desert areas, where the environment is very dry in the absence of moisture in the soil, wood can survive without decaying for thousands of years. A good example for this is the discovery of many wooden materials (coffins, furnitures, figurines, etc...) in Egypt dated back to 3000 B.C. and even earlier (Western 1969: 178).

What the archaeologist is interested to know is the type of trees and shrubs utilized by past societies for their daily activities such as for fuel, for building, furniture, rituals. This data can give us a clue on local vegetation history and on ancient climates (Evans 1978:7). It can also give an idea of locally available or imported timber for craftsmanship purpose. Wood and charcoal residues, like all the organic materials, are also very important for carbon-14 dating (Western 1969: 178).

The structure of the wood is an essential identifying character of most trees and shrubs. Through analysis of wood anatomy, it is possible to separate one genus from another. Excluding ferns, trees and shrubs can be categorized into two groups; the gymnosperms (soft woods) are in general cone bearing and the angiosperms (hard woods). Exceptions to this category are palms, since their structure does not belong to gymnosperms and angiosperms. The transverse sections are used in the identification of hard woods. Hard woods of the temperate climate develop growth rings in concentric circles. Tropical and other climate woods may not demonstrate growth rings because of lack of a specific growth period (ibid. 178-179).

1.4 WHICH THEORY CAN BE TESTED BY PALEOETHNOBOTANICAL APPROACHES?

Paleoethnobotany being a recently emerging discipline lacks a clearly outlined set of theory. Its theories are often derived from the methods it adopted from other disciplines such as biology (and/or biosciences), anthropology, and archaeology (Dincauze 2000:331). This idea is best manifested in Fuller's definition of archaeobotany (2009:16) if one takes archaeobotany as a synoym for paleoethnobotany without giving too much emphasis to the anthropological component. According to Fuller 'Archaeobotany, simply defined, is the application of botanical methods and theory to archaeological problems and archaeological remains'. Fuller further explained that the Neolithic can be seen as 'a botanical revolution' since new plant species evolved as a result of anthropogenic impact when forests were cleared, soils cultivated and varieties of crops and weeds appeared.

It is, however, important to stress that until we see a progress in the methods of the science of archaeology and related disciplines, paleoethnobotany, at this time, is one of the most valuable approaches to address theories about the origin of human-plant interaction.

1.5 RATIONALE: PROBLEMS AND JUSTIFICATIONS

Archaeobotanical evidence for agriculture in Northern Nubia is limited. Despite a wealth of settlement and cemetery evidence from Lower Nubia, most works were carried out before sieving was routine or field flotation had been developed.

(Dorian Q. Fuller, in press)

This research is based on an assessment of archaeobotanical and ethnographic data from a region of Northeast Africa; Eastern Sudan and the lowlands of western Eritrea and Northwest Ethiopia. I have already examined thousands of archaeological materials from the site of Agordat, Western Eritrea as part of research requirement for M.A. degree in the years 2004-2006 (Beldados 2006). The purpose of the study is to reconstruct pre-historic subsistence patterns based on crop production and the environmental milieu in the region. The data from Ethiopia and Eritrea are highly fragmentary and do not provide us a direct clue on the onset of plant food utilization. A number of researchers have, however, pointed out that the Highlands of Ethiopia are independent centers of plant cultivation and domestication (Vavilov 1931, Simoons 1965, Ehret 1979, Brandt 1984, D'Andrea *et al.* 1999, Marshal and Hildebrand 2002, Butler 2003, Hildebrand 2003, Lyons and D'Andrea 2003, D'Andrea *et al.*, 2008, D'Andrea 2008). Most researches exclude the Northwestern lowlands and there are very few studies conducted in the region. To the Southwest, further south of the study area, a survey project has been underway since the year 1999 led by Victor Fernandez of the University of Madrid, Spain. The project has the objective of testing a hypothesis about contribution of the area of the present day Assosa (a border region between Ethiopia and the Sudan) to the introduction of the agro-pastoral economy into the highlands by ca. 6th millennium B.P. (2002 field season preliminary report). It is, thus, with the the intention of uncovering data for the rather neglected boarder lands that this research is initiated. The premise of the research work is on the Eastern most part of the Sudan and the Ethio-Eritrean lowlands might have been inhabited by people who had similar means of livelihood in prehistoric times between the mid and late Holocene.

I have argued in other works (Beldados 2004, 2006, 2007) that the pre-historic culture-history of the highlands and the adjacent lowlands of the Horn of Africa is *terra incognita*. In Eastern Sudan, there is a relatively better documentation of the cultural sequence of the Gash Group in site like Mahal Teglinos (Fattovich *et al.*, 1984, Fattovich and Piperno 1986, Fattovich 1989, 1993), for the people of Jebel Mokram Group, possibly related to the Medjay of the Egyptian sources (Sadr 1987, 1991) the Atbara and Khartoum regions (Haaland 1992), in sites belonging to the Butana area (Marks 1989, 1993, Marks and Fattovich 1989), and in areas along the Nile valley: Aneibis, El Damer and Abu Darbein (Haaland and Magid 1995). For the lowlands of Ethiopia and Eritrea (with the exception of the huge data available from Agordat) pre-historic cultural sequences were not reconstructed. The causes and consequences of the onset of early food production in the region have remained subjects that are rarely visited. As a result of the absence of evidence, the few works of research available see the prehistoric cultural processes in relation to or as extensions and exaggerations of Nubian and South Arabian cultures (Vogt and Buffa 2005:437). In view of the same trend, Vogt and Buffa (2005:437) wrote, 'researchers often compared the cultural development of Ethiopia and Eritrea before the Aksumites with the then better known ancient cultures of 1st millennium B.C. South Arabia.'

In line with the premise of this research, at least temporarily, it is thus, a necessity rather than a need to see together the cultural developments of the Northwestern lowlands of Ethiopia and Eritrea with the relatively better documented data available in the Eastern part of the Sudan for the following reasons:

a. The lowlands of Eritrea, Ethiopia and Eastern Sudan are characterized by a similar environmental condition and geologic set up;

b. The prehistoric and current inhabitants of the area were\are entertaining life from the same River Systems. All of the major Rivers; Gash, Atbara, Barka, Setit have their sources in the Eritrean highlands. The Mereb River changes its name into Gash when it crosses the Eritrean boarder. The Tekeze River is termed the Atbara on the other side of the Eritrean boundary. The cultural developments in the region were\are also shaped by these River Systems as Sadr (1988: 80-82) commented, the environment and the settlement pattern of the region are strictly related to the local hydrology;

c. Archaeological sources have indicated that the ancient inhabitants of the Gash Delta had a very strong role in the 'Socio-economic and cultural history of Northeastern Africa' (Fattovich 1994:50). Fattovich stressed that 'the investigation of this region must be regarded as a primary task for both Sudanese and Ethiopian archaeology' (ibid.);

d. The theories set on the origin of early plant food utilization have for long been observed as a continuation of cultural climax that was already achieved in the Nile Valley of the Sudan and the Eastern Desert (Haaland 1992, Magid 1989b,1990, 1991);

e. Ethnographic studies demonstrate that the present day inhabitants of North western Eritrea, the Beni Amir Bejas are still practising pastoralism and cultivation of cereals like Sorghum and Millet (Sadr, 1989, 1990, 1991). The current periodic population composition of the Eastern Sudan is also consisting of the same population group. It is, thus, possible to see contacts between peoples that may have had similar cultural development in the prehistoric arena.

5

1.6 ARCHAEOBOTANICAL/PALEOETHNO-BOTANICAL RESEARCH IN NORTHERN SUDAN: A HISTORY

Since C. Knuth (1826) studied the desiccated fruits, grains, and seeds which were recovered from the tombs of ancient Egypt, archaeoethnobotany has captured the interest of scientists in many fields of research such as genetics, botany, agriculture and archaeology.

(Magid 1989a: 459)

In Central Sudan, one of the earliest attempts to recover botanical remains from an archaeological site was made by Arkell in 1949. The sites investigated for archaeobotanical purposes were Khartoum Hospital and Gerif town (Arkell 1949: 108-110, Magid 1989a: 459). From the Neolithic site of Esh Shaheinab, Arkell, later, identified identical macrobotanical remains to the ones in Khartoum Hospital site (Arkell 1953: 80). The plant seeds recovered from the sites of Khartoum Hospital and Esh Shaheinab were non-carbonized *Celtis integrifolia* Lam. Arkell argued that the fruits of this tree were collected and carried to the site for consumption. From the west side of the River Nile in two areas of the Esh Shaheinab site (Islang and Nofalab) carbonized remains of *Elaeis guineensis Thumb.* and *Zizyphus sp.* were recovered. The earliest Khartoum site, Saggai, has provided a date that ranges between 7410±100 B.P. and 7230±100 B.P. (Magid 1989a: 461).

This was a period in which people relied on broad spectrum resources, both terrestrial and aquatic (pastoralism, fishing and hunting). According to Magid (1982:98 see also 1989a:461), the wild Sorghum, S. *Verticiliflorum Stend.* (Stapf.) identified from the site of Esh-Shaheinab was utilized and the domesticated version of the same progenitor is the major food crop in the Sudan currently.

Kryzyaniak (1978:160) interpreted possible plant gathering and cultivation from range of plants recovered from the pre-historic occupation site of Kadero 1. Several plants belonging to the Graminaeae family were identified as imprints on pot sherds from the site of Kadero 1. The same site has also provided fossilized seeds like C. *integrifollia* Lam., and *Hyphaene thebaica (L.) Mart.*

Both *Celtis integrifolia Lam.* and wild sorghum S. *Verticiliflorum Stend.* (Stapf.) were commonly available in almost all of the occupational sites east of the River Nile (like Zakyab, Umm Direwiya, Kadero 1). For instance, according to the archaeobotanical data, 5 impressions of wild sorghum S. *Verticiliflorum Stend.* (Stapf.) on pot sherds were identified from the site of Zakyab. Whereas, Umm Direwia and Kadero 1 provided 4 impressions each. Here also, the assumption of the presence of similar economic practice simultaneously across these sites is raised by Magid (1989a: 461) based on parallel evidence.

From the caves of Shaqadud several carbonized seeds were recovered belonging to a variety of species from deposits that range in time between 4200 years B.P. and 3600 years B.P. Seeds and fruits of *Zizyphus sp. Lam.* and *Grewia Sp.* (Forsk.), seeds of *Pennisetum sp.* (Brum.) *Stapf.* and *Hubbard*, a grain of *Sorghum sp. Stapf.*, seeds of *Panicum trugidum Forsk.*, seeds of *Solanum dubium L., Setaria sp.,* and *Crotalaria sp.* were all identified from Shaqadud caves (Magid 1984: 28). The area of Shaqdud is within the range of the wild sorghum growing area according to Harlan and Stemler (1976).

Sorghum sp. Moench, Setaria sp. Beauv, Echinochloa sp. Beauv (abundant plant types at Nabta playa), all belonging to the Graminae family, were recovered as pottery impressions in Blue Nile area in the early and Middle Holocene context. *Setaria sp. Beauv* is still utilized by desert inhabitants in Egypt and the Sahara. The recovery of these plants indicates that the climate was more humid than the present (Magid 2003). *Sorghum verticilliflorum*, for instance, needs a minimum of 500 millimetres of annual rain fall; the clayey alluvial soil being the most conducive type for sorghum (Haaland 1981: 197).

For Eastern Sudan our knowledge is even scarcer. Plant impressions from pottery from a survey of *Shurab el Gash*, about 15 kilometers South of Kassala at a locality called *Jebel Abu Gamal* (or Mahal Teglinos) and from test excavations at Mahal Teglinos (K1), near the Northern end of Jebel Kassala and where the beginnings of the granite outcrops of Eritrea are observable, were analyzed by Costantini (1982: 30-33). The result of the analysis rendered domestic sorghum (*Sorghum cf. bicolor*), *Seteria cf. glauca*, cf. *paspalum sp. Jebel Abu Gamal* is dated to the 2nd millennium B.C. based on comparative studies of pottery.

A year after the 1982 publication, Costantini *et al.* (1983: 23) reported the identification of imprints of a sample of the Middle Eastern domesticate barley, *Hordeum sp.* and several fruit stones of *Zyziphus sp.* from the site of Mahal Teglinos, excavation units KI and KII. On the identification of *Hordeum sp.*, in particular, Magid, (1989a: 464), raises a number of questions about whether this sample is imported or locally cultivated? If it is locally cultivated how could barley grow in the Kassala area of a Savannah grass land with warm winters and summer rains? If this is imported, is there any other associated material culture evidence? And also why did the inhabitants of Kassala look for (cultivate) barley in the presence of wild growing sorghum?

Palaeoenvironmental speculations were made for Southern Atbai based on the analysis of botanical materials by Wickens (1982:23-51). The result of the investigation showed that during the early Holocene (Ca. 10,000-5000 B.C.) the environment of the area was more of a deciduous savanna woodland.

Among the more recent views on the model of use/adaptation of different crops in ancient Nubia and

Sudan, Fuller (in press) came up with a pattern in time for the prevalence of winter crops and summer crops in Northern Sudan based on the limited archaeobotanical data available. According to the sources, during the period of the A-Group, end of the fourth millennium B.C., barley and emmer wheat were under cultivation. Rather fragmentary archaeobotanical evidence compiled together showed that at the time of the C-Group and Kerma, mid-3rd to mid-2nd millennium B.C., the same winter crops had flourished. The archaeobotanical evidence for the early periods is completely devoid of indigeneous sub-saharan crops. The same trend can be seen in Egypt, where there is better documentation of the archaeobotanical evidence, and the highlands of Ethiopia and Eritrea. At the beginning, cultivation of the winter crops in Northern Sudan probably followed the same pattern as the original Egyptian agricultural system, which was based on retreating Nile floods.

Recent studies demonstrate that the adoption of sorghum in the Northern part of Sudan was a slow process. A fully domesticated morphotype of sorghum dominantly existed in the Meroitic period. The wild progenitor, however, was investigated and identified as impression on pottery as early as 6010±90 BP from the site of Umm Direwia (see chapter V of this volume). The dietary and agricultural importance of sorghum boosted only at the end of Meroitic period and continued to show progress in the post Meroitic period. An increasing importance of such summer crops in the post Meroitic times is evidenced by the isotopic study of samples from the cemetery of Wadi Halfa region. The study indicated a change towards the use of C-4 crops like sorghum and the millets (Fuller in press).

Synthesizing the archaeobotanical works done in Northern Sudan and based on analysis of other archaeological sources on ancient agricultural systems, Fuller (in press) tried to draw the economic base for the establishment of the state of Qustul-Ballana. During the 4th century A.D. the state of Nobadia had flourished in Lower Nubia and the archaeological culture that came in to view during the same centuries in the region was called Qustul-Ballana or the X-Group. He argued that the beginning of double cropping, concentration on cash-crop production (cotton and grapes) by employing an irrigation system resulted in the increase of the demographic figure (due to need for new labour) and the accumulation of wealth, which are essentials for creating an independent political entity. New source of wealth achieved by better irrigation and enlarged cultivable land (the saqia effect) and due to utilization of more efficient double cropping (the savanna crop effect) was partly responsible for the demise of the economic control of the Meroitic center. He further argued that the other possible factor that made the Meroitic center even more fragile was the simultaneous occurrence of increased aridity in Northeast Africa as evidenced by the decrease of Lake Abhe in Ethiopia, for instance. These incidents might have forced the inhabitants to a more pastoral way of existance abandoning settled life.

1.7 THE STATUS OF ARCHAEOBOTANICAL/ PALEOETHNOBOTANICAL RESEARCH IN THE HIGHLANDS AND ADJACENT LOWLANDS OF NORTHEAST AFRICA

As much as Vavilov and Harlan are credited for popularizing the highlands of Ethiopia as a rich source of genetic diversity for plants and as the probable center for the origin of agriculture, the works of the Italian agronomist Rafaelle Ciferri in the 1930s and 40s was not less important. But, most researches dealing with botany, archaeobotany and the origin of ancient agriculture fail to mention his contribution to the field.

Ciferri (1939) argued that the Ethiopian Center is unique in the world for the study of plant diversity and ancient agriculture. The area possesses a very rich variety of wheat, which makes it ideal for the study of the evolution of the plant. In his article, *Wheat and other grains indigeneous to Ethiopia*, (1939) he calls for a combined effort employing multi-disciplinary approaches to document the floral diversity of the country. He states that the information we have on Ethiopia before this period (1930s) was based on isolated reports of explorers and travelers accounts. What is required is documenting the phyto and zoo-geography of the country and study in depth the effects of the mountainous terrain set up, the climate, the ecology and the pedogenic processes (Cifferri 1939:337).

Ciferri has intensively documented most of the indigenous crops of Ethiopia in his works; *Il Neuch o Guizotia dell'Africa Orientale Italiana* (1942), *Frumenti e Granicoltura Indigena in Etiopia* (1939), *L'Istituzione del "Triticum abyssinicum" per i Frumenti Indigeni d'Etiopia* (1943). One of the earliest studies on Sorghum, *I Sorghi o "Durre" dell'Africa Orientale Italiana* (1942) and *La cerealicoltura in Africa Orientale: Generalità botanico-agraria sui sorghi* (1942) was conducted by the same author.

Some five kilometers from the main stelae field of Aksum, at Gobedra, a quarry area for Aksumite obelisks, Phillipson (1977) excavated a rock shelter in which he recovered an un carbonized/un charred finger millet (*Eleusine coracana*). The millet seed was first attributed to 5180 B.C.±165. Later, however, the seed was determined to be intrusive and was not in the same context with the stratum dated to 5180 B.C.±165.

D'Andrea *et al.*, (1999) attributed the lack of ethno-archaeological and archaeobotanical researches in Ethiopia and Eritrea to the long years of political insecurity that the region had experienced than lack of scholarly interest. Although ethnoarchaeological research began in the Sahara in the late 1980s, they state that it is still in its incipient stage in Ethiopia and Eritrea. Efforts have been taken by (Phillipson 1994, 1995, 1996; Bard and Fattovich 1995; Fattovich 1995; Bard *et al.*, 1996; Bard *et al.*, 2000; Boardman 2000) to rectify the situation. With such a combined effort plant seeds were identified from pre-Aksumite and Proto-Aksumite contexts such as Chick pea (*Cicer artietinum*), barley (*Hordeum vulgare*), tef (*Eragrostis tef*), lentil (*Lens esculentum*), linseed (*Linum usitatissimum*), free-threshing wheat (*Triticum aestivum/durum*), emmer wheat (*Triticum dicoccum*) (D'Andrea *et al.*, 2011: 369).

A new cultivated species of pea (*Pisum abyssinicum*), known otherwise as the Ethiopian pea, has proved to be a separated species of the common pea (*Pisum sativum*) which was thought to have been introduced from Southwest Asia into the Horn of Africa. The wild species and the evolution of this species are unknown. It is, however, believed that the species has evolved either in Ethiopia or Yemen. The Ethiopian peas, which are dated around 400 AD, are also recovered from a Roman site in Egypt. The recovery of this separate species, according to Butler (2003: 37-47) gives insight us into separate development in Ethiopia or into a regional contact with Egypt further in the north or a South Arabian connection in the east.

Guidelines for distinguishing grains of *tef* from the archaeological context is prepared by D'Andrea (2008:547). The main objective of this guideline is primarily to show how to separate the domesticated *tef* seed from *Eragrostis pilosa*, its wild progenitor. There is an overlap in grain sizes in wild and domesticated forms and both could not survive charring at 300°C (D'Andrea, 2008:547-566). According to her experiment, *tef* is found to be less resistant to high temperature exposure unlike crops to large grain size such as wheat and barley. The domestication history of *tef* is also observed to be dissimilar to other cereals. Selection based on preference for large grain sized cereals and continous cultivation of these species might not be dictating factors for prehistoric cultivators. The determining factors for them were, probably, relatively more branching and increased number of seeds with in a small cultivated plot.

Paleoethnobotanical study has been conducted around Asmara at ancient Ona sites that are dated back to the 1st millennium B.C. The objective of the study was to reconstruct the prevailing agricultural economy during the 1st millennium B.C. The sampling method was based on the recovery of floral remains from one liter soil sample from every excavation level. The analysis provided emmer and free-threshing wheat (Triticum *dicoccum* and T. *durum/aestivum*), hulled barley (*Hordeum vulgare*), a grain of tef (*Eragrostis tef*), lentils (*Lens culinaris*), Linseed (*Linus usitatissimum*). The sites are dated between 350 and 800 B.C. (D`Andrea *et al.*, 2008).

Surface collection of potsherds (n=1469, weight for rim sherds=39.8 kilograms) from the site of Agrodat were examined in the store room of the National Museum of Khartoum, Sudan by Beldados (2006: 58-59) for plant impressions. Eleven of these (weight=942 grams) are thought to bear plant impressions. Although the identification process is still ongoing, eight potsherds are found to have cavities similar to those of plant impressions (mainly grains), the majority of them belong to seeds of different genus of Gramineae. One of those seed impressions belong to a wild taxa of *Sorghum*. Advanced laboratory examination is yet to be made in order to confirm the preliminary results (Anwar A-Magid, preliminary report). It is important to remember here that the site of Agordat and the whole Valley of Barka are within the geographic range of wild sorghum growing areas.

One of the eight potsherds selected for plant impression examination is burned on its interior surface. Magid (Pers. Comm.) commented that the burning of the sherd is due to the inclusion of some plant materials as temper. Besides, the smoothening\burnishing of some of the sherds is done also using plant materials as can be seen on the surface of the ceramics. A typical comparison can be done here with the ceramics of the Jebel Mokram Group where fiber tempering and crudeness are diagnostic characteristics (Sadr 1988:90).

The oldest record for the presence of wild sorghum in the archaeological context came from the Mesolithic sites in the Atbara area, Abu Darbein, El Damer and Aneibis (Magid 1995, Haaland 1999). Whereas, the earliest evidence (around 4000 years BP) for domesticated sorghum is recovered from Southern Arabia. Since wild sorghum does not grow in Southwest Asia, Haaland (1999) argued that either the domesticate or the wild species originated in Africa. Supporting the argument raised, Magid (1989b) discussed that to prevent back crossing the gene pool has to be isolated from the morphologically wild progenitor. This can happen by a conscious transportation of the wild seeds from its natural environment.

Fuller (in press) does not accept the idea of Haaland and Magid arguing based on current archaeobotanical knowledge for self- pollinating species (wheat and barley) and cross pollinating species such as rice. The suggestion that the domestication of sorghum in Africa is delayed or obstructed by cross pollination unlike the case for wheat and barley is not valid. Fuller stressed that 'if cultivation of sorghum had begun, we would expect some evidence for shift towards domesticated morphotypes'.

Most paleoethnobotanical studies from Ethiopia and Eritrea demonstrated preference for Middle Eastern domesticates over the indigenous crops. Wheat and barley, for instance, have developed their own indigenous forms after their introduction into the highlands of the Horn of Africa (see Harlan 1969). Archaeobotanical evidence has revealed the long presence of domesticated wheat and barley in the other side of the Red Sea. Costantini (1984) selected 300 pot sherds from the site of Wyi in Yemen which is dated to 3700±80 B.P. for archaeobotanical investigation. Twenty of these bear impressions of barley, sorghum, millets, oats and cumin. Costantini (1984) argues that with the abundance of evidence that has been acquired from Yemen, the area should have better considered part of the primary, Ethiopian-Sudanese center for the origin and spread of

Table 1.1 Aksumite kings who have minted their coins with two wheat stalks decoration

Names of Kings	Period	Number of coins with two stalks wheat
Endubis	c. A.D. 270-330	48
Aphilas	✓	17
WZB (Wazeba)	✓	2
Ousanas	✓	12
Ezana (Before conversion to Christianity)	✓	20
Ezana (After conversion to Christianity)	c. A.D. 330-540	10
Anonymous	✓	1
Ouazebas	✓	21
Eon	✓	8
Anonymous	✓	6

cultivated plants. He further argues that the Yemeni mountainous area is part of the Sudanian Region Phytogeographically characterized by plant species like "Nubo sindian and Eritro-Arabian provinces" (Costantini 1990: 188). Vavilov (1957) had already categorized the mountainous Arabia as belonging to the same climatic dimension as the Ethiopian Highlands. Unlike the later, however, the Yemeni highlands were seen as secondary center for the origin of cultivated plants (Vavilov 1951).

Preference for Middle Eastern domesticates can also be seen in the state sponsored coins minted during the Aksumite period. A significant number of Aksumite kings used to mint coins decorated with two wheat stalks which curve around to meet above the head of the King (Munro-Hay 1984: 43-127). The table 1.1 summarizes names of kings and amount of coins minted during their reigns with two wheat stalks engravings.

A recent study has shown that the southern highlands of Ethiopia are also important for the study of indigenous crops. Hildebrand *et al.*, (2010), for instance, investigated the Holocene archaeology of Southwest Ethiopia concentrating in Keffa area, a region with a unique environmental setting from the rest of the surroundings with cool, humid and forested tropical highlands. The elevation of the area ranges from 500 to 2000 m with different resource distribution in a limited space. The region was considered to be center of domestication for crops like Coffee (*Coffea arabica*), *enset* (*Ensete ventricosum),* anchote (*Coccinia abyssinica*, a plant belonging to the pumpkin family and with consumable tuber and fruit), some varieties of Yam and possibly Oromo potato (a local variety of potato), Finger millet (*Eleusine coracana*) and Tef (*Eragrostis tef*) (Hildebrand *et al.*, 2010:256 and Hildebrand and Brandt 2010:44). One of the excavated rock shelters in Kaffa, Kumali, rendered plentiful macrobotanical remains. Although the identification process of the recovered plant specimens is still underway, the presence of Musaceae (either wild/domesticated *Ensete ventricosum* or domestic Musa) and two fragments of *Coffea arabica* is reported on top of a layer dated to 1740 B.P. In addition, the site of Kumali with abundant botanical remains represented a good

example of the possibility of plant preservation in humid areas (Hildebrand *et al.*, 2010:284).

1.8 ETHNO ARCHAEOLOGICAL STUDIES ON PLANT FOOD UTILIZATION: REVIEW OF THE RESEARCH

Contrary to the strong warning of Harlan (1969) and the applauded comment forwarded by Costantini (1990:188), focus on the study of crop production and exploitation and ethno-archaeology has been extremely minimal. Both of these authors explained the potentials of the region in its botanical resources and diversity. Harlan in his alerting statements stated that we have to tap the virginity of Ethiopian highlands for the study of agricultural origins and crop diversity before it disappears due to the effects of modernization. Costantini, on the other hand, stressed the phytogeographical potentials of "Nubo Sindian and Eritro-Arabian provinces." Specifically on ethno archaeological documentations of plant food utilizations and related subjects, researches were conducted by D'Andrea *et al.*, (1999), Hildebrand (2003), Lyons and D'Andrea (2003), Daniel (2004) and Abawa (2009). In the paragraphs ahead a review of these researches is presented.

D'Andrea *et al.* (1999) undertook ethnoarchaeological study of traditional farming systems in Northern Ethiopia, Tigrai Regional State, on a small farming community at a locality called Adi Ainawalid, Northwest of Mekelle. The objectives of their study were observing features of traditional farming activities with the intention of formulating testable models of the characterstics and evolution of ancient farming communities in the area. Interview and observation of crop processing of some cereals and legumes, documenting domestic architecture and craft technology were the methods they employed in their study. These approaches were expected to shed light on the impact of crop processing activities on the composition of archaeobotanical assemblages and general observation of site formation processes for a better assessment and interpretation of the evidence. The study indicated that the temporary nature of kitchen buildings and the presence of portable stoves at Adi Ainawalid resulted in limited and fragmentary accumulations of charred plant residues in living quarters. In addition, charred plant body parts that can be preserved in residential areas are results of sweeping and discarding (D'Andrea *et al.*, 1999: 101-122).

Apart from interest in traditional farming practices and archaeobotany, their project had an objective to contribute a share on the preservation of biodiversity. They emphasized that due to natural and anthropogenic impacts, the traditional farming system in Northern Ethiopia is under threat. Unless efforts are quickly made in land race preservation, crop germ plasm and indigenous knowledge of farmers about plants are greatly diminishing and vanishing (ibid. 104).

On the basis of Ethno-archaeological approaches, Hildebrand (2003:242) studied wild plants in Southwest Ethiopia which the local people are still utilizing with the objective of understanding the subsistence calendar of the society and looking for possible scenarios that could lead to the utilization of the resources. She stated that some farmers use wild Yams by replanting the species in their agricultural plots and this process might be the first stage towards the domestication of the plant. In the final analysis Hildebrand single out climate, environment and seasonality as push factors that may lead to plant domestication in Southwestern Ethiopia.

Lyons and D'Andrea (2003) conducted an ethnoarchaeo-logical comparative study on the use of ovens and griddles and the preservation of gluten ingredients in bread. A griddle is a large circular utensil made of ceramic. This cooking utencil is very commonly used in Ethiopia and Eritrea for baking bread and 'injera'. In their study Lyons and D'Andrea argued that African indigeneous crops like sorghum, *tef*, finger millet and pearl millet lack gluten substances unlike wheat and barley. Griddle cooking practice seems to have created a favorable condition for the long preservation of wheat and barley. Based on analysis of technology and cousine, they proposed that before the introduction of Middle Eastern crops, indigenous plants were already in use in the highlands of Ethiopia. The absence of evidence in the archaeobotanical record can be explained in terms of griddle cooking practices that favor the preservation of wheat and barley over African cereals (Lyons and D'Andrea 2003:515)

An Ethnoarchaeological study on the production and use of Niger seed or *noog* (*Guizotia abyssinica* (L.) Cass.) *and mech* (Guizotia scabra (Vis.) Chiov), its probable wild form, was conducted by Daniel (2004: 7-91). The purpose of the study was to understand the beginning of traditional agricultural system in highland Ethiopia. The study has recorded the technological, cultural, economic and social aspects related to this oil plant. The research has revealed that the tools used in the processing of the plant do not show evidence for the presence of noog in the archaeological record. The charring experiment demonstrate that noog require a lower temperature than

most plants demand which is between 250 to 350°C under oxidized atmosphere and 300 to 350°C under reduced condition (low oxygen exposure).

In an attempt to have an idea on the origin of agriculture in Ethiopia, Abawa (2009:74-84), studied the cultivation of *tef* in Gojjam highlands of Northwestern Ethiopia based on ethno archaeological methods. Through the ethnographic study, he documented the processes involved in the cultivation and consumption of *tef*. He has also compared the processes observed in *tef* with other major cereals growing in the region. The result of the research demonstrate that there are deep rooted cultural and ritual practices associated with the cultivation of *tef* and that these firmly established cultural and ritual aspects on indigenous edible plants of Ethiopia predate the introduction of crops from outside.

1.9 METHODS

The first work for the compilation of this volume started by the study of pot sherds stored in the Archaeology Laboratory of the University of Naples "L'Orientale", *Departmento di Studi e Ricerche su Africa e Paesi Arabi* (Department of African and Arabian studies) using x 10 magnifying glass. In due course more than thirty one thousand pot fragments from the sites of AAS1, AAS2 (*Amm Adam station),* from excavation units KI, KII, KVI at Mahal Teglinos (K1), EG3, JM2 (close to the *Jebel Mokram), KG5, KG16, KG23, KG93, KG96,* (in the area of *Kashim el-Girba)* and *SEG11, SEG42* (with in *Shurab el-Gash*) were examined. The Mahal Teglinos collections are results of excavations whereas the rest are all surface collections from surveys. Further investigation of the samples with plant impressions using high power microscope was conducted at Bio-archaeological Research Centre, National Museum of Oriental Art, Rome, Italy. In the same laboratory grains and fruit stones (n=742), soil samples (ca. 6 kilos) and more fragments of pot sherds (n=1023) from previous field seasons (1980-1995) were analysed as components of the research.

This was followed by ethnographic studies of pottery making groups in Northwest Ethiopia and in Kassala, Eastern Sudan. The final step of the data collection process was test excavation at Mahal Teglinos, Kassala and survey at Kassala and the nearby localities (the details of these data acquisition processes are presented under sections 1.9.1 and 1.9.2, 1.9.3 and 1.9.4 below). The ethnographic studies are compiled in chapter II. The result of the archaeobotanical work is presented in chapter IV, VI and VIII whereas, chapter VII summarizes the survey and excavation works conducted in Eastern Sudan.

1.9.1 Archaeobotany

As stated above the archaeobotany work was done in the Archaeology Laboratory of the University of Naples "L'Orientale" and at Bio-archaeological Research Centre of the *Museo Nationale di Orientale.* In these two laboratories, all the systematic works of quantifying, screening, analyzing with low power magnifying glass and Stereo microscope, making temporary and permanent casts, sieving soil samples and comparing the botanical specimen with comparative plant collections were completed.

1.9.1.1 *Identification of grain\seed impressions*

The identification process was consisting of the following steps:

1. Drawing the positions of the impressions using pencil and paper;

2. Making temporary casts for a short term analysis of the samples using Das, black which is permanently soft even after long exposure to air;

3. Permanent cast was done with Das, white air hardening modeling material;

4. Taking pictures of the impressions using scanning electron microscope, SEM;

5. Comparing the identified impressions using photographic data base and real seed collections for a possible scientific nomenclature up to genus and species levels. For photographic comparison references like, the *Digital Seed Atlas of the Netherlands*, *An Illustrated Taxonomy Manual of Weed Seeds* (Delorit, 1970) and *Manual for Testing Agricultural and vegetable Seeds* (Agriculture Hand Book N0. 30, 1952) were consulted;

6. Dry sieving was used for recovering botanical remains from soil samples using 2.8 mm, 2 mm, 1 mm, 0.5 mm and 0.25 mm mesh sizes. The utilization of various mesh sizes helped to recover plant remains ranging from macro to micro;

7. To calculate and measure the dimensions of grain/seed/ fruit stone impressions a Leica Qwin soft ware is used. The name Leica Qwin is used both for the machine (microscope, Leica MST39) and the program (the soft ware). Calculating the size of the imprints helped us to notice differences among the wild, cultivated and domesticated varieties.

For samples which are not impressions, like the fruit stones, the stages of analysis were relatively easy. However, step 4 and 5 were common for all.

1.9.2 Ethno-archaeological Approach

In Ethiopia, two sites were selected in Northwestern most point where there are group of people who still practice pot making as an occupation and these are the only available sites in relative proximity to the Gash Delta archaeological sites from where the archaeobotanical data is collected. Ethnographic and ethnobotanic studies were conducted at four localities: *Akatin* and *Grathitsa* within the *Salaklaka* Administrative locality and *Adrar* and *Kushet Adrar* within *Indabaguna* local administration. In these sites the whole process of pottery making, from clay extraction to manufacturing stages were documented in field notes and photographs, GPS coordinates were taken, individual and group interviews were also conducted. The same process was repeated in the ethnographic and ethnobotanic study of the site of pottery production at Reba, in the outskirt of the city of Kassala in Eastern Sudan.

1.9.2.1 *Interview*

At *Akatin*, in addition to on site observation of the pottery making process, individual and group interview was also conducted. The group interview was consisting of me and three other women pot makers. The same process was also undertaken at *Kushet* and *Kushet Adrar*. At the last two sites, participants in the interview were four sisters who practice the same occupation. At the site of Reba a group interview was made with four men pot makers. The participants shared extensive information on clay types, temper materials or inclusions, pots, and some locally available plant species which they use during the process of manufacturing of pottery (for burning and burnishing) as well as the edible crops that they grow for consumption and market purposes. This led to an appreciation of their indigenous knowledge of botanical resources.

The coordinates of all of the sites studied, especially major reference points like excavation site, clay extraction sites, manufacturing sites and market centers were taken in 3D (latitude, longitude and altitude) using Garmini 225 W GPS instrument. Besides, almost each and every Stage of the pottery making process and the excavation process was documented with digital camera.

1.9.3 Survey

The survey that was conducted at Kassala and the nearby localities was based on the information acquired from the antiquity officers of the National Corporation for Antiquities and Museums, Khartoum. An intensive survey was made in four different localities and samples that manifested plant impressions were collected for further analysis.

1.9.4 Test Excavation

The site for excavation at Mahal Teglinos, Kassala, was selected due to observation of large exposed baked clay full of vegetal remains brought to light by wind and endangered of destruction if not rescued. At first the site was suspected to be a fire place. Later, after excavation, it was possible to see that it was an accumulation of baked clay originally plastering a storage pit, as no evidence of burned material was recovered. Levels were set using total station. The total size of the excavation spot was two meters by two meters at the beginning and this was reduced to a meter by two to expose the target. A total of 70 centimetres deep was excavated and two living floors were distinguished separated by soft sandy soil. The upper living floor, badly eroded, was related to the storage pit. To recover macrobotanical and faunal remains, soil from each stratigraphic layer was sieved using 0.5 mm mesh size. Findings were counted and samples were taken for analysis.

1.10 OBJECTIVE AND SIGNIFICANCE OF THE STUDY

The archaeobotanical analysis of the pottery collections and soil samples from Eastern Sudan and the ethnographic and ethnobotanic study of women pot makers from Northwest Ethiopia and men pot makers from Eastern Sudan have the following basic objectives:

1. Re-construction of the subsistence pattern of the pre-historic inhabitants of the area;

2. Reconstruction of the vegetation history of the study area;

3. To see the continuity of plant food utilization from the pre-historic times to the present;

4. To observe the prevailing environmental condition from about 6,000 years B.C. (mid-Holocene) to ca. 200/300 A.D. and compare this with the present day environment;

5. To document indigenous knowledge on botanical resources using ethnobotanical methods and use this asset for conservation of the natural heritages and comment on other advantages of the herbal resources. Documenting genetic diversity is crucial since the loss of biodiversity through deforestation, land degradation, erosion, resettlement and political instability has recently reached a climax.

Chapter II
AN APPROACH TO THE PREHISTORIC SETTING: ETHNO-ARCHAEOLOGY IN NORTHWEST ETHIOPIA AND NORTHEAST SUDAN

The variability in the physical geography of Ethiopia has resulted in different climatic zones in the country, which has an enormous implication for plant diversity and human adaptation. This idea is well expressed by Stemler and Harlan in their publication of 1977 (446-460).

> The country known to us as Ethiopia is an anomaly on the African Continent. Ethiopia's historical heartland is the home of Monophystic Christian kingdoms and Semitic Amhara cultivators of wheat, barley, and *teff (Eragrostis tef (Zucc.) Trotter)*. It is a cool highland plateau bounded by the Great Rift Valley, warm mid-elevation highlands, hot savannas, and lowland desert. The contrast in natural environments in Ethiopia is paralleled by contrast in economic systems and human cultures (Stemler and Harlan 1977: 446).

2.1 NORTHWEST ETHIOPIA, ETHNO-ARCHAEOLOGY AT *SALAKLAKA*

An ethnoarchaeological field study was conducted at *Salaklaka*, an administrative territory in Tigrai Regional State (Region -1) some 35 kilometers to the northwest of the historical city of Aksum or around an hour and half drive from it. *Salaklaka* is selected for the study because the area is known historically for centuries as home of women potters which had been their major occupation.

The other reason why *Salaklaka* was selected is due to its relative proximity to the Eastern Sudan from which I have been studying archaeobotanical analysis of plant impressions on potteries and seeds and fruit stones from soil samples. The objective of conducting the ethnographic study is to understand and pin point the various stages in which plant impressions could be formed in the process of manufacturing pottery. Two localities namely *Akatit* and *Grat hitsa* were chosen for

the simple reason of availability of women who still practise traditional pottery making.

2.1.1 *Akatit*

Akatit is situated at 14°.06.000 North latitude and 038°.28.912 East longitude. The elevation of the area is 2005 meters above sea level (m.a.s.l.) accuracy being 17.2 meters. The area is surrounded by high mountains which could range in elevation between 2600 to 2900 m.a.s.l. Granite stones, out of which, almost all of the houses of the local inhabitants made, is the dominant rock type of the area. The same stone type is observed across Northwest Ethiopia all the way to the Eastern part of the Sudan, Kassala. Piles of granite stones have been observed at Aksum, Shire and Kassala areas (Beldados 2004: 46-47, Constatini *et al.,* 1982: 17). Aksumite obelisks, one of the nine world heritage sites recorded by UNESCO for Ethiopia, are carved out of granite stones.

Tef (Eragrostis tef) is the dominant cereal that grows in the area. It is also the most preferred staple crop for the inhabitants at *Salaklaka*. Other than *tef,* maize (*Zea mays*) and *dagussa* (local name) or finger millet (*Eleusine coracana*) are the crop types that are under cultivation in the locality. The two Middle Eastern domesticates wheat (*Triticum dicocum/monoccocum*) and barley (*Hordeum vulgare*) seems to be absent in this area. All of my informants told me that they do not cultivate wheat and barley. *Zigba* tree (*Podocarpus gracilior*), *Gulo* (*Ricinus L. euphorbiaceae*), *kinchib* (*Anogeissus leiocarpus*) also grow in the area.

I have conducted a group interview at *Akatin*. Participants of the interview were *Weizero* Roman Hailesilasse and *Weizero* Workalem Biruh. Both of them inherit pot making from their mothers. As in other parts of Ethiopia, pot making is the task of women. What is unique in this area is that pot making is not a despised occupation.

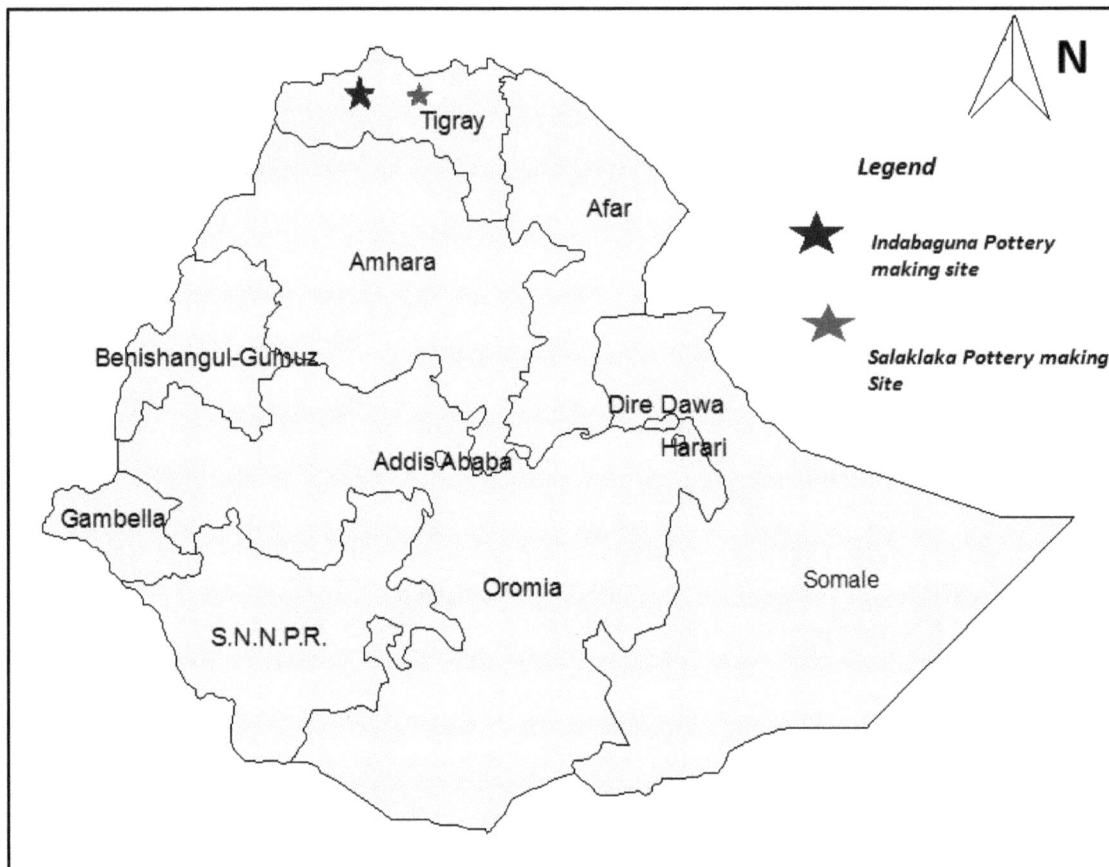

Figure 2.1 A map showing Salaklaka and Indabaguna, Tigrai Regional State

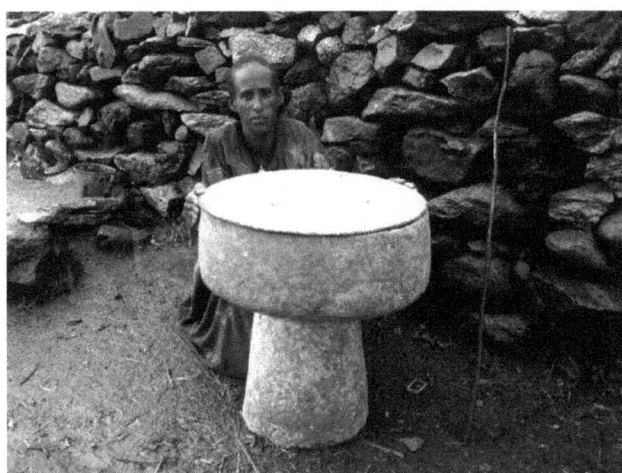

Figure 2.2 Picture showing mesob
(a container made of clay soil and straw)

In this particular site clay is molded to make different utensils which are important for home use; griddles, big and small jars, cooking pots, Coffee pots, incense burners, vessels, big and small storages containers and *Mesob*[1] (see the figure 2.2). While making the pottery, they use two different types of clay soils, the black and

[1] Mesob is a container for baked bread and 'injera' made of clay soil and straw at Salaklaka and Indaabaguna localities of Tigrai Regional State. In other parts of Ethiopia this container is made out of dried straw only.

white clay soils as they call it. According to them, both of the clay soils have their own characters in the making. The white clay consists of two-third of the mix while the black constitutes the remaining one-third. For the question why the proportion of the white clay is larger than the black, they explained that if the black soil is larger in proportion, the pot will break easily. For them the white clay is naturally sticky and strong. However, I have been able to observe that the white soil has a good proportion of sand particles to the extent that they were not expected to add extra inclusions. The source of the black clay soil is a kilometer away whereas to get the white clay soil they have to travel up to four to five kilometers.

2.1.2 *Grathitsa* Site

Grathitsa is a locality within *Salaklaka*. It is situated at 14°.1147 latitude and 38°.4811 longitudes. The elevation of the area is 2004 m.a.s.l. accuracy being 23.5 meters. In and around the site crops like *Ater bahir* (*Vicia faba*) and *Tef (Eragrotis tef*) grow for consumption and for market.

Weizero Hiwot Gebre Maryam, forty one, has been practicing pot making for the last twenty years. She acquired the knowledge of pot making from an old woman living in the same village. *Weizero* Hiwot make griddles, big and small jars, cooking pots of various sizes and coffee pots for household use and for market. For the making of these utensils they use two types of clay soils, red clay and white clay. The source area of the white clay is at the top of a nearby hill which is an hour and half away on foot whereas the red clay soil is ten minutes walk from the manufacturing area.

Firing the griddle is done using cattle dung (the same practice is observed in the ethnographic case study at Kassala) and using plants available in the area like *Agam (Carissa edulis), Koslet (Zizyphus sp.), Lahay (Acacia lahai), Tahses (Dodonea viscosa), kelmit (Cadaba rotundifolia).*

2.1.3 Ethnography at *Indaabaguna*

Indabaguna is an administrative territory within the Tigrai Regional state. It is 20 kilometers to the west of Shire Administrative Zone. It is dominantly inhabited by the Kunama people. The Kunama are dominantly pastoralists and they settled in a relatively lowlying area. Other than Tigrigna, the language of the region, they speak their own different language called Kunama or Kunamigna. Within *Indabaguna* two sites were selected for ethnographic study namely, *Adrar* and *Kushet Adrar* based on the presence of women who still practise traditional pot making.

2.1.3.1 *The Site of* Adrar

The site of *Adrar* is located within 13°.9539 latitude and 38°.1805 longitudes. The elevation of the area is 1777 m.a.s.l accuracy being 16.2 meters. In the area finger millet (*Eleusine coracana*), tef (*Eragrotis tef*), *Ater*/Pea (*Pisum sativum*), Noog/Niger Seed (*Guizotia abyssinica*), *Selit (Amh.)/Intatii (Tig.) (Salvia merjamie)* grow as food and cash crops. But, wheat and barley are not growing at *Adrar*.

At Adrar *wizero* Nigisti Haftishyimer and her family are the only pot makers. She is forty two years old. She and her sisters inherited the tradition of pot making from their mother who in turn acquired this knowledge from her mother. *Weizero* Nigisti has been in this occupation for the last thirty years. The mother of *Weizero* Nigisti who is seventy years old now still practise pot making.

Weizero Nigisti makes griddle, big jar, cooking pot and coffee pot for both house hold use and market. The clay source is at a place called *Guwita* one hour away from where she lives. She uses three different types of clay: the black, the red and the white. Here, meshed sand particles are added as inclusions to give strength to the pot. While making a stand (a case for cooking pot and storage facility), she uses straw, a by-product of *tef* to add reinforcement (see figure 2.3).

The baking of the pots id done using cattle dung and straw. Burnishing/smoothening for big jars is made by kinchib (*Anogeissus leiocarpus,* see picture of this plant under section 4.2), digwidiguna (*Lannea fruticosa*) (a plant species collected from the nearby low lying plain, desert like environment), flour of finger millet (the use of the flour of finger millet is unique to *Indabaguna*). Burnishing of the griddle is done by *Adri (Brassica carinata),* Gulo (*Ricinus communis*), *selit (Salvia merjamie),* noog (Guizotia *abyssinica*).

2.1.3.2 Kushet Adrar

Kushet Adrar, also known as *Tabia Lemlem,* is the second site within *Indabaguna* where ethnographic study was conducted. It is situated within 13°.9567 latitude and 38°.1683 longitude. The elevation of the area is 1808 m.a.s.l. with the accuracy of 34.3 meters. The vegetation of the area is consists of *Gaba (Zizyphus spina-christi), Ahwi (Cordia africana),* metere (*Buddleja polystachya*), *Agam (Carissa edulis),* Ch'ea (*Acacia albida,* A. *tortilis,* A. *amythetophylla*), *Am-amgemel (Heliotropium ovalifolium),* Momona (*Acacia albida*), *Kulkwal (Euphorbia abyssinica).* In the nearby there is a river called *Mayet* which flows all round the year. Peasants in the surrounding grow finger millet *(Eleusine coracana),* sorghum (*Sorghum durra*), maize (*Zea mays*), different species of *tef (Eragrostis tef),* Noog (*Guizotia abyssinica*), Intati (*Salvia merjamie\Liniumusitatissimus*), *Ater (Pissum sativum), Ater bahir (Vicia faba), Ayni ater (Pissum sativum),* berbere\Peper *(Capsicum abyssinicum)* for market and household consumption. Wheat does not grow in this area whereas barley is rarely sown and cultivated.

Figure 2.3 A standing case for cooking pot and storage facility (a and b)

At *Kusht Adrar/Tabia Lemlem* the pot makers interviewed were sisters; Atsede Habtishyimer, 25 and Letecheal Habtishyimer, 28. Both of them were sisters of *Weizero* Nigisti residing in the different locality of Adrar. They have been engaged in this occupation since childhood. They make cooking pots, griddles, coffee pots and jars for household use and for market. Here also three different types of clay soils are used (the black, the red and the white). All of these clay soils are found within a maximum of 20 minutes walk radius from the settlement and manufacturing site. The manufacturing area is 4 to 5 metres in front of their house.

Firing is done by covering the pots with dried cattle and donkey dung. Burnishing of jars and cooking utensils is done with *Kinchib* (*Anogeissus leiocarpus*), flour of finger millet (*Eleusine coracana*) and *Digwidiguna* (*Lannea fruticosa*) and for griddles with by *Gulo* (*Ricinus communis*) and *Adri* (*Brassica carinata*).

2.2 POSSIBILITIES FOR THE OCCURRENCE OF PLANT IMPRESSIONS

The following six points on the possibilities of the occurrence of plant impressions on pottery are result of ethnographic observation at *Salaklaka* and *Indabaguna*:

1. Plant seeds or parts of plant bodies could be collected together with the clay soil. The clay source areas at *Salaklaka*, for instance, are found within relatively forested places;

Figure 2.5 Pottery in the process of manufacturing on a surface full of plant residues (a and b)

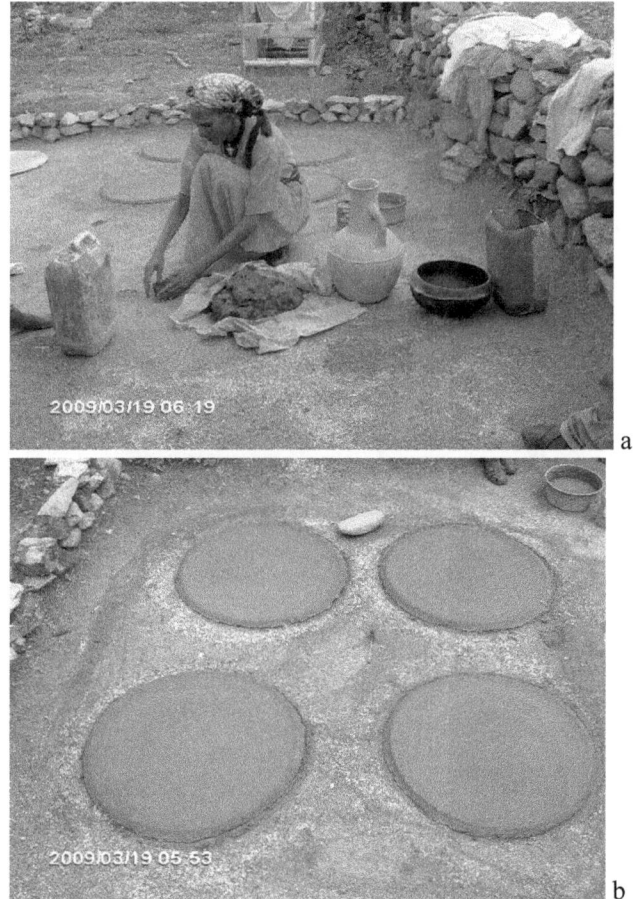

Figure 2.4 Clay Soil extraction

2. Plant impressions could also occur in the manufacturing plot during the process of making pots and especially when the pot is in a wet stage. At the site of *Akatin* there were by-products of *tef* (*Eragrostis tef*) on the surface of the manufacturing plot (see figure 2.5);

3. Another possibility by which plant impressions could occur is during the process of firing the pots. In both sites at *Salaklaka* they use plant items that are dry

enough and that are found in the surrounding to fire the pots. These plant species include *Agam* (*Carissa idulis*), *Kosli* (*Zizyphus sp.*), *Lahay* (*Acacia lahai*), *Tahses* (*Dodonea viscosa*) and *Kelmit* (*Cadaba rotundifolia*). In addition they use dried cattle dung. The by-products of *tef* (*Eragrostis tef*) are used to ignite the fire. These plants and the ceramic firing process are demonstrated below in figure 2.6;

4. Burnishing could also result in impressions in plant bodies. At *Akatin* different plants are used for burnishing different utensils made of clay. The small and big jars, for instance, are burnished using a plant called *Kinchib* (*Anogeissus leiocarpus*) Griddles are burnished using *Gulo* (*Ricinus Communis*) and *Gomen Zer* (*Erucastrum abyssinicum*). The same species are used for burnishing in Gondar area, Amhara Regional State (Region -3) to the Southwest of Tigrai. Cooking pots are also burnished by *Gomen Zer* (See the part on the biological characteristics of plants that could result in impression);

5. Plant impressions could also occur during the time of production. When some clay utensils are made plant materials are deliberately applied to add strength. This is the case in the production of large storage facilities and *mesobs* (a container for *injera*). At *Salaklaka*, in both of the sites in which ethnographic study was

Figure 2.6 Pictures taken from a ceramic burning site at Salaklaka (a to d)

conducted, by- products of *tef*/straw are added for re-enforcement. In traditional iron smelting sites where they use a furnace for smelting the iron, the furnace is made using clay, mud and straw. After manufacturing the external parts of the storage facilities the containers are often smoothened from time to time to avoid cracks by wet animal dung. It is quite possible that plants consumed by the cattle could be an additional means of impressions while smoothening the container;

6. Sometimes the clay will be covered by textiles or broad plant leaves and is kept for a long period of time (up to a year) for a usage at another time. Here, also it creates a possibility for the occurrence of plant impressions either from the leaves used to cover the wet clay or from other sources. Wetness increases the probability of getting impressions.

2.3 PLANTS THAT MAY RESULT IN IMPRESSION: PHYTOGEOGRAPHICAL, MORPHOLOGICAL AND CYTOGENETIC OBSERVATION

The ethnographic study conducted at *Salaklaka* and *Indabaguna* helped to select plant species that could possibly result in impression. Plants like *Agam* (*Carissa idulis*), *Kosli* (*Zizyphus spina-christi*), *Lahay* (*Acacia lahai*), *Tahses* (*Dodonea Viscosa*), *tef* (*Eragrostis tef*) and *kelmit* (*Cadaba rotundifolia*) were commonly utilized in the four localities for baking of the molded clay while

making pottery. Whereas, plants that are used for burnishing/smoothening are Kinchib (*Anogeissus leiocarpus*), Gulo (*Ricinus communis*), Adri (Tg.) or *gomen zer* (Am.) (*Brassica carinata*), Digwidiguna (*Lannea fruticosa*), Intati (Tg.) or *Teliba* (Am.) (*Salvia merjamie*), selit (*Sesamum indicum*), Noog (*Guizotia abyssinica*).

2.4 PLANT SPECIES USED FOR FIRING POTS

2.4.1 *Lahai (Acacia lahai steud.* and *Hochst)*

Acacia lahai steud. and *Hochst.* (figure 2.7), *lahay* (Tg.) or *Tikur girar* (Am.) is a species within the Fabaceae family. It is a small tree which varies in size between 2.5 and 4 meters high. It is a spreading shrub in most parts of the highlands of Ethiopia. The conducive environmental horizon for this species is the altitudinal range of 1800 and 2500 m.a.s.l. with in the tropics. It has long stipular spines, yellowish bark which shallowly fissure, inflorescence yellow spike and yellowish flowers. Around Adwa, Aksum and Shire Inde sillasie (major cities within Tigrai Regional State), the tree is part of the remnant of the natural vegetation (Tadesse 1991).

2.4.2 *Dodonea viscosa*

Tahses (Tig.), *Kitkita* (Amh.) is a species within the Sapindaceae family (Kelecha 1977). The origin of this plant is considered to be Australia, New Zealand and the tropical parts of the world. It is a small tree which is

Figure 2.7 Acacia lahai steud. *and* Hochst

Figure 2.9 Carissa edulis

between 3.5 to 4.5 meters tall. The leaves are often linear and glossy on the average 5-12 cms long and 1-2 cms wide. There are many varieties of this species. Out of the diverse varieties the green ones are more cold resistant than the red-yellowish viscosa plants. On the average the frost resistance of this species can vary between 15 to 26°F (Herbareum archives, AAU). At *Salaklaka*, ethnographic site of *Grathitsa*, this plant species is used to bake the pottery together with other plant species.

Figure 2.8 Dodonea viscosa

2.4.3 *Carissa edulis*

Agam (in Amh. and Tig.) is a plant in Apocynaceae family (Kelecha 1977). A shrub, 1-3 meters high, mostly dark green in color. It has paired thorns and leaves are elliptical in shape. The fruits are dark when ripe and are between 5 to 7 mm in diameter. They grow along rivers and hill sides. The branches are sometimes used to construct fences (Herbareum archives, AAU). At *Grathitsa* ethnographic site, in Tigrai *Carissa edulis* is used for baking the wet clay (figure 2.9).

2.4.4 Eragrostis *tef*
Gramineae (family) → Eragrostideae (subfamily) → *Eragrostis* (Genus) →*tef* (species)

There are about 350 species of *tef* in tropical and sub-tropical areas of the world. It is an annual or perennial plant. It grows as a cereal crop only in Ethiopia and is cultivated throughout the country up to an altitudinal range of 2500 m. Because of the variety and similarity of many species Eragrostis is a difficult genus to name. A more credible identification of this genus is based on the observation of spikelet disarticulation. E. Pilosa is accepted to be the wild progenitor of the cultivated cereal *tef* (Hedberg and Edwards, 1995: 110). There are almost no data on the domestication history of *tef*. It is, however, assumed that *tef* was most probably domesticated in the highlands of Ethiopia because of the distribution of its wild ancestors. Experiments demonstrate that there is an overlap in grain sizes in wild and domesticated forms and both cannot survive charring at 300°C (D'Andrea 2008). In many pottery making sites throughout Ethiopia, pottery is fired using straw or by-products of *tef*. In addition, it is also used as a strengthening component while storage facilities are made from clay soil.

2.4.5 *Zizyphus sp.*

Kosli (Tig.) *kitel* (Amh.) is a generic name in both languages for all varieties of leaves. Zizyphus is a genus that has about 40 species. It is a herb within the rhamnaceae family. These varieties grow in warm temperate and in sub-tropical areas. The leaves are deciduous for some species and evergreen for some others. They can also be between 4 to 6 cms long. Fruits can be red, brown or black with 1 to 1.5 cms in diameter. They are sometimes edible (El Amin 1990: 295). *Zizyphus* and its variety of species are commonly used for firing pottery in both sites where ethnographic study is conducted. It is also used as a source of fire for baking *injera* and other food staffs (for more characterstics of this species see chapter VI).

Table 2.1. A table showing plants used for burning pots across sites

No.	Plant types	*Akatit*	*Grat hitsa*	*Adrar*	*Kushet Adrar*
1	*Acacia lahai steud. and Hochst*		√		
2	*Dodonea viscose*		√		
3	*Carissa edulis*		√		
4	*Eragrostis tef*	√	√	√	√
5	*Zizyphus spina Christi*	√	√	√	√
6	*Cadaba rotundifolia*	√	√		

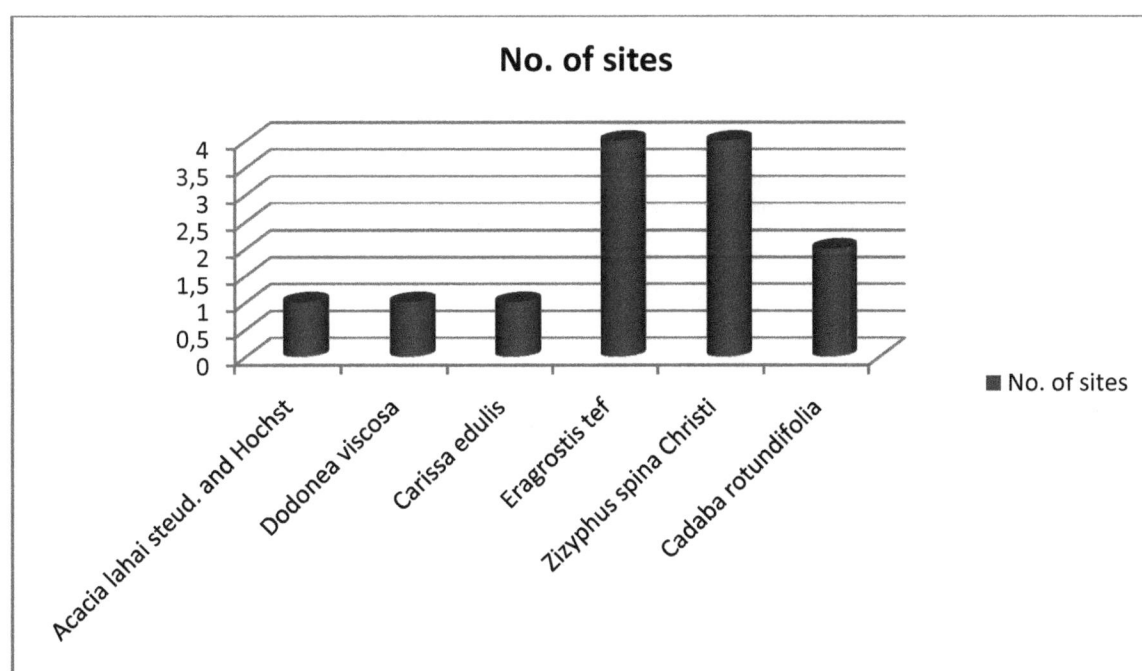

*Figure 2.10 A graph showing the number of sites where the different locally
available plant species are used for firing their pots*

*Table 2.2 A table showing the number of sites that used
locally available plant species for firing
their pots*

No.	Plant types	No. of sites
1	*Acacia lahai steud. and Hochst*	1
2	*Dodonea viscose*	1
3	*Carissa edulis*	1
4	*Eragrostis tef*	4
5	*Zizyphus spina Christi*	4
6	*Cadaba rotundifolia*	2

2.4.6 *Cadaba rotundifolia*

Kelmit (Tig.) is a plant of tropical East Africa within the Capparidaceae family. It is a shrub with many branches. It can grow up to 2.5 meters tall. Leaves are commonly elliptical and are between 3 to 3.8 cms long and 2.5 to 3.5 cms wide. Fruits are cylindrical in shape and are up to 5 cms long and 6 mm wide. The color of the plant ranges between green and light brown. (Elffers *et al.*, 1964:1). *Cadaba rotundifolia* is recognised as a toxic plant that can cause liver and kidney damage, diarrhea and salivation as well.

2.5 PLANTS SPECIES USED FOR BURNISHING

2.5.1 *Brassica carinata*

Brassica carinata (figure 2.11) locally known as *adri* (Tg.) or *gomen zer* (Am.) is a species within Brassicaceae family. It is a herb, 30-150 cm tall. Seeds are between 1to 1.5 mm and are dark brown. It grows in many parts of the tropics, Africa, Asia and America. The altitudinal range in which this plant grows is between 1350 and 2600 meters in Ethiopia. Both the leaves and the seeds of the plant are important. The leaves *gomen* (Amh.) can be consumed cooked as a vegetable whereas, the seeds *gomen zer* (Amh.) are used to oil the griddle while making injera. The plant has about 370 genera and 3500

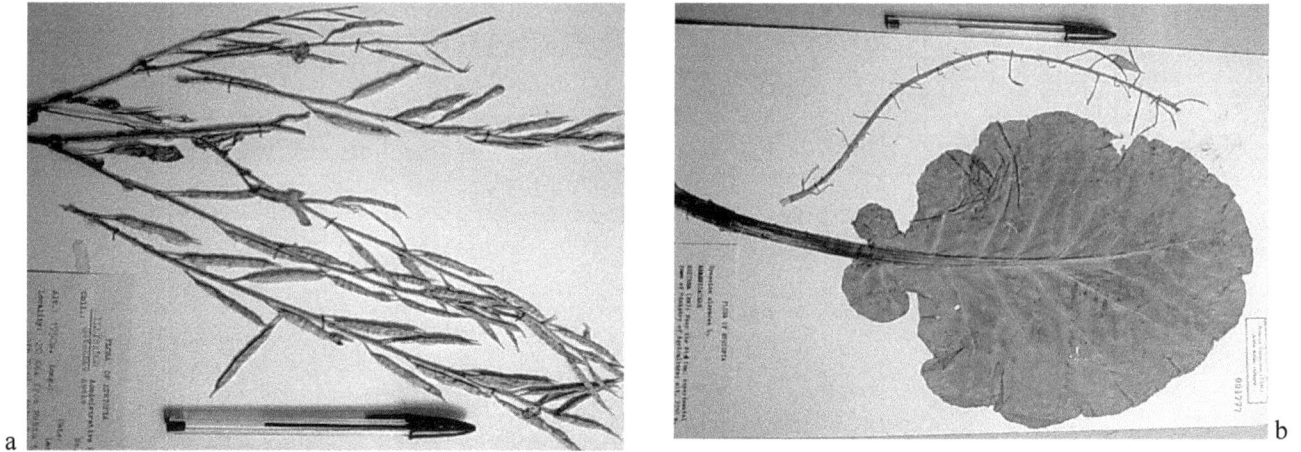

Figure 2.11 Brassica Carinata *(a. the seed and b. the leaf)*

species in general growing in the Meditterranean area, Asia and some parts of North America (Jonsell, 1983, 45-47).

2.5.2 *Ricinus communis*

Ricinus communis is a species within the Euphorbiaceae family, *Gulo* (Amh.). It is classified as a shrub within the tropics and a herb when it is adventive in the temperate region. The male plant has more branches than the female. The stem of the plant can grow up to 5 meters tall. When the plant ripes, it explodes, open and drops its seeds. The seed has a high degree of oil content, it can be used as a lubricant and as a medicine. Both the seed and the leaf of this plant can be used in the burnishing and smoothening of pottery. The seed mixed with the seeds of cotton is used for burnishing whereas the leaf is used for both smoothening and decorating/painting the pottery (Willis, 1973: 998).

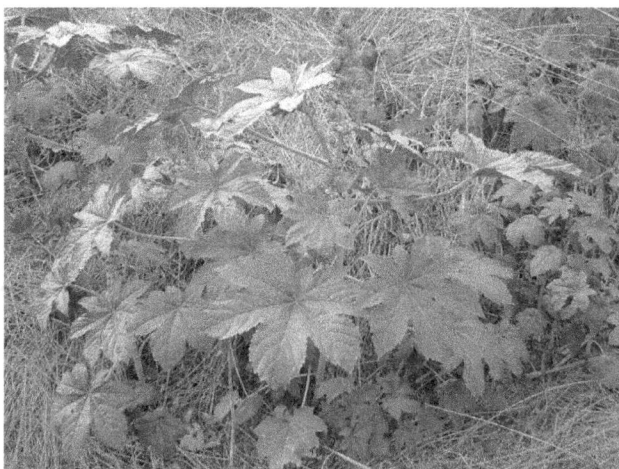

Figure 2.12 Ricinus communis
(Photo: Wikepedia Free Encyclopedia)

2.5.3 *Salvia merjamie*

Intatii (Tig.) and *Teliba* (Amh.) is a plant in the Labiatae family (Willis 1973:1022). It is a perennial herb. This plant might be indigenous to the highlands of East Africa, stretching from the Ethiopian highlands in the north to Tanzania in the south. It also grows in Yemen on the other side of the Red Sea. The altitudinal preference of this species ranges between 1800 to 3900 m.a.s.l. The species name merjamie is taken from the Arabian name of the plant *meriyamiye (http://en.wikipedia.org/wiki/ Salvia_merjamie)*. Salvia merjamie can grow up to 0.6 to 0.8 meters tall. The leaves are basal and possess hairs on both surfaces. The leaves are 2 inches wide and 6 inches long. It is an oil plant. Pot makers at *Grathitsa, Adrar* and *Kushet Adrar* ethnographic sites use *Salvia merjamie* for burnishing or smoothing their products.

Figure 2.13 Salvia merjamie

2.5.4 *Anogeissus leiocarpus*

Kinchib (Tig.) or *Anogeissus leiocarpus* is a plant within the combretaceae family (Kelecha, 1977). It is an evergreen tall tree indigenous to the savanna grass lands of tropical Africa. It often grows at the edge of the rainforest or along riverbanks. This plant is common in Cameroon and Senegal in West Africa and in the highlands of Ethiopia in east Africa. It grows within the altitudinal range of 500 to 2000 m.a.s.l. This plant can grow up to 30 meters tall. Leaves are elliptical in shape and are between 3-8 cms long and 1-3.5 cms wide. Fruits are reddish brown and yellowish, 5-7 mm long and 6-10 cms across. The wood is used for construction, firewood and charcoal. The gum is used to glue materials together. The leaves and bark are used as dye in fabric (Herbareum archives, AAU). In all of the four pottery making sites the gum is probably utilized to burnish the pot. It has a very strong sticky substance (figure 2.14).

Figure 2.14 picture of Kinchib (Anogeissus leiocarpus) *long utilized for burnishing pots at Indabaguna*

2.5.5 Lannea *fruticosa*

Digwidiguna (Tig.) is a species within the Anacardiaceae family. It is a savanna tree that can grow as tall as 8 meters. The bark is dark grey and black in color. Flowers are often yellowish and grow usually before the leaves (Herbareum archives, AAU). According to my informants in Northern Ethiopia, this plant species is used to burnish pots during the process of manufacturing.

2.5.6 *Sesamum indicum*

Selit (in both Amh. and Tig.) is a species within Pedaliaceae family. This plant is indigenous to sub-Saharan Africa. It also grows in a relatively smaller number in India. Archaeological evidence demonstrates that this plant was first domesticated in Southern India and there are indications that the plant was cultivated in the Indus Valley between 2250 and 1750 B.C. (Bedigian 2003: 17-36). The flowers of this plant can be yellow, purple and blue. *Sesamum indicum* grows annually to 50 to 100 cms tall. Leaves can be between 5 to 15 cms in length and up to 5 cms broad. This plant has very rich oil seeds. The seeds can have white and dark black color. In pottery making sites of Salaklaka, this plant is used for burnishing pots in the process of manufacturing.

2.5.7 *Guizotia abyssinica*

Guizotia abyssinica or *noog/nug* (Amh.) is one of the major indigenous, edile crops in Ethiopia. It is a species within the Asteraceae family. It is an annual herb cultivated for its edible oil and seeds. Its wild progenitor, known locally as *mech*, is commonly available in the highlands of Ethiopia. In Ethiopia *noog* grows dominantly west of the Rift Valley. This plant is cultivated in Sudan, Uganda, Congo, Tanzania, Malawi, Zimbabwe, South Africa (Daniel, 2004:23). G. *abyssinica* also grows in the southern part of India. In the archaeological

Table 2.3. A table showing the type of plants utilized for burnishing in the ethnographic study sites

No.	Plant types	*Akatit*	*Grat hitsa*	*Adrar*	*Kushet Adrar*
1	*Brassica carinata*			√	√
2	*Ricinus communis*	√	√	√	√
3	*Salvia merjamie*		√	√	
4	*Anogeissus leiocarpus*	√	√	√	√
5	*Lannea fruticosa*			√	√
6	*Sesamum indicum*	√	√		
7	*Guizotia abyssinica*			√	

Table 2.4. A table showing the summary of plant use for burnishing

No.	Plant types	No. of sites
1	*Brassica carinata*	2
2	*Ricinus communis*	4
3	*Salvia merjamie*	2
4	*Anogeissus leiocarpus*	4
5	*Lannea fruticosa*	2
6	*Sesamum indicum*	2
7	*Guizotia abyssinica*	1

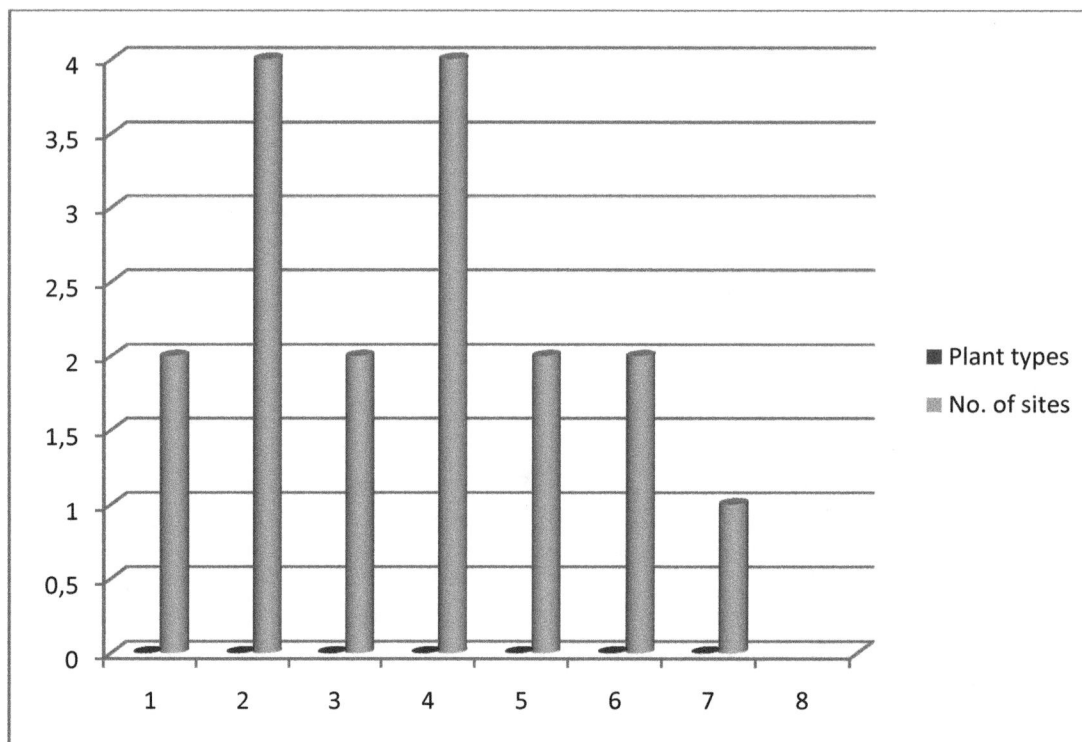

Figure 2.15 A graph showing plant types for burnishing pots across sites
Key: 1. Brassica carinata; 2. Ricinus communis; 3. Salvia merjamie; 4. Anogeissus leiocarpus;
5. Lannea fruticosa; 6. Sesamum indicum; 7. Guizotia abyssinica

context *noog* is recovered at Aksum, (Ona Nagast) by D'Andrea (1997) and from the rock shelter of Anqher Baahti by Finneran (2001).

2.6 ETHNO-ARCHAEOLOGY AT KASSALA, EASTERN SUDAN

Kassala, the administrative city of the State of Kassala, is located some 350 kilometers to the east of Khartoum, the capital city of the Republic of the Sudan. The center of the city of Kassala is found to the east of the Gash River. Taking into account the semi-desert climatic condition of the area, it is highly probable to assume that the river has been an important attraction for the establishment of the city and for the establishment of settlements in ancient times. The city has also become an important trade center since it is located along the high way Khartoum-Port Sudan. The granite hills and mountains of Jebel Taka, Toteel (Kassala Mountains) and the Jebel Mokram are the grace of the city to the Southeast and Northeast direction respectively. Further North from Kassala lies the Gash Delta, a fertile region flourishing every year thanks to the waters of the River Gash and the hot, flat territory of the Eastern Desert of the Sudan characterized by a similar geographic and environmental set up all the way to the border of Egypt. The Eastern Desert is predominantly found between the Nile River to the west and the Red Sea coast to the East. To the west of Kassala, there is the Atbara River and the Butana Grassland (the area between the Atbara River and the Nile River).

The average elevation of the Kassala area is around 500 meters above sea level. This elevation increase by 200 meters more at the granite outcrops of Jebel Kassala. The Jebels are part of the low lying extensions of the Eritrean highlands (Sadr 1991:25-26).

On the way to Kassala from Khartoum one has to cross the small towns of *Wad Medani, Gadarif, Kashim el-Girba* and *Shouak*. Except for the green plants along the sides of the Atbara River between the town of *Shouak* and the city of Kassala, most of the area is predominantly composed of Sahelian vegetation, short shrubs with maximum height of between 1 and 1.5 m. Sorghum is the widely cultivated crop in most places of Eastern Sudan (see the type of the modern variety of cultivated sorghum (*durra*) in figure 2.16). Camels which are known for their best adaptation to the desert environment are commonly observable in the aforementioned towns together with cattle and sheep. In general, the eastern part of the Sudan is a flat land with some hills standing out here and there.

With irrigation from the Gash and Atbara Rivers in Kassala and the surrounding areas cereals, fruits and vegetables are cultivated. Some of the cultivated cereals, fruits and vegetables that were documented during the ethnographic study include Sun flower (*Helianthus annus*), Cow pea (*Vigna unguiculata*), Sesame (*Sesamum indicum*), Cotton (*Gossypium barbadene*), Peanuts or ground nuts (*Arachis hypogaea*), Hot pepper (genus *Capsicum*), Onions (*Allium cepa*), Okra (*Abelmoschus esculentus*), Cluster bean (*Cymopsis psoraloides*), millet (either *Pennisetum glacum* or *Eleusine coracana*),

Figure 2.16 Modern variety of cultivated Sorghum (S. durra)

Sorghum (*Sorghum spp.*), Chick pea (*Cicer arientinum*), Broad bean (*Vicia faba*), Orange (*Citrus sinensis*); Bannana (*Musa paradisiaca*), Water melon (*Citrullus lanatus*), Papaya (*Carica papaya*), and Lemon (*Citrus limon*).

Kassala and its environs are inhabited by various population groups who claim their descent separately. The major inhabitants of the area are the Beja (including the Beni Amir and the Hadendewiya), the Rashaida, the Halenga, Hawsa, Al-Habab, Shukriya and Halfawin. The Rashaida claim their descent from the other side of the Red Sea, the Arabian Peninsula as migrants of a century or more ago. In terms of numbers, the Beja, who live both in Eastern Sudan and the western lowlands of Eritrea, constitute a majority. For the Beni Amir pastoral communities, in particular, seasonal movements across boundaries have been the normal trend from time immemorial. As stated in chapter I of this volume, the western lowlands of Ethiopia and Eritrea and Eastern Sudan, share the same river systems and similar geographic setting. Prehistoric and historic cultural manifestations also demonstrate similarity in the archaeological record (Fattovich 1993).

According to historical sources, Kassala which is now within the political boundary of the Republic of the Sudan was for a long period of time (second half of the 19th century) administered by a number of foreign countries and colonial powers (L'Africa Italiana al Parlamento Nazionale, 1882-1905: 589). Ever since the establishment of the the town of Kassala in 1840, it was occupied by different foreign forces such as the coalition of Turkish and Egyptian powers, the Mahdists, Anglo-Egyptians and Italians (Sadr 1991:26).

2.6.1 Plants as temper materials: ethnographic observation of pottery making at Reba Site

The Reba site is found immediately on the outskirts of the city of Kassala on the direction of the Northeast. It is situated at the right side of the highway that connects Khartoum with Port Sudan. The GPS coordinates of the area is 15° 2656N latitude and 36° 25.41E longtudes. The physical geography of the area is similar to the Eastern Desert of the Sudan characterized by a hot, flat and open area with sporadic shrubs and acacia as the only naturally growing vegetations. Sorghum (the modern variety, Durra) is also cultivated to the North and Northwest of the site by the Beni-Amir pastoralist communities.

The site is part of the sphere of influence of the Beni-Amir Beja. The pot makers, however, are not original settlers of the area and do not have affinity with the Beni-Amir Beja Group. They are migrants from the central and Southern part of Sudan. Unlike in Ethiopia, in general and the ethnographic sites of *Salakala* and *Indabaguna* in particular, pottery making here at Reba site is the occupation of men. Pottery making is their major occupation. In addition, in contrast to the women pot makers of Northwest Ethiopia, they do not stress their ancestry in the same area practicing the same occupation. They produce large vases (see figure 2.17), water jars and chicken and pigeon houses, where they lay their eggs. All of these products are produced for sale to the inhabitants of the city of Kassala.

The pot makers reside at the manufacturing area and where there is at the source of the clay. The physical effort employed to acquire and extract the clay soil is, thus, very minimal. Previously produced broken pot sherds are also smashed into tiny pieces and re-used again. In most cases, the clay is mixed with animal dung

a

b

Figure 2.17 Large vases and water containers at the manufacturing site

Figure 2.18 A picture showing smashed animal dung mixed with straw

deliberately added as a temper. The abundant presence of the chaff of sorghum and varieties of *Millet sp.* in the archaeo-botanical analysis of plant impressions on pottery from the Gash Delta confirms such deliberate inclusions, i.e., the ethnographic studies support the result of the archaeobotanical analysis.

Once the manufactured objects are produced, they will be left in an open space in the sun to dry for seven days. Decoration of the products is made by a modern plastic comb in a combed wavy line design on the neck of the water jars and the vases and with patterns of crossed lines (sees the decoration pattern and the tool used in figure 2.19).

and straw (see figure 2.18). If dung and straw are not available or are scarce, they opt for the chaff of Sorghum, by products of the threshed crop. For the purpose of utilizing chaff and to support their livelihood, the pot makers also cultivate sorghum. Except for animal dung, straw and chaff, sand and other inclusions are not

Following drying what comes next is firing the utensils in a pit, which is done for two days more. All plant materials that is dry enough to burn can be used in the firing process, straw and the *Ziziphus* genera being the commonly utilized ones. Dried animal dung is also used for firing the pots. Supporting the ethnographic data again, fruit stones of Ziziphus sp. are one of the most commonly identifiable pieces of evidence in the archaeo-botanical study of plant impressions and soil samples from different sites of the Gash Delta (figure 2.20).

a

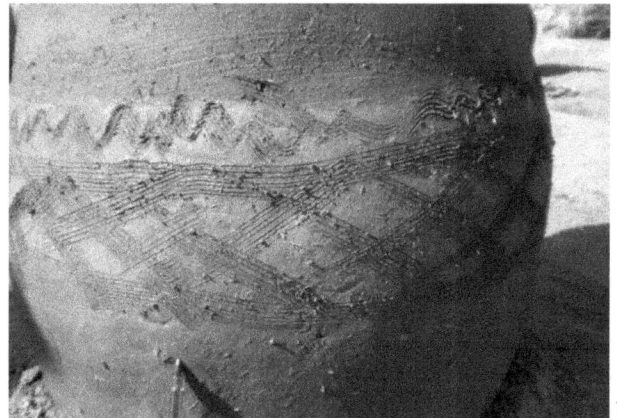

b

Figure 2.19 The tool (a) and the decoration patterns made by the tool (b)

a

b

Figure 2.20 Picture showing firing pit (a) and the process of drying (b)

Chapter III
THE STUDY AREAS:
THE GASH DELTA CULTURAL GROUPS

3.1 GEOLOGY AND PALEOENVIRONMENT OF THE GASH DELTA

Except for the Nile Valley and a few oases, Southern Egypt and most of northern Sudan are all desert and practically uninhabited...The banks of the Barka, Gash, Atbara, Setit and the Blue Nile are the Popularity of the Nile proper.

Sadr 1988:65

Climatic fluctuations follow a periodic cyclical pattern. Each periodic oscillation leaves behind its signatures on planet Earth. The signatures are evidence for reconstructing Paleoenvironment. Based on various approaches many researchers have attempted to document a history of paleo environment of the world in general and that of Africa in particular. Among those whose works on the paleoenvironment of Africa (more specifically the Sahara and the Rift Valley Lakes) gave us a good background knowledge are Warren 1970, Butzer 1975; 1981; 1982, Street and Grove 1976, Street 1980, Livingstone 1980, Gasse 1977, Gasse and Street, 1978, Gasse *et al.*, 1980, Wondrof *et al.*, 1970, 1980, Williams *et al*, 1982, Bonnefille and Mohammed 1994, Mohammed *et al.*, 1996, Mohammed and Bonnefille, 1998, Lamb *et al.*, 2000, Benvenutti *et al.*, 2002, Hoelzmann *et al.*, 2004. Due to the scope of this research, however, the environment of the very recent past is only addressed in this work.

Based on the study of the geomorphology of Central Sudan, Waren (1970:154-180) identified four climatic oscillation periods that occurred within the last 20,000 years. The first period is characterized by a very dry climate in which wind and rainfall belts were moved southwards about 450 km further than they are found at present. Sand particles were also assumed to have travelled south up to 10°N. According to Wickens (1975:45), this phase could be paralleled with the climatic conditions of the period 20,000 to 15,000 B.P.

The second period is generally a wet stage which could be roughly correlated to the years 15,000 to 7,000 B.P. It was during this period that the Paleo-White Nile Lake existed which was supposed to have 40 km width at its upper and 20 km width in its lower levels. This lake was assumed to have concentrated at the meeting place of the White and the Blue Niles and the zenith of its extension had been between 650 and 500 km south to *Malakal* and *Melut*. This period also correlates with the fresh lake deposits that Williams and Adamson reported as existing around 10 km to the west of the Nile in 1973 (498-508). Radiocarbon dates for these deposits range between 8400±150 and 6990±100 B.P. The elevation of these lakes was more than the highest elevation of the Nile. This discovery demonstrates that there was a time of abundant rainfall in the Sudan that could create water levels as high as or above the top levels of the Nile. In other words it is a good testimony for the argument which states that the Nile water levels were not entirely the function of the amount of rainfall in the highlands of Ethiopia and Eritrea (ibid:46).

The third phase characterizes a relatively short dry period, between 7000 and 6000 B.P. At the time, the wind and rainfall line had moved south by about 200 km and was accompanied by a northward return of the wind. Due to the instability of the climatic condition, plants were very sluggish to conquer areas of high altitude (ibid.).

The last phase, period IV, represents a wet climate ranging in time between 6000 and 3000 B.P. According to Wickens, the Neolithic settlement at *Esh Shaheinab*, situated about 50 km to the North of Omdurman, flourished during this wet phase. The assessments of Waren and Wickens of the climate of the northern part of the Sudan for the last 20,000 years is largely supported by recent more regional syntheses of Gasse and Roberts (2005) and Hoelzmann *et al.*, (2004). A summary of their research findings is presented in the following paragraphs.

At the time of the early Holocene (Ca. 10,000-5000 B.P.), North Africa had gone through a pluvial climate. This period is known as the 'African Humid Period' (AHP) which is characterized by a period in which the Sahara was humid and green (Gasse and Roberts 2005: 317; Hoelzmann et al., 2004:228). At the time lakes flourished in many parts of the present day Sahara Desert (Sadr 1991). A reasonable amount of data is documented by many Paleo-lake records in north and eastern Africa. In Ethiopia most lakes increased their levels including the ones in the Rift Valley. The four major Rift Valley lakes: Abiyata, Shala, Ziway and Langano had merged together to create a macro lake phase. The change from dry to a wetter condition was a result of the increase of the African and Indian monsoon which occurred due to the temporal alteration of the earth's orbit (Hoelzmann et al., 2004).

The Holocene climatic oscilliations of the Gash Delta had similar effects to those that of the Horn and North Africa (Fattovich, 1993). Most of the sediments around the Gash Delta were deposited during the Holocene period. Botanical evidence demonstrates that in Southern Atbai decidous savanna woodland was growing during the early Holocene. The vegetation changed to Savanna during the mid-Holocene dry phase (Sadr 1991:30). Around the 5th millennium B.P., the area experienced a period of climatic drying. This is indicated by the presence of huge accumulations of Pila, an amphibious snail which requires seasonal inundation, in the site which is dated back to the 5th and 4th millennium B.P. On the other hand, the presence of reed rats and monkeys in some sites like the KG14 (a Butana Group) indicate the existence of forest near the River Atbara and an estimated amount of rainfall larger than 500 mm per annum (Fattovich et al., 1984). In Southern Atbai, too, there was a dry phase with an annual rain fall of about 100 mm per annum, a marked decline from 1000-800 mm during the early Holocene (10,000-5000). The Butana flat plain is about 520 kilometers wide. There are two major river systems that cross this area, the Atbara and the Gash Rivers, which seasonally transport and deposit large amount of silt from the highlands of Ethiopia. At present, this area is the eastern most boundary of the Sahel belt experiencing hot climate with Ca 150 mm of average yearly rainfall (Abbas et al., 1989: 473).

Geomorphological study of the Kassala area demonstrated the gradual shift of the Gash River in the direction of the north-east from the original east-west trend during the mid- Holocene. The same study has also shown that before the change of the course, the Gash River used to join/flow to the Atbara River during the early Holocene or by the end of the Pleistocene. The final destination of the combined Rivers (Gash and Atbara) was the Nile. The change in the course of the river occurred between 5000 to 4000 B.P., a transitional period from the Neolithic humid phase to the post-Neolithic arid phase (Sadr 1991: 32-33).

When the course of the river changed, it created a space for the settlement of the Butana people who moved from the Atbara northwards to *Shurab el Gash*. This has also resulted in the establishment of the Gash Group culture as a result of interaction with the Kerma. The possible outcome of the shift according to Fattovich (1993) is that it reduced the distance from the Middle Nile valley area to Northern Ethiopia and facilitated the midway role of the people of the Gash Delta in the trade contact between Egypt and Horn of Africa. Some of the trade items from northern Ethiopia and Eritrea had also to pass through the same people. Based on the archaeological data it has also become possible to deduce the fact that *Shurab el Gash* was largely settled by the Gash Group people. Due to similarity in material culture, the same people are believed to have spread up to Erkowit (the Red Sea coast in the North) and Agordat in the East in Eritrea. The present position of the Gash River was achieved around 4000 B.P. as evidenced from the morphology of the area (ibid.). The hydrological shift of the Gash River was very rapid with immediate effect on the environment of the area and on the settlement pattern of the Southern Atbai. According to Fattovich et al., (1984), up to ca. the 3rd millennium B.P., large game animals like giraffe, elephant, buffalo and rhino had inhabited the Eritrean-Sudanese lowlands and the area between the Atbara and the Gash Delta. These big savanna mammals prefer a humid grass land environmental condition.

During the period of the post-Neolithic arid phase, around the middle of the 3rd millennium B.P. and after, drier conditions were recorded on the steppe between the rivers Atbara and the Gash Delta. This was accompanied by an increase in settlement areas and the overall non-appearance of Pila shells in the environmental record (Fattovich et al., 1984). There were, however, large settlement sites along the main rivers long before this period. But, during this period the settlements increase in number. At Kassala large settlements were there before the appearance of domestic cattle in the archaeological record, subsistence being mainly based on aquatic resources.

At present broadleafed plants grow only adjacent to the Gash River. The current hot lowland territory between the Eritrean and Ethiopian highlands and the Atbara River obtain between 200-400 mm of rain fall per annum. This can support vegetations like acacia and scrub (Sadr 1991:25).

3.2 THE GASH DELTA CULTURAL GROUPS: THE STUDY AREAS

Decades of research on the study of the archaeology of the Gash Delta have resulted in the classification of the cultural groups of the area into six major entities. These are:

1- the Amm Adam Group (Ca. 8th-7th millennia B.P.),

2- the Malawiya Group (7th-6th millennium B.P.),

3- the Butana Group (Ca. 6th-5th millennia B.P.),

4- the Gash group (Ca. 5th-4th millennia B.P.),

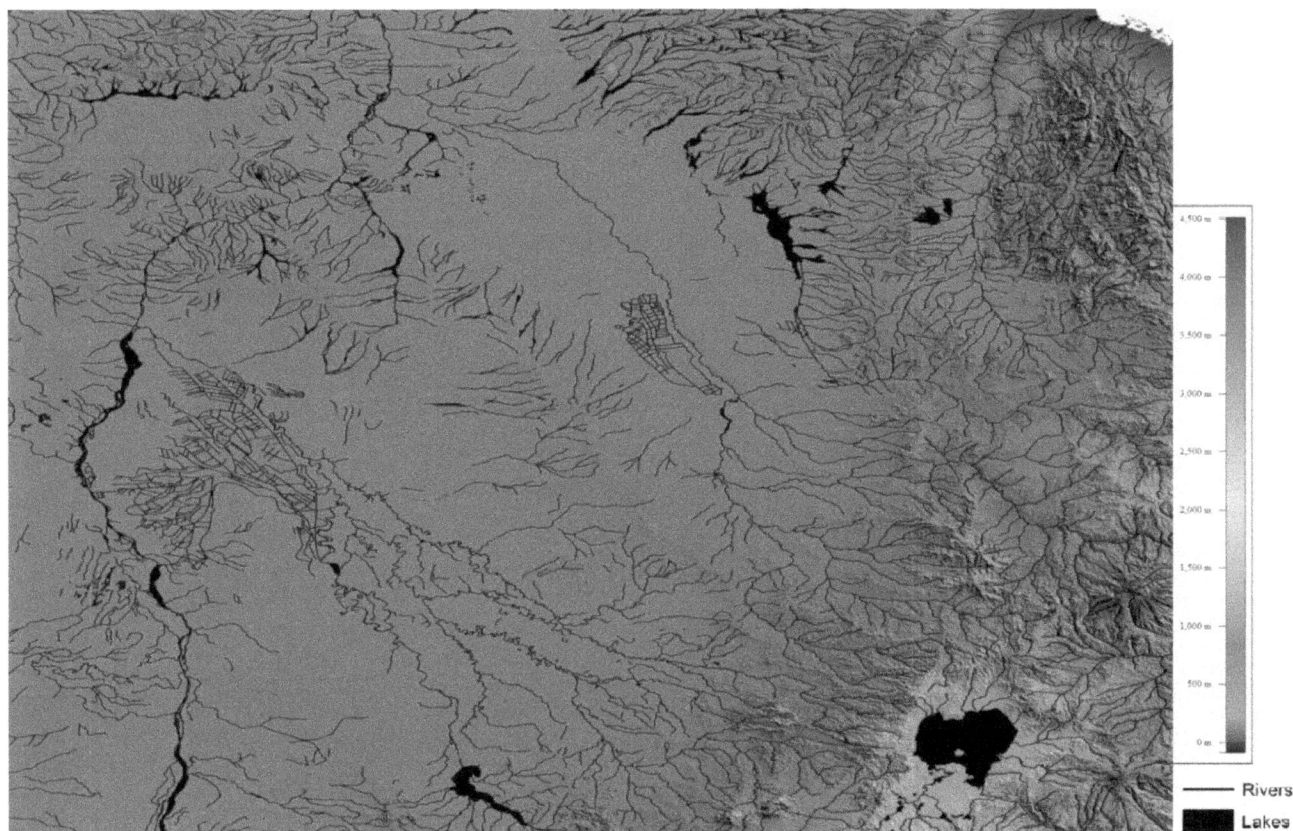

Figure 3.1 Geomorphologic map of Kassala and its environs

5- the Jebel Mokram Group (Ca. 4th-3rd\2nd millennia B.P.),

6- and the Hagiz Group (Fattovich 1989: 481; 1993). Detail description of these five major cultural groups is presented below. See map 3.1 for the geographic centers of the aforementioned five cultural groups.

3.2.1 The Amm Adam Group

The Amm Adam Group flourished between about 8th-7th millennia B.P. and represents the oldest stage of the cultural sequence in the Gash Delta. This is, probably, the stage in which process of peopling the delta started. The cultural tradition of Amm Adam can be paralleled with what is known as the Pre-Saroba site of the *Kashm el-Girba* area (KG14). Near Kassala, two sites with distinct ceramic tradition that belongs to this stage were discovered. The data acquired from this period, however, are still insufficient (Fattovich 1989:483).

The sites of Amm Adam are identified north of the Gash Delta (three sites) and west of the Delta near Ukheiderat and Jebel Ofreik, where it is represented by a number of sites. All of these sites are situated in the flat alluvial plains of the Delta. What is typical of this tradition are the ceramics decorated with knobs. The sherds have also some elements that are similar to the Khartoum Horizon style, Central Sudan. But, this ceramic tradition is separate from the ceramic traditions of the Nile Valley (Fattovich and Piperno 1982, Fattovich 1989:484).

Triangular and rectangular bands of knobs mostly along the rim and in a wavy line model, cord impressed horizontal or slanting lines along the lips and rims, rocker stamped wolf tooth style, are some of the most common types of pottery decoration techniques and patterns that belong to the Amm Adam tradition (Fattovich 1989: 484). The knobs consist of holes closed with clay balls.

The economy of the inhabitants was largely based on the utilization of aquatic resources. This is deciphered from the bone barbed harpoon collected from some of the sites and this is comparable to the Early Khartoum sites. In addition, analysis of faunal remains from the same site rendered an indication of the presence of wild grazing antelopes and aquatic animals like hippopotamus, fish, buffalo, warthog (ibid.).

The Amm Adam sites are not dated using the radiometric system. However, based on comparison with the Early Khartoum and Pre-Saroba sites a dating is suggested that ranges between 8,000 and 6,000 years B.P. (ibid.).

3.2.2 The Malawiya Group

The Malawiya Group marks the beginning of the evolutionary stage of the Atbai Ceramic Tradition which is termed as the Saroba Stage. The Group was first observed in the *Kashm el-Girba* area. Almost all of the sites that belong to this Group are situated between the Atbara River and *Shurab el-Gash* (Marks and Fattovich 1989: 455-456). The ceramics of the Malawiya Group are

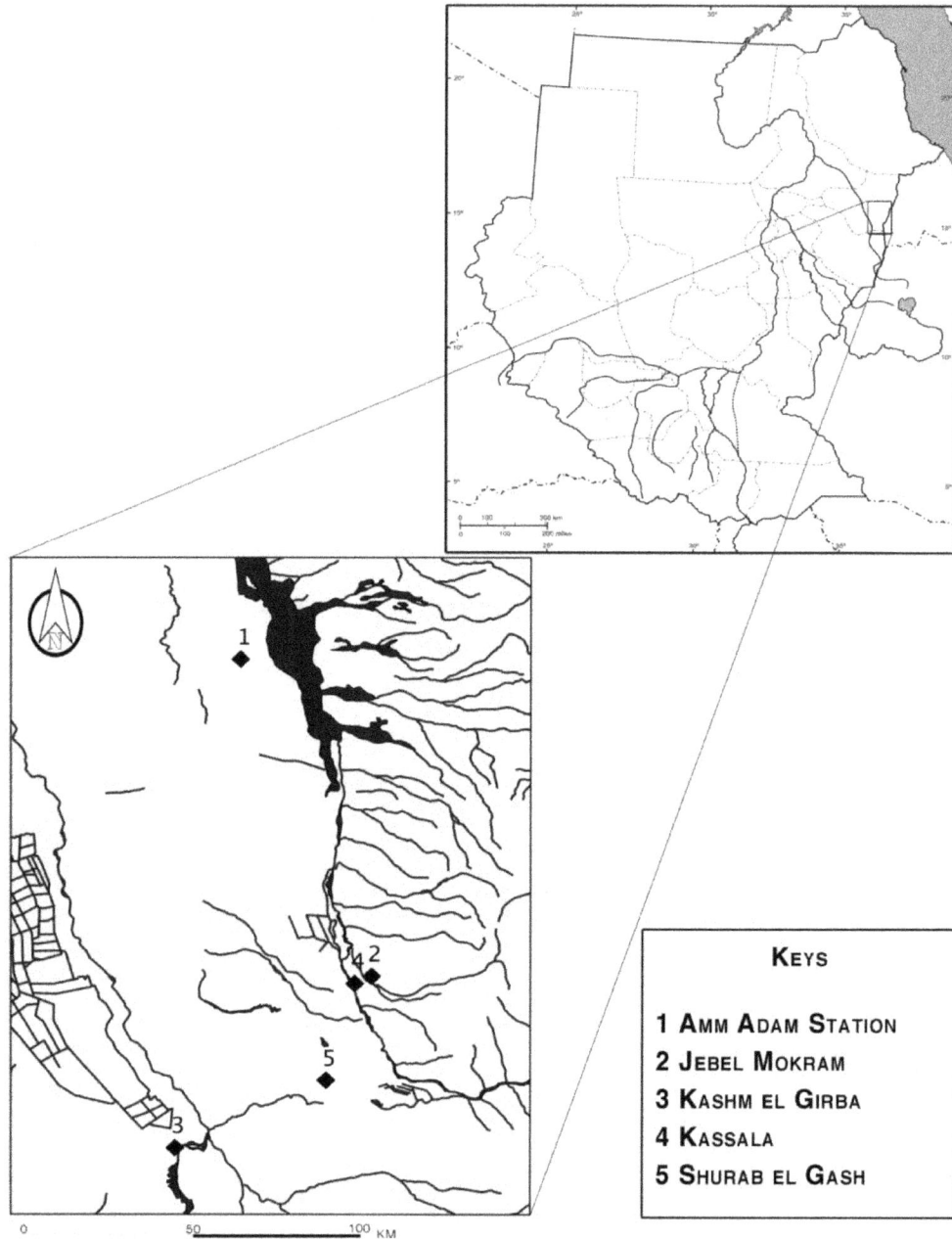

Figure 3.2 The geographical location of the main sites of the cultural groups in this study

often decorated in punched and rocker stamped wolf tooth motifs.

Most of the sites are identified in the steppe along an old river bed of the Gash. The sites have rendered no animal bone remains to comment on subsistent pattern and the paleo-ecology. However, large accumulations of *Pila* shells are reported which shows an environment with seasonal transgression of a flood. Based on the evidence from *Khashm el Girba*, it is possible to deduce that the inhabitants of these sites were hunter\gatherers who were dependent partly on the available savanna and riverine vegetations and partly on the aquatic resources (Fattovich 1989: 486).

The ceramics from the Malawiya Group can be comparable with the Khartoum Horizon style whereas,

the motifs have no affinity with the cultural groups that had flourished along the Middle Nile. The dates provided for this Group are between 5th to 4th millennium B.C. based on comparison with *Khashm el-Girba* (ibid.).

3.2.3 The Butana Group

The Butana is a flat featureless plain extending from the Nile to the Abyssinian Plateau.

Abbas S.A. *et al.*, 1989:473

The Paleoenvironment of the Butana area as briefly described in section 3.1 was more of a savanna habitat as can be reconstructed from the faunal remains recovered from the sites. The bones of wild animals, fish, crocodile, hippopotamus, and an array of bovids of different size were documented (Ibid.).

This site was first reported by Shiner (1971). The main sites of the Butana Groups are to be found in the *Kashm el-Girba* area. Near Kassala, from *Jebel Tukulabab* to *Shurab el-Gash* twenty four sites were identified as belonging to the same tradition. The main characterstics of the pottery assemblages recovered from these sites is that the majority are of thread tempered. The Butana Group, the Gash Group and the Agordat Group are manifestations of the second evolutionary stage of 'the Atbai Ceramic tradition' known as the Kassala Phase. According to Fattovich (1989:487) 'regional variants of the same basic tradition'.

3.2.4 The Gash Group

The nucleus of the Gash Group people was Eastern Sudan. Adjacent to the Gash Delta around 32 Gash group sites have been identified. The main site of these groups is Mahal Teglinos, near Kassala and has provided sherds that have affinities with the C-Group and Kerma. On the basis of social organization, sequence of cultural deposits and cultural changes observed within the Gash Group, Fattovich (1993) has suggested four distinct periods. These include; the proto-Gash Group (3000-2500 B.C.), Early Gash Phase (2500-2300 B.C.), Middle Gash Group (2300-1900 B.C.) Classic Gash Group (1900-1700 B.C.), Late Gash Group (1700-1500 B.C.) and Terminal Gash phase (1500-1400 B.C.).

At the time of the Proto-Gash Group, settlements were more permanent as can be deduced from the thick layer of cultural deposit at Mahal Teglinos. During this phase the hunting of wild games seems to have been the main subsistence base of the people in the Gash Delta. At the time of the Early Gash phase, the Butana Group people moved east wards and occupied the *Shurab el Gash* area following the change of the course of the Gash River. This process probably facilitated the interaction of the Gash Group people with the Kerma. The contact between the two cultural groups might have resulted in reviving the Gash Group proper. This phase marked the shift from Butana to Gash cultural phase.

Since 2000 B.C. monolithic stelae were used as funerary markers. Probably one of the oldest burial stelae was recovered during this period. Fattovich (1993) considered the site of Mahal Teglinos (K1) to be ceremonial based on the worship of the dead. The Gash Group cultural influence was also seen at Eriba, further north towards the Red Sea Hills. The subsistence pattern was based on both the utilization of wild species and on pastoralism. In terms of administrative structure, the Gash Group people were hierarchical. The recovered ceramic seals indicate that the inhabitants at Mahal Teglinos were organized at the chiefdom level. There was evidence for cultural interactions with the C-Group and Kerma culture of the Middle Nile Valley region (Fattovich *et al.*, 1984).

The Gash Group reached its maximum territorial extent to the east inhabiting most of the Eritreo-Sudanese boarder areas and to the north up to the Red Sea coast during the Classic Gash Group Phase. Comparable cultural manifestations like that of the Gash Group were observed at Agordat, Aqiq, and Erkowit. At the same period, the sphere of influence of the *Shurab el Gash* area increased by two more temporary settlements. The subsistence base of the Gash Group people during this phase was animal husbandry and cultivation of crops. It was also during this time that the economic interaction between Nubia, the highlands of the Horn of Africa and Egypt became strong. The 'Circuit' of trade might also have involved Somalia and Southern Arabia. The midway role for this trade contact between Egypt and the highlands of the Horn of Africa was probably taken by Mahal Teglinos (Fattovich 1993).

The Terminal Gash is the last phase of the Gash Group cultural tradition, marked by the absence of an archaeological record. However, on the basis of the little evidence from Mahal Teglinos, it is possible to see the presence of interaction with peoples of the Pan-Grave culture and that of the C-Group from II\b phase. A reduction in settlement areas and the decline of trade with the highlands of the Horn and Egypt were probably reasons for the absence of evidence. This decline, on the other hand, might have facilitated the expansion and control of the Gash Delta by the people belonging to the Pan-Grave Culture (Fattovich *et al.*, 1984; Fattovich 1993).

3.2.5 The Jebel Mokram Group

The archaeological evidence revealed that the Jebel Mokram Group had inhabited southern Atbai from about the mid 2nd millennium B.C. to the mid 1st millennium A.D. In terms of chronology the Group is further divided into Mokram (Ca. mid 2nd millennium B.C. to Ca. early 1st millennium B.C.) and the Late Mokram Group (Ca. early to mid 1st millennium B.C.). After the late Kassala Phase (Ca. 1500-750 B.C.), the Gash Group material culture evidence had been replaced by the Mokram Group. The ceramics of the Mokram Group have affinity with that of the Pan-Grave culture (Sadr 1991: 47-48).

Together with the Mokram Group, a new stone tool technology has also appeared in the record like distinctive "T" shaped polished axes and stone bracelets. Sadr (1988:90 see also 1991:45) commented that these new stone tool technologies were made of 'imported Porphyry' (reddish purple stone containing large sized crystals, predominantly fieldspar). Highly refined polished axes with metal prototypes and stone bracelets are also common in the Barka Valley of Agordat as can be observed in the collections of Arkell (1954) housed in the National Museum of Khartoum (Beldados 2006: 49).

In comparison with the Gash Group, the subsistence pattern at this stage was not that much changed. There is evidence for the presence of cattle (Sadr 1991: 48). The archaeobotanical data has also revealed that Sorghum and Millet were cultivated at the time (Costantini *et al.* 1983:17-19). In addition, there was direct evidence for Sorghum and Millet in the Teka Phase (Ca. 750 B.C. to 350 A.D.).

3.2.6 The Hagiz Group

The Hagiz Group marks the final phase of the 'Atbai Ceramic Tradition'. This Group was first categorized as the Jebel Teka Group by Fattovich and Pipperno (1986). Along the Gash Delta around seventeen sites were identified belonging to the same Group in Jebel Mokram and *Shurab el-Gash* areas. During the Teka Phase, the ceramics were again similar to the Mokram. The only exception at this time is that mineral tempering is substituted by a mix with fiber tempering. (Fattovich 1989: 497). The technique of using fiber as temper material is also observable among the ceramics of the Agordat collection (Beldados 2006: 58-59). The first pastoralists of the Southern Atbai, the Hagiz Group, were dominant at this stage. The main diagnostic elements of the Hagiz Group ceramics are crudeness and fiber tempering. Like that of the Gash Group they decorate their pottery using rim band motifs and scraping. Pre-Aksumite types of pottery fragments were also observed in the sites belonging to the Hagiz Group demonstrating their contemporaneousness (Sadr 1991:49-50).

Chapter IV
ARCHAEOBOTANICAL STUDY OF
THE EASTERN SUDAN COLLECTIONS

A total of 31,814 sherds from different sites of Eastern Sudan namely, AAS-1 and AAS-2 (*Amm Adam Station*), KI, (*Mahal Teglinos* and excavation units KI, KII, KIII), KG5, KG16, KG23, KG93, KG96, (from *Kashim el-Girba* area*),* EG3, JM2 (near *Jebel Mokram),* and SEG11, SEG42 (from *Shurab el- Gash)* were examined in the laboratory for plant impression analysis (for the location of the area where the sites are see map 4.1). Thirty three of these were thought to bear plant impressions that can be diagnosable and hence subjected to further examination using stereo microscope. The thirty three sherds were selected based on the assumption that their cavities are similar to the cavity that seeds/grains leave

behind. In almost all of the *Jebel Mokram* collections there are impressions of various parts of plant bodies' observable on both the interior and exterior surfaces and along their edges. Such kind of impression is difficult for identification. The same pattern could also be seen in many of the *Kashim el-Girba* sherds and in some of the Kassala collections. The table below (Table 4.1) summarizes the number of sherds with plant impressions, the sites from which they were collected and their relative chronology. The chronology is evaluated on the basis of the typological assessment of the sherds submitted to archaeobotanical investigation.

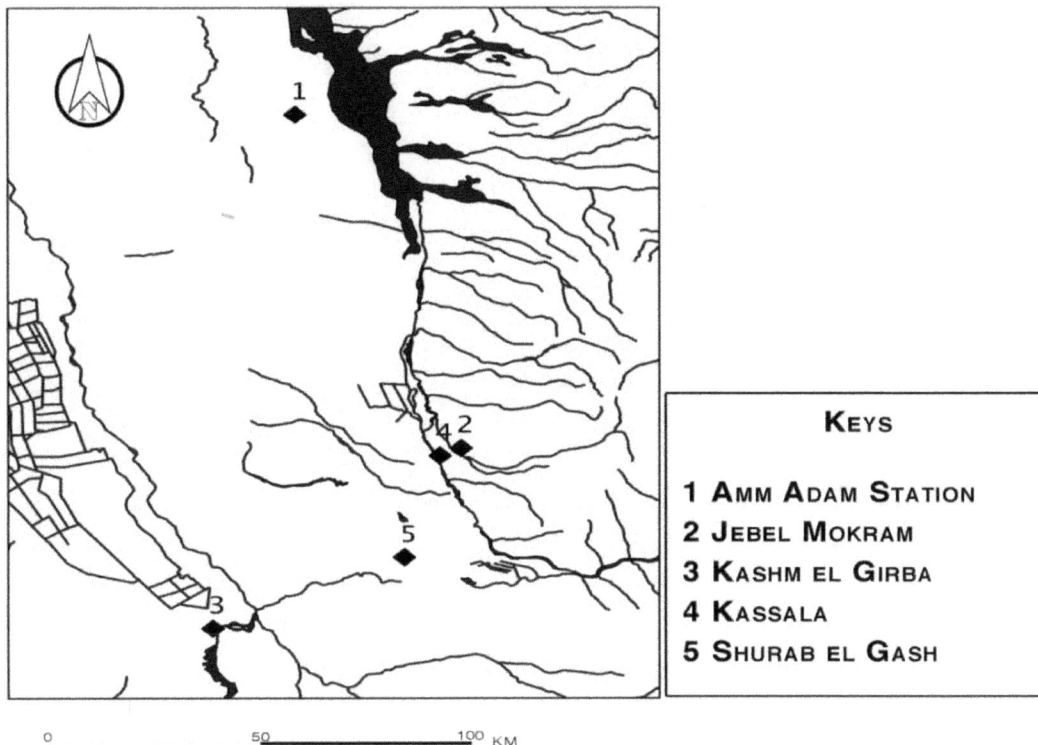

KEYS

1 AMM ADAM STATION
2 JEBEL MOKRAM
3 KASHM EL GIRBA
4 KASSALA
5 SHURAB EL GASH

Figure 4.1 The geographical distribution of the main centers in this study

Table 4.1 A table showing sherds with plant impressions: their inventory number, chronology and cultural affiliation

No.	Code and Inventory number	Site	Cultural affiliation and Chronology of the assemblage
1	AAS 1, #363	Amm Adam Station	Amm Adam Group (5000-4000 B.C.)
2	AAS 1 #212, #183	Amm Adam Station	Amm Adam Group (5000-4000 B.C.)
3	KG 96 A-L6-8 #663	Kashim el Girba	Butana Group (ca. 3500-2500 B.C.)
4	KG 23 SE-slope	Kashim el Girba	Butana Group (ca. 3500-2500 B.C.)
5	KG 96 A-M6 1	Kashim el Girba	Butana Group (ca. 3500-2500 B.C.)
6	KG 23 SE-Slope	Kashim el Girba	Butana Group (ca. 3500-2500 B.C.)
7	KG 93 B1-4 643	Kashim el Girba	Butana Group (ca. 3500-2500 B.C.)
8	KG 96 66-10 641	Kashim el Girba	Butana Group (ca. 3500-2500 B.C.)
9	KG 16 32-8 395	Kashim el Girba	Butana Group (ca. 3500-2500 B.C.)
10	KG 96 A-L6-8 636	Kashim el Girba	Butana Group (ca. 3500-2500 B.C.)
11	KG 5	Kashim el Girba	Butana Group (ca. 3500-2500 B.C.)
12	KG 23 C-C3-15	Kashim el Girba	Butana Group (ca. 3500-2500 B.C.)
13	K1 II 11 # 63	Mahal Teglinos	Middle to Late Gash Group (ca. 2000-1500 B.C.)
14	K1 II 11 # 100	Mahal Teglinos	Middle to Late Gash Group (2000-1500 B.C. ca.)
15	K1 II 11 # 41	Mahal Teglinos	Middle to Late Gash Group (ca. 2000-1500 B.C.)
16	K1 II 11 # 44	Mahal Teglinos	Middle to Late Gash Group (ca. 2000-1500 B.C.)
17	K1 II 11	Mahal Teglinos	Middle to Final Gash Group (ca. 2500-1400 B.C.)
18	K1 II 15	Mahal Teglinos	Classic to Late Gash Group (ca. 2000-1500 B.C.)
19	K1 II 11 # 46	Mahal Teglinos	Middle to Late Gash Group (ca. 2000-1500 B.C.)
20	K1 II 11 # 21	Mahal Teglinos	Middle to Late Gash Group (ca. 2000-1500 B.C.)
21	K1 I 13 # 138	Mahal Teglinos	Final Gash Group (ca. 1500-1400 B.C.)
22	K1 I 6	Mahal Teglinos	Final Gash Group (ca. 1500-1400 B.C.)
23	K1 I 15 # 34	Mahal Teglinos	Final Gash Group (ca. 1500-1400 B.C.)
24	K1 I 6 # 28	Mahal Teglinos	Final Gash Group (ca. 1500-1400 B.C.)
25	K1 I 1 # 39	Mahal Teglinos	Final Gash Group (ca. 1500-1400 B.C.)
26	K1 I 5	Mahal Teglinos	Final Gash Group (ca. 1500-1400 B.C.)
27	K1 I 15 60	Mahal Teglinos	Final Gash Group (ca. 1500-1400 B.C.)
28	EG3		Early Jebel Mokram (ca. 1500-1000 B.C.)
29	JM2	Jebel Mokram	Early Jebel Mokram Group (ca. 1500-1000 B.C.)
30	SEG 11	Shurab el Gash	Late Jebel Mokram/Hagiz Group (half-late 1st mill. B.C.)
31	SEG 42 GS	Shurab el Gash	Hagiz Group (first centuries A.D.)
32	SEG 42 RS	Shurab el Gash	Hagiz Group (first centuries A.D.)
33	SEG 42 R5	Shurab el Gash	Hagiz Group (first centuries A.D.)

Table 4.2 The number of sherds with plant impressions across sites

Sites	No. of sherds with plant impressions
AAS-1	2
KG5, KG16, KG23, KG93, KG96 (Khashim el Girba)	10
KI (K I)	7
KII (KI)	1
KIII (KI)	7
EG3, JM2 (Jebel Mokram)	2
Shurab el Gash I (EG 1)	1
Shurab el Gash II (SEG 42)	2

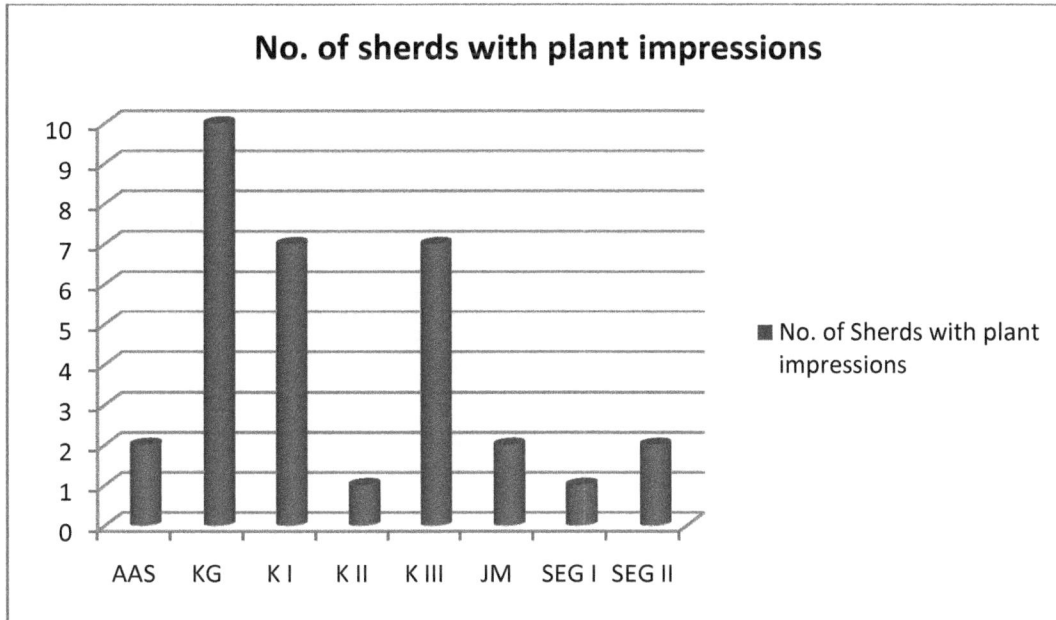

Figure 4.2 A graph showing the number of sherds with plant impressions across sites
AAS- Amm Adam (5,000-4,0000 B.C.); KG- Khashim el Girba, Butana Group (Ca. 3,500-2,500 B.C.); K I- Mahal Teglinos, Classic to Late Gash Group (Ca. 2,000-1,500 B.C.); K II- Mahal Teglinos, Classic to final Gash Group (Ca. 2,500-1,400 B.C.); K III- Mahal Teglinos, Final Gash Group (Ca. 1,500-1,400 B.C.); JM- Jebel Mokram, Early Jebel Mokram (Ca. 1,500-1,000 B.C.); SEG I- Shurab el Gash, Late Jebel Mokram\Hagiz Group (half-late 1st millennium B.C.); SEG II- Shurab el Gash, Hagiz Group (1st centuries A.D.)

Table 4.3 A Percentage of sherds with plant impressions across sites

Sites	No. of sherds with plant impressions	Number of sherds with plant impressions in percentage
AAS-1	2	6%
KG5, KG16, KG23, KG93, KG96 (Khashim el Girba)	10	30%
Kassala I	7	21%
Kassala II	1	3%
Kassala III	7	21%
EG3, JM2 (Jebel Mokram)	2	6%
Shurab el Gash I	1	3%
Shurab el Gash II	2	6%

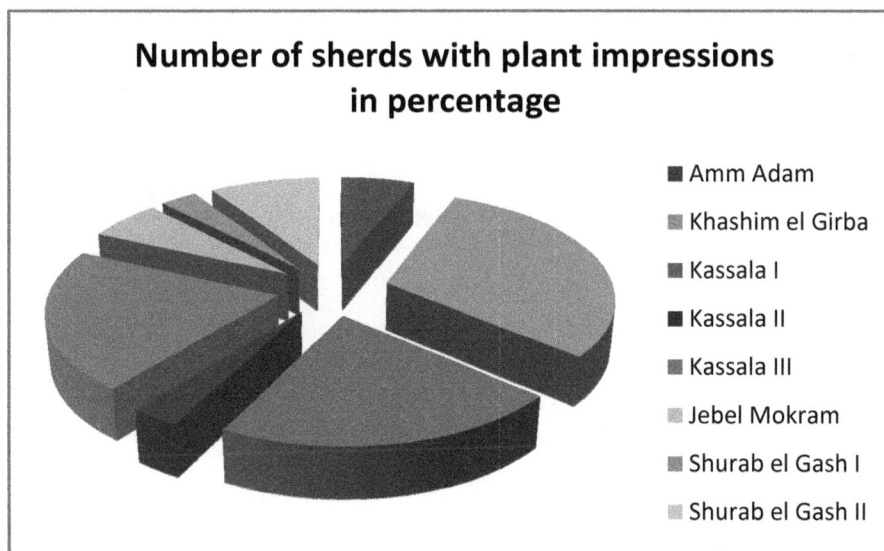

Figure 4.3 A pie chart showing the percentage of sherds with plant impressions across sites

4.1 ARCHAEOBOTANICAL STUDY ON AMM ADAM (AAS-1) SHERDS

Two sherds were selected out of a total of 178 collected from surface of the site of Amm Adam in the years 1980 and 1982 by Rodolfo Fattovich. This is 1.1 percent of the total. Based on typology the Amm Adam materials are dated between Ca. 5000 and 4,000 B.C. The Amm Adam ceramics are mainly reddish and brownish in color and composition of the fabric comprises clay and mineral inclusions like coarse grained quartz, quartzite and sand particles. The ceramics are knobbed, rocker stamped, combed and scrapped. Vegetal remains are generally very low. Thickness of the sherds is below 1 cm.

i. AAS 1, #363
Amm Adam Group (5000-4000 B.C.)

This sherd demonstrated low vegetal remains on ventral and dorsal surfaces and along the edges. There is one impression on dorsal edge which is similar to grain cavity but difficult to identify. It has very high proportion of inclusions; quartz, quartzite and sand particles (see the microscopic detail of the sherd in Fig. 4.1.1). Thickness of the sherd is 0.7 cms. The impression is not identifiable.

Figure 4.1.1 Microscopic detail of Amm Adam sherd

ii. AAS 1 #212, #183
Amm Adam Group (5000-4000 B.C.)

A close examination of the suspected imprint using a stereo microscope demonstrated no vegetal remains on all surfaces except an insect imprint, known as eletra, characterized by straight lines of microscopic dots (see picture 4.1.2) on dorsal surface. Similarly, Costantini and Audisio (2001: 149) had identified holes, burrows and bite traces of spermatophagous (*Coccoptrypes dactyliperda*) beetles on date palm stones from a Bronze Age site of RAS AL-JINZ (RJ-2), Sultanate of Oman. The insects' attachment on the date palm stones is to complete their biological cycle. Similarly, a high proportion inclusion of quartz, quartzite and sand particles are visible and the thickness of the sherd is 0.7 cms.

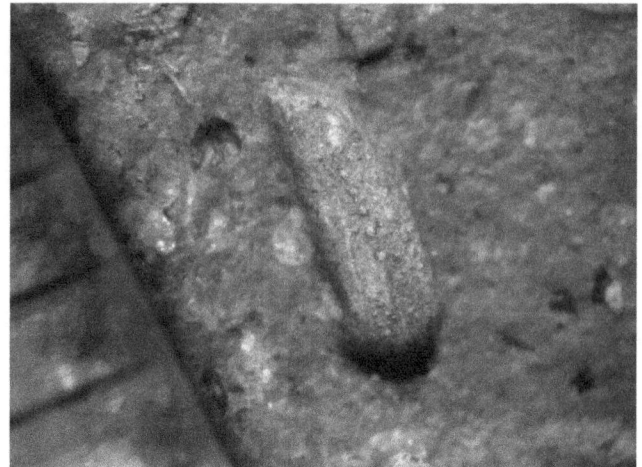

Figure 4.1.2 Microscopic image of eletra

4.2 ARCHAEOBOTANICAL ANALYSIS OF THE KASHIM EL-GIRBA SPECIMENS

Ten sherds were selected out of a total of 6,600 collected from the surface from the region of *Khashim el-Girba* since 1971 by Anthony E. Marks. This is 0.6 percent of the total. Based on typology the *Khashim el-Girba* material is dated between Ca. 3,500 and 2,500 B.C. Sherds from *Khashim el Girba* are red, brown and grey in color and the composition of the fabric comprises clay soil and chaff and glumes with seeds belonging mainly to *Panicum sp.* and *Setaria* sp. Charred chaff and seeds are dominantly observed along the edges of the selected sherds. The thickness of the sherds ranges between 1 and 1.4 cms. Due to the shape and the size, it is possible to suggest that most of the plant impressions, on the five of the sherds, belong to *Panicum sp.* (KG 96 A-4 6 -6, KG 96-B1-6 643, KG 96 82-8 395, KG 23-SE-slope, KG 96-66-10 641). The specimens are compared with examples in the Digital Seed Atlas of the Netherlands, page 138 and the actual *Panicum sp.* (*Millet sp.*) grain varieties present in the Bio-archaeological laboratory of the Museum of Oriental Art, Rome. One of the sherds happens to be different from the rest in fabric, color and its imprints as summarized under KG 96A-L6-8 633. Two other (KG-5 and KG 23C-C3-15) are also different in composition and the imprints they bear.

The presence of abundant charred chaff and glumes of millets and other cereals as components in the composition of the *Khashim el-Girba* ceramics gives us insight into different possibilities in the process of manufacturing:

1- The availability of the dorsal and ventral glumes embracing the grain is probably an example of the usage of the whole grain before threshing together with the clay soil as components in the manufacturing. The charring of the grains might have happened while baking the clay;

2- Possibly already roasted seeds of *Setaria sp.* or *Panicum sp.*, left over from consumption or waste, were used as parts of the pottery making process.

The abundance of the charred grains in relation to chaff can also compel us to pose the question why did they use the edible seeds directly instead of utilizing the chaff, the wastes\by-products? Costantini, pers. comm., has looked at this question from the point of view of resource availability. He argued that, probably, the pre-historic inhabitants of the area had a rich source of millet to the extent that shortage of these grains was not their immediate problems. Had it been the case that the locally available millet crops were small and the resources poor, they would definitely have opted for chaff of millet only as inclusions to produce their ceramics. A detail of the archaeobotanical analysis of the Khashim el Girba sherds is presented as follows:

4.2.1 KG 5
Butana Group (ca. 3500-2500 B.C.)

Too many impressions are observable in this piece of sherd testifying that a lot of chaff is used in the making process. The chaff is not of the common cereals (wheat and barley). Since the impressions are smaller and finner, it happens to be very difficult to identify and classify them. In the internal part there is a ventral surface impress-sion of a cereal (Gramineae). In the same surface, there are two very small insect impressions. A thin section of the sherd demonstrated that the piece is consist of two parts: a reddish external and a dark, burned, full of chaff interior. The thickness of the sherd is 0.6 cms.

4.2.2 KG 23C-C3-15
Butana Group (ca. 3500-2500 B.C.)

Crude, unbaked clay with some vegetal impressions. At the center of the interior part there is an imprint of the rachis fragment of barley. The thickness of the sherd is 0.5 cms.

4.2.3 KG96-66-10 641
Butana Group (ca. 3500-2500 B.C.)

This rim sherd is very rich in plant impressions. 11 imprints are counted on the exterior surface, whereas the interior and the lip have got 4 imprints each. There are, therefore, a total of 19 grain impressions all over the body of the sherd belonging to *Panicum sp.* (Figs. 4.2.1 and 4.2.2). In addition, there are a number of charred grains observable by microscope. Along the edges, specifically, charred grains and chaff are visible. Chaff and fine sand particles are used as inclusions. Thickness of the sherd is 1.2 cms.

4.2.4 KG23-SE-Slope
Butana Group (ca. 3500-2500 B.C.)

A rim sherd possessing 13 imprints along its exterior surface, 7 on its interior and 6 along its edges, making a total of 26 vegetal imprints. This has also many charred grains and chaff along its edges. Inclusions are basically fine sand particles and chaff. There is a possibility that all of the imprints belong to *Panicum sp.* Thickness of the rim is 0.8 cms.

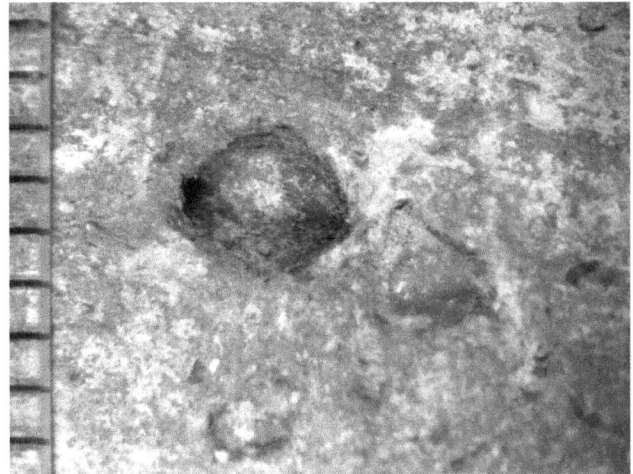

Figure 4.2.1 impression of Panicum sp., *the negative or the impression*

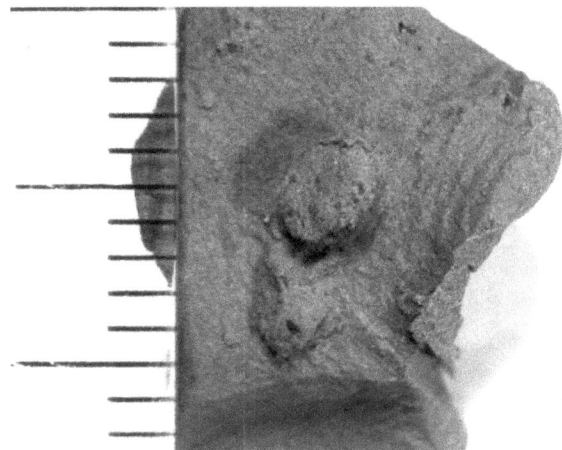

Figure 4.2.2 Impression of Panicum sp., *the cast\the positive*

4.2.5 KG 16-32-8 # 395
Butana Group (ca. 3500-2500 B.C.)

This sherd has 12 plant imprints on its external surface. Here also, fine sand particles and chaff is used as inclusions. Charred grains are present along the edges. The impressions almost all belong to *Panicum sp.* Thickness of the sherd is 0.6 cms.

4.2.6 KG 96A-L6-8 # 636
Butana Group (ca. 3500-2500 B.C.)

Although there is a general observable trend that almost all of the *Khashim el Girba* sherds are made using chaff of the Millets *(Panicum sp.* basically*)*, this piece happens to be different. It's fully reddish clay, unlike in most cas-es (grayish and brownish). The fabric comprises are basi-cally clay and chaff. Thickness of the sherd is 0.5 cm. This is a very unique and productive sherd in terms of varieties of plant imprints. On its ventral surface there are six imprints and three on its dorsal surface (see the posi-tion of the impressions in Fig. 4.2.3). Most of the vegetal impressions are comparable with specimens: 422-C, 422-

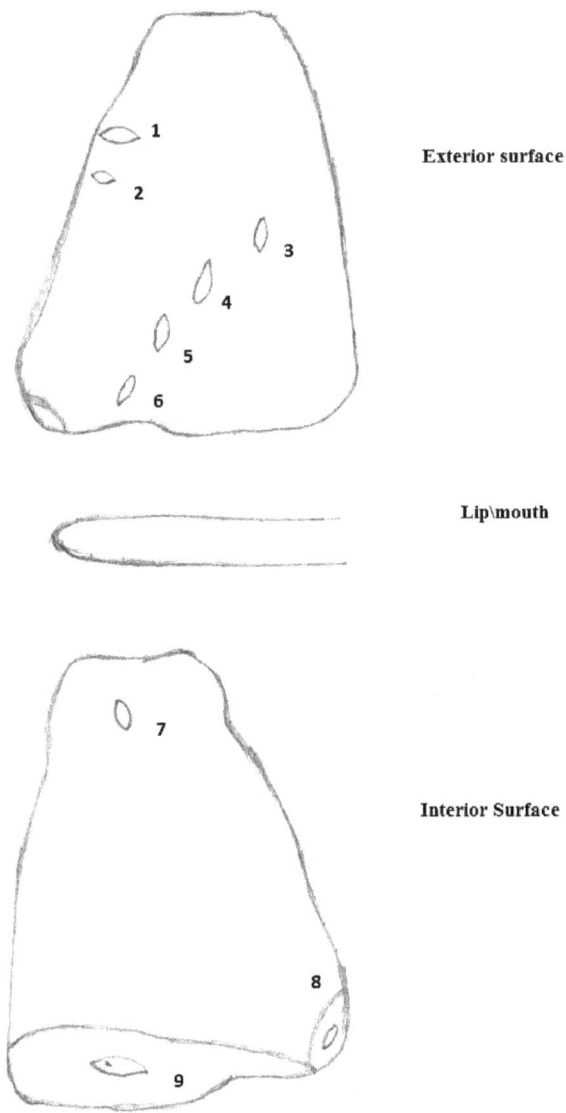

Figure 4.2.3 Positions of impressions
on sherd KG 96A-L6-8 # 636

7. Figure 4.2.6 imprint chaff cf. *Eleusine sp.*

8. Glume of Cereal, wheat\barley, un identified

9. Ventral surface of a half barley grain (see Fig. 4.2.7 and 4.2.8)

Figure 4.2.4 The cast of a grain impression of barley

Figure 4.2.5 The cast of Lolium sp. *as compared with the grain of the species*

D, and 442-E, *Hordeum vulgare* ssp. Distichon (hulled), page 148 in the *Digital seed Atlas of the Netherlands*. In many of the imprints mineral parts of the glume are observable.

Key on the impressions:

1. Ventral surface of barley grain (figure 4.2.4)

2. Part of dorsal surface of a cereal grain

3. Imprint of the ventral surface of barley grain and a glume of Gramineae

4. Imprint of grain of *Triticum monococum\diococum* in lateral ventral view

5. A *Lolium Sp.*, a weed of cultivated cereal (wheat and barley). The cast and the comparative plant specimen are shown in fig. 4.2.5

6. Glume of barley\wheat, unidentified cereal glume

Figure 4.2.6 Imprint chaff cf. Eleusine sp.

36

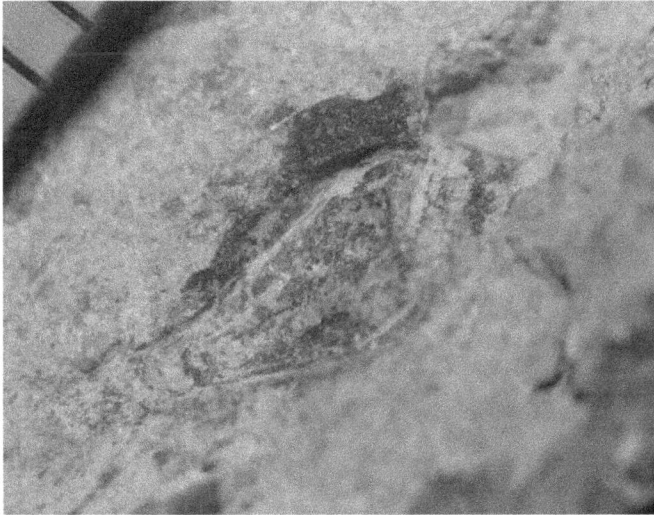

Figure 4.2.7 An impression of the ventral surface of barley

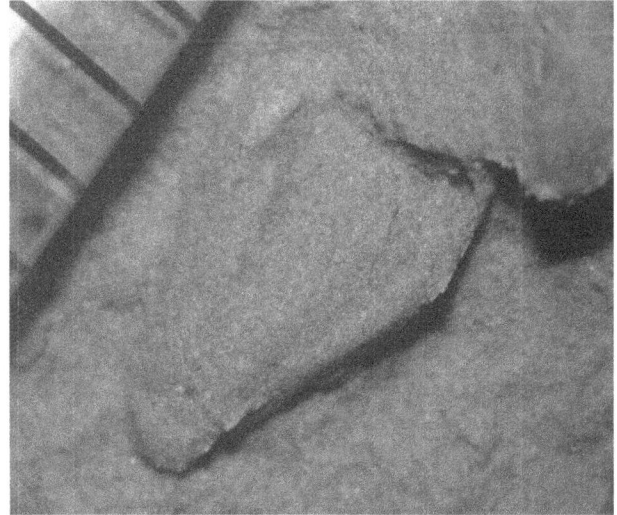

Figure 4.2.8 An imprint of the ventral surface of barley, the cast of the impression

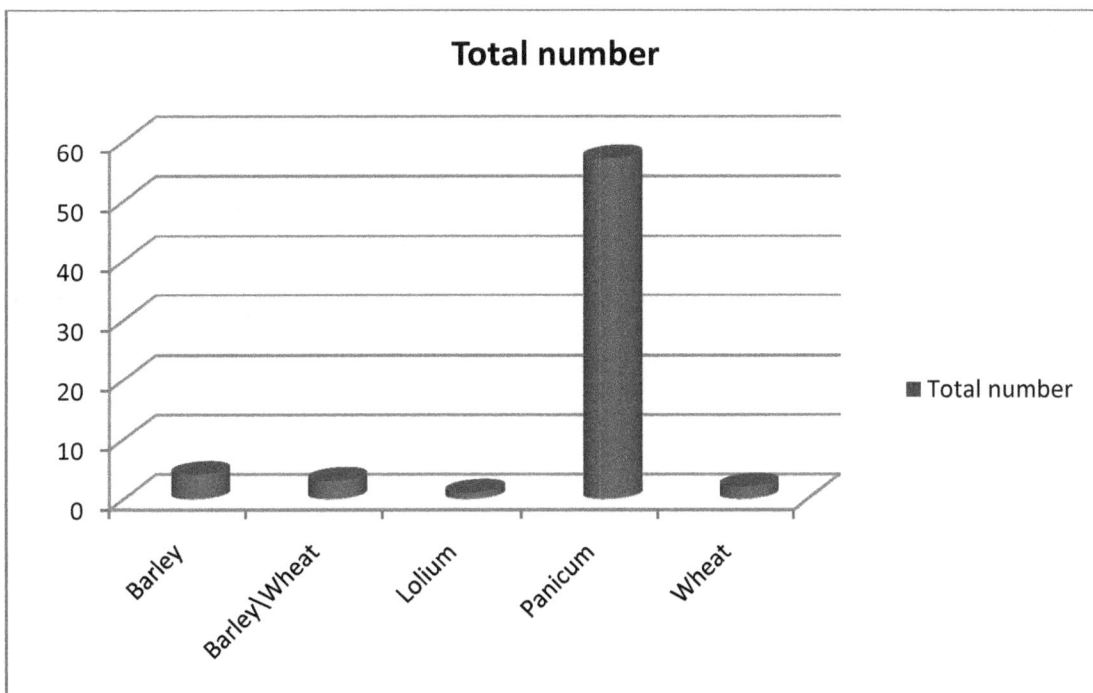

Figure 4.2.9 A graph showing the summary of impressions from Kashim el-Girba

Table 4.4 Summary of plant impressions from Khashim el Girba *Site*

No.	Plant types identified	Total number
1	Barley	4
2	?Barley\Wheat	3
3	Lolium	1
4	Panicum	57
5	Wheat	2

4.3 ARCHAEOBOTANICAL ANALYSIS OF THE KASSALA (KI) SHERDS

Fifteen sherds were selected out of a total of 22,163 excavated from the site of Mahal Teglinos, Kassala between 1980 and 1985 by Rodolfo Fattovich. This is 0.07 percent of the total. In broader terms the Kassala material is dated between 2000 and 1400 B.C. In this particular area they used chaff, as components in the composition of the ceramic not grains as in the case of *Khashim el Girba*. The components of the sherds are, thus, clay, chaff, quartz and fine sand particles. The colors of the sherds are black and dark grey. Thickness of the sherds on the average ranges between 0.5 to 0.7 cms. A detail of each sherd with plant impressions is presented below.

4.3.1 K1 II#15
Middle to Late Gash Group (ca. 2000-1500 B.C.)

Impressions are difficult to identify.

4.3.2 K1 II 11# 41
Middle to Late Gash Group (ca. 2000-1500 B.C.)

Few impressions on internal and external surfaces. At present the impressions are difficult to identify.

4.3.3 K1 II#100
Middle to Late Gash Group (ca. 2000-1500 B.C.)

Among the few impressions, it is possible to classify one of the impressions on the exterior surface, an impression of the lateral part of *Hordeum vulgare*, barley.

4.3.4 K1 II 11
Middle to Final Gash Group (ca. 2500-1400 B.C.)

The impressions are not identifiable.

4.3.5 K1 II 11 # 41?
Middle to Late Gash Group (ca. 2000-1500 B.C.)

Chaff are present, impressions not clear.

4.3.6 K1 II 11 # 63
Middle to Late Gash Group (ca. 2000-1500 B.C.)

At first the impressions were generally categorized as impressions of small millet. Detail analysis of the morphology of the impressions reduced the classification to *Eleuisine sp.* and *Phalaris sp.* due to the elongated shape of the glume. The rest *Panicum, Setaria, Paspalum* and *Echinocloa* have shorter glumes. On the external surface of the sherds five identifiable morphologies are recorded. Impressions number 1, 4 and 5 are three plate glumes whereas, 2 and 3 are single glumes of *Eleusine sp.* For further analysis, the sample is broken. Cross section of the broken surface demonstrated more imprints belonging to *Eleusine* sp.

4.3.7 K1 II 11 # 46
Middle to Late Gash Group (ca. 2000-1500 B.C.)

Similar glume impressions of small millet grains are available, *Eleusine sp.*

4.3.8 K1 II 11 # 21
Middle to Late Gash Group (ca. 2000-1500 B.C.)

A fruit stone impression of *Ziziphus spina-christi* is identified along the edge of the sherd. This is the genera utilized to fire the clay at the ethnographic sites of *Salaklaka* and *Indabaguna* in Ethiopia and at Kassala,

East Sudan (see chapter II of this volume). It is a source of vitamin in the absence of edible plants for some societies in times of drought. However, it is highly consumed by sheep and goats (Costantini pers.comm.). Another impression of *Phalaris* genera is also identified along the edge. The seeds of *Phalaris* are different in morphology than other small seeded millets, but the chaff is similar.

The third impression along the edge is a threshed imprint of *Eleusine sp.*, only the by-product without the grain. This impression has been compared with the chaff of *Eleusine sp.* from the comparative plant collections of the Oriental Museum of Rome, Bio archaeological laboratory (see fig. 4.3.1). The piece is full of chaff in addition to quartz and fine sand particles.

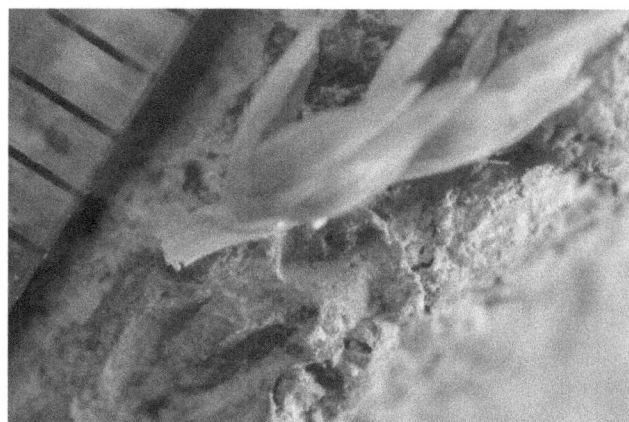
Figure 4.3.1 Image of the threshed imprint of Eleusine sp. *and the comparative plant specimen*

4.3.9 K1 II # 44
Middle to Late Gash Group (ca. 2000-1500 B.C.)

One impression of the dorsal and ventral glume of *Sorghum sp.* on the exterior surface is identified (see fig. 4.3.2). The chaff included in this sherd is in low percentage.

Figure 4.3.2 Image of the dorsal and ventral glume imprint of Sorghum sp. *and its comparative plant specimen*

Figure 4.3.3 Image of Setaria sp. *imprint and its comparative plant specimen*

4.3.10 K1 I6 # 28
Final Gash Group (ca. 1500-1400 B.C.)

Four very refined impressions of *Setaria sp.*, two on the interior and two on the exterior. *Setaria sp.* is identified from other millet genera because of its lined patterns on the grain on both ventral and dorsal surfaces. Some of the impressions have retained the charred glumes. The chaff is in low percentage and the impressions all in all are restricted on the surface.

4.3.11 K1 I 1 # 39
Final Gash Group (ca. 1500-1400 B.C.)

Two impressions belonging to *Setaria sp.* on the interior side of the sherd. In general this sherd demonstrated very few plant impressions. The low percentage seems to indicate that the grain impressions are occasional and not due to mix between clay and chaff.

4.3.12 K1 I 5 # 60
Final Gash Group (ca. 1500-1400 B.C.)

Only one plant impression on the exterior surface belonging to *Panicum\Setaria* genera.

4.3.13 K1 I 5
Final Gash Group (ca. 1500-1400 B.C.)

A very refined impression of *Setaria sp.* along the lip of the sherd (see fig. 4.3.3).

4.3.14 K1 I 6 #28
Final Gash Group (ca. 1500-1400 B.C.)

Only one impression of *Setaria sp.* in the internal surface.

4.3.15 K1 15 #3 4
Final Gash Group (ca. 1500-1400 B.C.)

On the lip of the exterior surface two *setaria sp.* impressions are identified (one ventral and the other dorsal impression). On the interior surface there is also one impression which is difficult to identify at the moment.

Table 4.5 Summary of plant impressions from Kassala (Mahal Teglinos) Site

No.	Plant (grain) impression identified	Total number
1	*Hordeum sp.*	1
2	*Eleusine*	7
3	*Panicum*	1
4	*Phalaris*	1
5	*Panicum\setaria*	1
6	*Setaria*	11
7	*Sorghum bicolor*	1
8	*Ziziphus spina-christi*	1

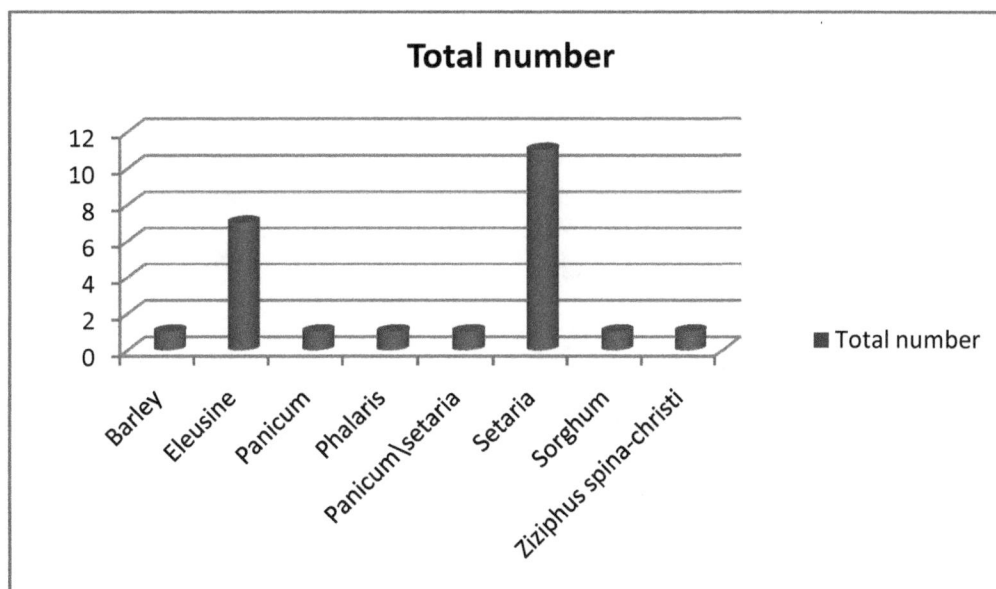

Figure 4.3.4 A graph showing types of plant impression from the site of Kassala

4.4 ARCHAEOBOTANICAL ANALYSIS OF THE JEBEL MOKRAM SHERDS

Two sherds were selected out of a total of 334 collected from surface from the site of Jebel Mokram between the years 1980 and 1995 by Rodolfo Fattovich. This is 0.6 percent of the total. The Jebel Mokram collections are dated between 1500-1000 B.C. These sherds are brown, grey and dark grey in color. The components of the ceramics are clay soil, fine sand particles and small percentages of plant materials.

4.4.1 JM 2
Early Jebel Mokram Group (ca. 1500-1000 B.C.)

Very few plant impressions are observable. The impresssions are of very small in size and are not very well pre-served. Most of the impressions belong to Panicoidaee, a group of *Panicum*. Thickness of the sherd is 0.5 cms.

4.5 ARCHAEOBOTANICAL ANALYSIS OF THE SHURAB EL GASH SHERDS

Three sherds were selected out of 2,931 collected from surface from the area of *Shurab el Gash* between 1982 and 1987 by Rodolfo Fattovich. The sherds with plant impressions constitute only 0.1 percent of the total. The occupational sequence of these sites ranges roughly between half of the 1st millennium B.C. to 1st centuries A.D. The sherds from *Shurab el Gash* are grey, brown and red in color and are rocker stamped, packed dotted. Zig zag lines and bands are also used as decoration motives.

4.5.1 EG 3
Early Jebel Mokram (ca. 1500-1000 B.C.)

This specimen is full of plant impressions. A lot of chaff were used while making the pottery (see the amount of chaff in fig. 4.5.1). The impressions are of a mix of glumes of *Pennisetum sp.* and *Eleusine sp.* The impressions of *Pennisetum* are longer in size and shape whereas that of *Eleusine* are shorter.

Figure 4.5.1 A picture showing the abundance of chaff in the composition of the ceramic

4.5.2 SEG 42 R-S
Hagiz Group (first centuries A.D.)

Very little evidence of chaff is observed on this sherd. But, on the external surface two impressions of *Panicum sp.*

4.5.3 SEG 42 G5
Hagiz Group (first centuries A.D.)

Very low percentage of chaff inclusions and the plant impression is not identifiable.

4.5.4 SEG 11
Late Jebel Mokram/Hagiz Group (half-late 1st mill. B.C.)

On the external surface only one impression of *Sorghum sp.* is identified (see fig. 4.5.2).

Figure 4.5.2 Impression of sorghum with its comparative plant specimen

4.5.5 SEG 42 R 5
Hagiz Group (first centuries A.D.)

On the interior surface a very refined impression of *Eleusine sp.* is identified (see fig. 4.5.3).

Figure 4.5.3 An imprint of Eleusine sp.

Table 4.6 Summary of plant impressions from
Shurab el Gash *Site*

No.	Plant impressions identified	Total number
1	*Pennisetum* glumes	Many
2	*Eleusin* glumes	Many
3	*Eleusine*	1
4	*Panicum*	2
5	*Sorghum sp.*	1

Chapter V
PHYTO-GEOGRAPHY, CHARACTER, MORPHOLOGY AND HISTORY OF THE IDENTIFIED PLANTS

The archaeobotanical study of the pottery collections from four areas and sites in Eastern Sudan rendered eight different plant species. From sites belonging to the *Kashim el Girba* area grain imprints like *Hordeum sp.*, *Triticum monoccocum/dicoccum*, *Lolium sp.*, and *Panicum sp.* were identified. The Kassala collection provided *Hordeum sp.*, *Eleusine sp.*, *Panicum sp.*, *Phalaris sp.*, *Setaria sp.*, *Sorghum sp.* and *Ziziphus spina-christi*. Imprints of *Panicum, Pennisetum, Eleusine* and *Sorghum sp.* were identified from the specimens of *Shurab el-Gash area* and a single sherd from *Jebel Mokram* exhibited very small imprints of *Panicoidaee* (see table 5.1). This chapter analyzes the characteristics of these crops, their life cycles, ecological preference (Phyto-geography) and related archaeobotanical information.

5.1 BARLEY, *HORDEUM SPP.*

Barley, the king of all crops!
Informant: Gabresilasse Abraha,
a farmer from Tigrai,
Northern Ethiopia

Barley and wheat were first domesticated in the Near East in the area known as the 'Fertile Crescent' (includes Jordan, Palestine, Lebanon, Syria, Southeastern Turkey, Western Iran and Iraq) around 8000 B.C. The archaeobotanical evidence from the same region demonstrates that the first barleys were the two-rowed barley. *Hordeum vulgare sp. spontaneum* is the wild ancestor of cultivated barley and it is commonly available in most places of the 'Fertile Crescent' (Ceccarelli and Grando, 2000: 51). Within the last 10,000 years barley has passed through a continuous manipulation by human beings to maximize its use for consumption and animal fodder. Currently barley stands fourth after wheat, rice and maize in the yield it provides and total area coverage. In Ethiopia, barley is the third important crop preceded by *tef* and maize (Asfaw 2000: 77).

In Northwest Ethiopia barley was supposed to have been in cultivation since about 3000 B.C. by one of the earliest inhabitants of the area, the Agaw people. In the southern part of Ethiopia, barley is seen as a sacred crop among the Oromo people. Botanists argue that the Ethiopian barley stock has gone through an independent line of evolution unlike the evolution of barley in Southwest Asia and the rest of the world. They argue that in Ethiopia *spontaneum* gene was cross fertilized and swallowed into the *vulgare* gene pool. Besides, current research pays particular attention to the diversity of barley types in Ethiopia, their disease tolerance behavior, germplasm conservation, ethnobotany of landraces as well as to possibilities to exploit such a diversity for breeding and rising modern barley cultivars, a potential that was already envisaged by Harlan four decades ago (Harlan 1969:83).

There are more than 180 agricultural varieties of barley today in the world and out of these 170 varieties are reported from Ethiopia. These varieties are classified into five groups; the *Viz. Convar. Deficiens, Distichon, Hexastichon, Intermedium, and Labile*. The *Deficiens* and *Labile* forms are indigenous to Ethiopia which can support the argument that a distinct evolutionary process in the morphology of barley has taken place in Ethiopia (ibid. 85-86).

In many parts of Northern highland Ethiopia farmers have a special place for barley giving the plant a unique and prestigious place among the crops. In local parlance it is named as *gebis yehil nigus*! meaning barley the king of all crops! One can ask how could a crop which is introduced from outside have acquired such a unique status? This labeling, however, has nothing to do with the autochthonous development or diffusionist idea. It has to do with the functional advantages of the crop. Barley as an ingredient is used in almost every beverage and food. Barley is an important component of *tella*, a traditional beer that is prepared at household level and *areke*, a traditional, distilled alcoholic drink. Barley is

Table 5.1 Summary of the archaeobotanical information from the sites of the Gash Delta

No.	Provenance	Site name	Chronology	Archaeobotanical Information
1	KG 5	Khashim el Girba	Butana Group (ca. 3500-2500 B.C.)	– Impression of a cereal, Gramineae
2	KG 23C-C3-15	√	Butana Group (ca. 3500-2500 B.C.)	– Rachies fragment of *Hordeum Vulgare*
3	KG96-66-10 641	√	Butana Group (ca. 3500-2500 B.C.)	– Impressions of *Panicum sp.*
4	KG23-SE-Slope	√	Butana Group (ca. 3500-2500 B.C.)	– Imprints of *Panicum sp.*
5	KG 96-82-8 395	√	Butana Group (ca. 3500-2500 B.C.)	– Imprints of *Panicum sp.*
6	KG 96A-L6-8 633	√	Butana Group (ca. 3500-2500 B.C.)	Imprints of – *Hordeum vulgare* – Cereals and glumes of Gramineae – *Triticum monococum\diococum* – Glume of barley\wheat, unidentified cereal glume – Ventral surface of wheat\ *Triticum Sp.* – Ventral surface of a half barley grain – *Lolium Sp.,*
7	KG 96 A-L6-8636	√	Butana Group (ca. 3500-2500 B.C.)	– Imprints of *panicum sp.*
8	KG 96 A-4 6 -6	√	Butana Group (ca. 3500-2500 B.C.)	– Imprints of *Panicum sp.*
9	KG 96-B1-6 643	√	Butana Group (ca. 3500-2500 B.C.)	– Imprints of *Panicum sp.*
10	K1 II# 100	Kassala	Classic to Late Gash Group (ca. 2000-1500 B.C.)	– Imprint of *Hordeum vulgare*
11	K1 II 11# 63	√	Classic to Late Gash Group (ca. 2000-1500 B.C.)	– Imprints of *Eleusine sp.*
12	K1 II 11# 46	√	Classic to Late Gash Group (ca. 2000-1500 B.C.)	– Imprints of *Eleusine sp.*
13	K1 II 11# 21	√	Classic to Late Gash Group (ca. 2000-1500 B.C.)	Imprints of – *Ziziphus spina-christi* – *Eleusine sp.* – *Phalaris sp.*
14	K1 II # 44	√	Classic to Late Gash Group (ca. 2000-1500 B.C.)	– Imprints of *Sorghum sp.*
15	K1 I6# 28	√	Final Gash Group (ca. 1500-1400 B.C.)	– Imprints of *Setaria sp.*
16	K1 I 1# 39	√	Final Gash Group (ca. 1500-1400 B.C.)	– Imprints of *Setaria sp.*
17	K1 I 5# 60	√	Final Gash Group (ca. 1500-1400 B.C.)	– Imprint of *panicum\Setaria* genera
18	K1 I 5	√	Final Gash Group (ca. 1500-1400 B.C.)	– Imprint of *Setaria sp.*
19	K1 I 5# 128	√	Final Gash Group (ca. 1500-1400 B.C.)	– Imprint of *Setaria sp.*
20	K1 15# 3 4	√	Final Gash Group (ca. 1500-1400 B.C.)	– Imprint of *Setaria sp.*

baked as bread. Barley is prepared as *besso* (traditional food prepared with hot pepper and butter and *besso* is also used as a non-alcoholic drink), *chiko* (a traditional food prepared by flour of barley and butter), *kollo* (roasted cereals), *Injera* (thin bread baked on griddle), *nifiro* (a boiled cereal), *genfo* (porridge), *atmit* (as a soup). It is believed that a person who consumes barley often is a healthy person.

Barley is a temperate cereal which is similar to bearded wheat. In Northeast Africa, excluding the Ethiopian highlands, most varieties of this crop have one grain in each spikelet and in each head there are two strips of grains parallel to each other. The leaves of barley seedlings do not have hairs unlike in wheat and they have soft auricles. In recent genetically modified barley, the glumes, which constitute the chaff are strongly attached to the seeds and are difficult to remove while threshing (DJ. Acland 1971: 17-18).

Barley grows best in areas where the amount of Rainfall is dependable and constant. The altitudinal preference of this crop is over 2100 meters or 7000 feet. Below this altitudinal range planting barley is not recommended due to low and unreliable rainfall. Barley cannot stand water logging and, thus, heavy soils are good for the growth of barley. Since moisture is not retained in sandy soils, such soil types are not preferred for barley (ibid.).

Previously from the site of Mahal Teglinos, Kassala, barley (*Hordeum sp.*) grains were identified as imprints in pottery by Costantini *et al.*, (1982). During the Late Neolithic and Bronze Age barley is reported from the site of Afyen, Toshka west, Buhen, Ukma and Sai, whereas, by the Napatan and Meroitic periods, the same crop is recovered from Qasr Ibrim, Qustul/Ballana, Kawa and Meroe (Fuller in press).

5.2 *LOLIUM SP.*

Lolium belongs to the Graminaea family. It is considered as a weed of cultivated cereals (mainly wheat and barley). *Lolium sp.* and other grasses are believed to have evolved during terminal Pleistocene as a result of hybridization while plants were migrating when the ice sheets were advancing and retreating. By ca. 8000 B.C. this plant had conquered forest and forest margin environment. The geographic origin of this plant, however, is not yet known (Simmonds 1976: 137).

At present *Lolium sp.* is no more a species of forest and forest margins. It is associated with agricultural activity. It is probably the first herbage grass that has later become a crop. The preferred habitat of this plant is nitrogen-rich and disturbed settings with high humus content. Simmonds (1976: 137) argues that *Lolium sp.* had probably covered a wide area in Europe following the westward migration of farmers during the Neolithic period.

A *Lolium* type of plant was recovered from a hearth site at Nabta Playa, the Western Desert of Southern Egypt, site 96E 4 (Barakat and Fahmy 1999:37).

5.3 SORGHUM: 'AN AFRICAN DOMESTICATE'

Sorghum is an important crop in drier parts of Northeast Africa. It can stand drought and water logged conditions. It can also provide a good product on sterile soils. Generally, the processing of sorghum including harvesting, threshing and cleaning are difficult and labor intensive. This plant has a very practical branched root system which is probably a good reason for its drought resistant nature. The roots of sorghum will not collapse in dry soil since the endodermis of the plant possesses large amount of silica. This mineral is sometimes observable as part of an imprint of the plant on pottery fragments (DJ Acland 1971).

The height of the stem of sorghum varies from species to species and may grow as tall as 4.5 meters. In addition, depending on the variety the heads, the panicles (may be open or intact), the glumes (large or small), the seed coat (strong or easily removable), the color (white, brown or red), and the endosperm (may be stronger or edible) could vary. Depending on the variety also sorghum could mature in between 3 to 8 months at an average altitude of 1100 m.a.s.l.

During its growing season sorghum needs at least 300-380 mm rainfall. It can also tolerate short period of water logging and, thus, grow well on heavy clay soils. In similar conditions to with bulrush millet, sorghum can give good yield in exhausted and over utilized environments. Sorghum is also strongly drought resistant due to the structure of the roots, its ability of reducing transpiration by closing its stomata and rolling its leaves. Many varieties of this crop adapt well in warmer conditions. It can also grow as high as 2400 m.a.s.l. (Ibid.)

Natural selection and human manipulation has resulted in five distinct races of sorghum, which are mainly identified from one to another by a careful observation of the morphologies of their spikletes. Out of the five different races, four are found in Ethiopia (Butler *et al.*, 1977: 325-327). These are:

1- *Sorghum bicolor*: this race has relatively small grains. The grains are totally covered by the glumes. It is characterized by primordial spikelete morphology.

2- *Sorghum guinea*: the guinea race is mostly grown in West Africa, where the amount of rainfall is high. The glumes are longer and have spaces in relation to the grains. It is distinguishd by discoid grains.

3- *Sorghum caudatum*: this race has a protruding part on the side of the grain on which the embryo is attached and the grains are defined by lack of symmetry. It is widely grown in Sudan and Chad and in other savanna lands of Northeast Africa.

4- *Sorghum durra*: the grains of this race have a leaf like shape with a protruding part at the top and a narrow cram at the bottom. The glumes are lined transversely. Durra is the most economically crucial sorghum in Ethiopia.

The fifth race, *Sorghum kafir*, is not cultivated in Ethiopia. This race requires an annual rainfall of more than 600 mm. It is well adopted to the southern part of the equator in Africa (ibid.).

The oldest evidence for sorghum is from Nabta Playa and is dated back to 8000 B.P. At Farafra, 82 grains and spikelets of *Sorghum Moench* were identified from the sites of 96E 4 and 96F 1, and 2 grains from Abu Ballas (Barakat and Fahmy 1999: 42). In Central Sudan from the site of Kadero I wild sorghum, *S. Verticiliflorum Stend. (Stapf.)* was recovered (Kryzyaniak 1978). From the site of *Jebel Abu Gamal* (belonging to Jebel Mokram Group), *Sorghum cf. bicolor* was identified as an imprint on pottery (Costantini *et al.*, 1982). Magid (1989a) has reported desiccated wild species of Sorghum from Shaqadud cave and as imprints in pottery from Umm Dariewa, Zakiab, Jebel Tomat and Rabak sites. From the site of Agordat in the Barka Valley of the lowlands of

Eritrea wild sorghum imprints were identified from pot sherds (Beldados 2007: 6-7).

In the highlands of Ethiopia and the adjacent lowlands to the Northwest Sorghum is utilized as *injera* by mixing with the flour of *tef*. In addition, it is also served as *Kollo, tella, kita, nifro*.

5.4 THE MILLETS

The millets are large genera of small seeded plants under the Gramineae family. These include *Panicum, Setaria, Paspalum, Phalaris, Echinocloa* and *Eleusine. Eleusine coracana*, finger millet, also termed African millet, grows from Nigeria to the west to Eritrea in the East and as far as Southwest Africa and Natal to the south. It is an important staple food in East and Central Africa and in some parts of India. This millet type is small in size with a diameter of 1-2 mm. The color is often reddish brown and sometimes whitish. One very good advantage of finger millet is that it can be stored for a long period of time. Without deterioration or damage it can stay up to ten years, a benefit against periods of famine (Purseglove 1976: 91).

Eleusine coracana is an indigenous crop to the highlands of Ethiopia. India is considered as the secondary center for the evolution of this crop. It was hypothesized that the crop was taken to the Indian sub-continent some 3000 years ago. Sorghum and bulrush millet were also considered to have been transported around this time (ibid: 92).

The flour of this plant can be consumed as porridge and bread. In Ethiopia, it is also prepared as *kita*, and *injera*. It is also germinated and dried for preparing beer and other local drinks.

Pennisetum americanum, P. typhoides, P. glaucum is popularily known as bulrush millet also pearl millet. It is an annual crop 0.5 to 4 meters tall. It grows in semi arid regions of Africa and India. It is commonly cultivated in the Sahel zone close to the Sahara in tropical Africa and the Sudan. This geographic range is almost similar to that of Sorghum growing areas. It requires lower amount of rainfall than sorghum with the northern limit having the 250 mm isohyte. In India, this variety possesses the fourth largest crop field next to rice, sorghum and wheat.

Bulrush millet is advantageous in drier environments in that it needs a low amount of rainfall, and grows in poor soils and sandy soils which cannot support other crops. The seed of Pennisetum is about 4 mm long and its color may vary between white, yellow, grey, and light blue (ibid.).

This millet variety can be consumed as porridge and bread. In Ethiopia, in particular, it is used as *kita*, and *injera*. It can also be deliberately planted as a fodder for animals.

Grains of *Pennisetum sp. (Brum.) Stapf.* and *Hubbard*, were recovered from the early Neolithic site of *Ehs-Shaheinab*, in Central Sudan (Magid 1984). In Egypt seven grains of *Pennisetum\Cenchrus* type were retrieved from site 96E 4, Farafra and at Nabta Playa (Barakat and Fahmy 1999: 42).

Echinochloa is the fastest growing of all the small seeded millets. It can mature within six weeks time. It is native to the old world, in tropical, sub-tropical and temperate zones. It is cultivated in Southeast Asia and is consumed as porridge by mixing the flour with the flour of rice. One of its varieties *Echinocloa frumentacea* common in India is awn-less and is genetically identical with the wild progenitor, *Echinochloa colonum*, native to Malaysia and Java. *Echinochloa frumentacea* is probably selected from *Echinochloa. Colonum* (Purseglove 1976: 308).

Echinocloa P. Beauv. is the most common grass at Nabta Playa. The recovered grains in most cases are naked. In sites like 96E 3, 96E 4 and 96 F and at Hidden Valley, all within Nabta Playa 18 grains of this species were recovered. In addition, at Eastpans site, 40 grains of the same taxa were retrieved (Barakat and Fahmy 1999:41).

From the site of *Nag el-Deir* a number of grains of *Echinocloa colonum* were identified in the intestines of an ancient mummy dated 4000-3500 B.C. This evidence was interpreted as an indicator of the cultivation of this cereal for the purpose of consumption. A number of researchers used to argue that this plant was not cultivated in Pre-dynastic Egypt but rather consumed wild. The same arguement was confirmed later by Fahmy (1995) when he recovered a wild spikelet, belonging to predynastic Hierakonpolis (3800-3500 B.C.). The morphology of this species is elliptical with a flat front and curved back. The maximum width of the grain is found at the middle of the grain (ibid.).

Setaria which is also known as Foxtail millet is very commonly cultivated in North Africa, Southeastern Europe and Asia. *Setaria italic* is widely planted in India and is the most preferred millet type in Japan. Its wild progenitor is unknown. However, it is considered that *Setaria viridis*, a common old world weed, is the wild ancestor of *Setaria italic*. In China, this variety was one of the five sacred plants around 2700 B.C. and China is considered as its probable place of domestication (Purseglove 1976: 309).

Apart from the identifications made in the course of analysis of sherds from the site of Kassala in this volume, *Setaria sp.* was also identified as impression on pottery from the same site earlier by Costantini *et al.*, 1982:30-33 and D'andrea 1991:16. In central Sudan, from Ehs-Shaheinab site (Islang and Nofalab) the same genus is recognized (Magid 1984, 2003) (see table 5.2 below). The same genus is also reported from Abu Darbien, in Central Sudan, within the time ranges of 7700±140, 7860±190 and 8500±100. Some 29 desiccated grains of *Setaria sp.* were recovered from Nabata Playa from site 96E 4 and 96F 1 at Farafra and other 13 from

Table 5.2 Summary of Archaeobotanical Information gathered from different sites of Northern Sudan and the highlands of Ethiopia and Eritrea

No.	Analyzed by:	Site Name	Chronology	Archaeobotanical Information
1	Arkell (1949)	Khartoum Hospital and Gerif town	The earliest Khartoum site, Saggai, is dated between 7410±100 B.P. and 7230±100 B.P.	-non carbonized *Celtis integrifolia Lam.*
2	Magid (1989a)	Esh-Shaheinab		-non carbonized *Celtis integrifolia Lam.*
3	Magid (1989a)	Ehs-Shaheinab site (Islang and Nofalab)		-carbonized remains of *Elaeis guineensis Thumb.* and *Zizyphus sp*
4	Kryzyaniak (1978)	Kadero 1.		*C. integrifollia Lam.*, and *Hyphaene thebaica (L.) Mart.*
5	Magid (1989a)	Zakyab and Umm Direwiya.		*C. integrifolia Lam.* and wild *sorghum S. Verticiliflorum Stend. (Stapf.)*
6	Magid (1984)	Shaqadud cave	Between 4200 and 3600 years B.P.	– fruits *of Zizyphus sp. Lam.* – *Grewia Sp. (Forsk.)*, – seeds of *Pennisetum sp. (Brum.) Stapf. and Hubbard*, – a seed of *sorghum sp. Stapf.*, – seeds of *Panicum trugidum Forsk.*, – seeds of *Solanum dubium L.*, – *Setaria sp.*, – *Crotalaria sp.*
7	Magid (2003)	Blue Nile area		– *Sorghum sp. Moench,* - – *Setaria sp. Beauv,* – *Echinochloa sp. Beauv*
8	Costantini *et al.,* (1982)	Mahal Teglinos (Kassala)	2nd millennium B.C.	– *sorghum cf. bicolor* – *Seteria cf. glauca, cf.* – *paspalum sp.*
9	Costantini *et al.,* (1982)	Kassala 1 and 2 (Mahal Teglinos)		– barley, *Hordeum sp.* – several fruit stones of *Zyziphus sp.*
10	Mgjid (1989a)	Abu Darbien	7700±140	– *Panicum sp.* – *Setaria sp.* – *Crotularia sp.* – *Capparis sp.* – *Ziziphus spina-christi* – *Celtis integrifolia*
11	Magid (1989a)	Abu Darbien	7860±190	– *Setaria sp.* – *Ziziphus spina-christi* – *Celtis integrifolia*
12			8500±100	– *Setaria sp.* – *Celtis integrifolia*
13	Magid (1989a)	Shaqadud cave site	4123±86	*Setaria sp.*
14	Magid (1989a)	Shaqadud cave site	Between 3615±88 and 4123±86	Carbonized and desiccated plant remains of – Wild sorghum sp. – *Panicum turgidum* – *Pennisetum sp.* – *Sida alba* – *Cratalaria sp.* – *Solanum dubium* – *Grewia tenax* – *Ziziphus spina-christi* – Cruciferae – Leguminaceae
15	Magid (1989a)	Umm Direwia	Between 5600±110 and 6010±90	Impression in pottery of – *Setaria sp.*
16	Magid (1989a)	Umm Direwia	6010±90	Impression in pottery of – Wild sorghum sp.

No.	Analyzed by:	Site Name	Chronology	Archaeobotanical Information
17	Magid (1989a)	Umm Direwia	4950±80	Impression in pottery of – Staked spikelet of wild sorghum – Lower glume of wild sorghum
18	Magid (1989a)	Zakiab	Between 5350±90 and 5660±80	Impression in pottery of – *Setaria sp.* – Wild sorghum sp. – bracts
19	Magid (1989a)	Jebel Tomat	Between 1770±80 and 4140±90	Impression in pottery of – *Setaria sp.* – *Panicum sp.* – *Sesamum sp.* – Wild sorghum
20	Magid (1989a)	Rabak	Between 4490±100 and 6020±150	Impression in pottery of – Wild Sorghum sp. – Cucurbitaceae
21	D'Andrea *et al.*, (2011)	Aksum	Pre and proto Aksumite context	Seeds of – Chick pea (*Cicer artietinum*) – Barley (*Hordeum vulgare*) – Tef (*Eragrostis tef*) – Lentils (*Lens esculentum*) – Linseed (*Linum usitatissimum*) – Free-threshing wheat (*Triticum aestivum\durum*) – Emmer wheat (*Triticum dicoccum*)
22	D'Andrea *et al.*, (2008)	Ona Culture, around Asmara	1st millennium BCE	Seeds of – emmer and free-threshing wheat (*Triticum dicoccum* and T. *durum/aestivum*), – hulled barley (*Hordeum vulgare*), – tef (*Eragrostis tef*), – lentils (*Lens culinaris*), – Linseed (*Linus usitatissimum*).

Abu Ballas. *Setaria P. Beauv.* was thought to have been cultivated as a cereal in predynastic Egypt (Barakat and Fahmy 1999; 41-42).

Panicum is another variety of millet within the Gramineae family. It has many diploid and tetraploid varieties in Asia. One of its species, *Panicum miliaceum* has been cultivated from ancient times. It was considered as one of the preferred items on the menu in the Roman Empire. This crop, however, is less important in South and Southeastern Asia. It is considered that this species was first domesticated in East Asia. It is difficult to pin point its probable progenitor.

Panicum adapts very well to arid environments. It requires a low amount of water for its growth. It can give product in too hot climatic condition where short rainy seasons are available. Unlike other cereals it can give yield in humus low poor soils. In the desert it is seen as an important fodder grass and its branches are gathered for fuel (Barakat and Fahmy 1999: 40).

A number of naked seeds of *Panicum turgidum* were recovered from Nabta Playa, southern part of the Western Desert of Egypt by Wasylikowa and Martens (1995) and the context is dated to 8000 B.P. Twenty one grains of the same species were identified from Farafra, another site within Nabta Playa, dated to 7030-6750 B.P. and 32 more grains were retrieved from Abu Ballas (6200-6000 B.P.) (ibid.).

5.5 WHEAT, *TRITICUM SPP.*

The world's foremost plant!
Feldman 1976: 120

Wheat is one of the earliest crops that human beings used to cultivate some 10,000 years ago. Both archaeological and botanical evidence suggest that einkorn (*Triticum monococcum*) and emmer (*Triticum dicoccum*) were domesticated in the 'Fertile Crescent' of the Near East by about 10,000 years B.P. The study of the evolutionary history of wheat focus primarily on the economic and cultural importance of wheat over the past ten thousand years and the rich variety of forms it possesses (Nesbitt 2001: 37). There are almost 17,000 different varieties of wheat today in the world. The growth of wheat is restricted to higher altitudes. This plant is mainly cultivated in Southern Russia, the central plateaus of the United States of America, Canada, the Mediterranean area, North China, India, Southwestern Australia and Argentina (Feldman 1976: 120).

Based on the number of chromosomes available wheat is classified into three main groups. These are einkorn, emmer and bread wheat (Vavilov 1951). Many recent varieties of wheat belong to the hexaploid *Triticum aestivum*. It has a high gluten content in its endosperm and is preferred for bread making. *Triticum turgidum var. durum* is a tetraploid variety of wheat and grows mainly in relatively drier regions like the Mediterranean basin. This variety has a larger grains and low-gluten and is preferred for macaroni and semolina. Diploid varieties are economically less important (Feldman 1976: 122-123).

Around Asmara, in Eritrea, from the ancient site belonging to the Ona Culture emmer and free-threshing wheat (*Triticum dicoccum* and *Triticum durum/aestivum*) were recovered by flotation technique (D'Andrea *et al.*, 2008). The Ona sites are dated to the 1st millennium BCE. In Ethiopia from the site of Aksum free threshing wheat (*Triticum aestivum/durum*) and emmer wheat (*Triticum dicoccum*) were recovered from pre and proto Aksumite contexts (D'Andrea *et al.*, 2011:369). In Northern Sudan *Triticum sp.* was recovered from the sites of Afyeh, Ukma, and Sai in Late Neolithic context. In Napatan and Meroitic periods *Triticum sp.* was identified in sites of Qasr Ibrim, Qustul/Ballanna, Kawa and Meroe and *Triticum dicoccum* were reported from Qasr Ibrim and Kawa. *Triticum durum* and *Triticum aestivum* were both identified from Qasr Ibrim (Fuller in press).

5.6 *ZIZIPHUS SPINA-CHRISTI*

Ziziphus spina-christi in general is an ever green shrub or herb. There are many varieties of this plant classified at separate family level. The Rhamnaceae family grows along the Nile banks and low lying plains. The Chenopodiaceae family of *Ziziphus* is commonly available in low lying plains as a weed in cultivable plots. The Cruciferae family is an annual or perennial herb that grows widely in low lying plains, as a weed in cultivable lands and in aquatic environment. The Cucurbitaceae family is an ascending herb that grows in a wide range of different habitats. The Leguminaceae family, are another variety of Ziziphus, which are dominantly herbs or shrubs that rise in a wide range of different habitats. The other widely recognized family of Ziziphus is the Molluginaceae, classified as herbs that grow in shallow clay and silt soils (Magid 1989b: 317).

The earliest archaeobotanical evidence of this plant goes back to the Early Khartoum (c. 9000-6000 years B.P.) in Central Sudan. Apart from the current investigation from Kassala, one impression of a seed of *ziziphus spina-christi (L.)* wild was recovered from the site of Abu-Darbien. Costantini (Pers. Comm.) argues that it is a source of vitamin in the absence of edible plants for some societies in times of drought. It is, however, consumed commonly by sheep and goats.

Chapter VI
GRAINS AND FRUIT STONES FROM K1, MAHAL TEGLINOS, KASSALA, AND THEIR WIDER IMPLICATIONS

Some 700 carbonized, non-carbonized and desiccated grains and fruit stones were analyzed in the Bio-archaeological Laboratory of the National Museum of Oriental Art, Rome with the intention of understanding the paleoenvironment and vegetation history of the Kassala area and the nearby territories of Northeastern Africa. The collections are results of excavations conducted at Mahal Teglinos (K1) in the year 1991and were kept in 50 test tubes. The labeling of the excavation was K1 V (trench number V). All of the macrobotanical remains were recovered by dry sieving. The GPS cocordinates of the site where the excavation was conducted is 15°26.57N and 036°25.72E. The result of the analysis of these collections is presented in this chapter.

1- Test tube number: 7
   Provenance: K1?
   Identification: – 78 complete fruit stones of?
        (not yet identified)
        – 4 half fragments of fruit stones
        (unidentifiable)
        – 2 very well made beads

2- Test tube number: 15
   Provenance: K1 A-L 7
   Identification: – 4 beads
        – 16 fragments of *Celtis integrifolia* fruit stones
        – 3 burned fragments of *Ziziphus sp.*

3- Test tube number: 27
   Provenance: K1 A-H 5
   Identification: – 15 fragments of fruit stones of *Celtis integrifolia*

4- Test tube number: 28
   Provenance: K1 A-E 10

Identification: – 14 fully preserved fruit stones of *Celtis integrifolia*, some are damaged, others are fragments. Most are mineralized. Two of them are burned

5- Test tube number: 29
   Provenance: K1 A-C 5
   Identification: – 1 complete fruit stone of *Celtis integrifolia*
        – 1 fragment of *Celtis integrifolia*
        – 3 fragments of insect holes (unidentifiable)

6- Test tube number: 30
   Provenance: K1 A-B 7
   Identification: – 1 well preserved fruit stone of *Celtis integrifolia*
        – 4 half fruit stones of *Celtis integrifolia*
        – 1 fragment of *Ziziphus spina-christi*, charred
        – 1 fish bone

7- Test tube number: 31
   Provenance: K1 A-E 5
   Identification: – 1 incomplete fruit stone (unidentifiable)

8- Test tube number: 32
   Provenance: K1 A-F 8
   Identification: – 3 beads
        – 4 fragments of *Vigna unguiculata*
        – 6 fragments of *Celtis integrifolia* fruit stones
        – 7 fragments of *Ziziphus spina-christi.*

9- Test tube number: 33

Provenance: K1 A-L 4
Identification: – 2 small fragments of *Ziziphus spina-christi*
– 1 petrified piece (clay)

10- Test tube number: 34
Provenance: K1 A-A 7
Identification: – 3 fragments of *Ziziphus spina-christi* fruit stones
– 1 complete fruit stone of *Celtis integrifolia*
– 15 fragments of *Celtis integrifolia*

11- Test tube number: 35
Provenance: K1 A-H 4-5
Identification: – 6 well preserved fruit stones of *Celtis integrifolia*
– 1 burned fragment of *Celtis integrifolia*

12- Test tube number: 36
Provenance: K1 A-K 2
Identification: – 2 fragments of *Celtis integrifolia* fruit stones
– 1 fragment of *Ziziphus spina-christi*

13- Test tube number: 37
Provenance: A-L 6
Identification: – 1 fragment of *Celtis integrifolia*
– 1 insect remain
– 1 fruit stone of *Ziziphus spina-christi*

14- Test tube number: 38
Provenance: K1?
Identification: – 1 fruit stone of *Celtis integrifolia*

15- Test tube number: 41
Provenance: K1 E-B 24
Identification: – 3 damaged fruit stones of *Ziziphus spina-christi*
– 17 fragment fruit stones of *Ziziphus spina-christi*
– 1 well preserved fragment of cowpea, *Vigna unguiculata*

16- Test tube number: 42
Provenance: K1 A B-E 22
Identification: – 2 burned fragments of *Ziziphus spina-christi*

17- Test tube number: 43
Provenance: K1 A-E 9
Identification: – 5 well preserved fruit stones of *Celtis integrifolia*
– 7 damaged seeds of *Celtis integrifolia*
– 1 burned fruit stone of *Ziziphus spina-christi*
– 12 damaged seeds of *Ziziphus spina-christi*

18- Test tube number: 44
Provenance: K1 A-G 10
Identification: – 5 well preserved fruit stones of *Celtis integrifolia*
– 14 damaged fruit stones of *Celtis integrifolia*
– 7 burned fragments of *Celtis integrifolia*

19- Test tube number: 45
Provenance: K1 A-A8
Identification: – 2 fruit stones of *Celtis integrifolia*
– 4 damaged and burned seeds of *Ziziphus spina-christi*
– 5 small, immature fruit stones of *Ziziphus spina-christi*
– 3 fragments of legumes, *Vigna unguiculata*

20- Test tube number: 46
Provenance: K1 A-E 11
Identification: – 8 well preserved fruit stones of *Celtis integrifolia*
– 4 half fruit stones of *Celtis integrifolia*
– 5 burned and damaged seeds of *Ziziphus spina-christi*
– 1 fruit stone of *Ziziphus spina-christi* with evidence of rodent teeth gnawing
– 2 fragments of *Vigna unguiculata*

21- Test tube number: 47
Provenance: K1 A-B 11
Identification: – 8 complete fruit stones of *Celtis integrifolia*
– 9 damaged fragments of *Celtis integrifolia*
– 1 completely burned seed of *Ziziphusspina-christi*
– 1 seed of *Vigna unguiculata*
– 1 charcoal piece

22- Test tube number: 48
Provenance: K1 ACB 15
Identification: – 1 half fragment of *Celtis integrifolia*
– 7 damaged and burned fruit stones of *Ziziphus spina-christi*
– 2 unidentified fruit stones, one of which is well preserved.

23- Test tube number: 49
Provenance: K1 A-E 12
Identification: – 12 damaged fragments of *Ziziphus spina-christi* fruit stones out of which 2 well preserved
– 3 fruit stones of *Celtis integrifolia*
– 1 unidentifiable fruit stone

24- Test tube number: 50
Provenance: K1 AC-B 23

Identification: – 2 half fruit stones of *Ziziphus spina-christi*
– 10 damaged fragments of *Celtis integrifolia*
– 2 desiccated fruit stones of *Vigna unguiculata*

25- Test tube number: 51
Provenance: K1 A-A9
Identification: – 5 well preserved fruit stones of *Celtis integrifolia*
– 11 damaged fruit stones of *Celtis integrifolia*
– 2 very small whole fruit stones of *Ziziphus spina-christi*
– 1 fragmentary fruit stone of *Ziziphus spina-christi*
– 1 remain of an insect

26- Test tube number: 52
Provenance: K1 A-H9
Identification: – 8 charred remains of *Ziziphus spina-christi* fruit stones

27- Test tube number: 53
Provenance: K1 A-L9
Identification: – 4 well preserved fruit stones of *Celtis integrifolia*
– 8 damaged fruit stones of *Celtis integrifolia*
– 1 burned fruit stone of *Ziziphus spina-christi*
– 1 fragment of *Ziziphus spina-christi*

28- Test tube number: 54
Provenance: K1 A-B 12
Identification: – 1 fruit stone of *Celtis integrifolia*
– 1 half fruit stone of *Celtis integrifolia*
– 1 burned fruit stone of *Ziziphus spina-christi*
– 5 fragments of *Ziziphus spina-christi*

29- Test tube number: 55
Provenance: K1 A-H9?
Identification: – 1 fruit stone of *Celtis integrifolia*

30- Test tube number: 55
Provenance: K1 AB-E 14
Identification: – 2 well preserved fruit stones of *Celtis integrifolia*
– 3 half pieces of *Celtis integrifolia*
– 5 burned fragments of *Ziziphus spina-christi*
– 3 remain of legumes, *Vigna unguiculata*

31- Test tube number: 57
Provenance: K1 B-E 13
Identification: – 4 fruit stones of *Celtis integrifolia*

– 2 well preserved fruit stones of *Ziziphus spina-christi*
– 1 half broken fruit stone of *Ziziphus spina-christi*
– 1 damaged fruit stone of *Vigna unguiculata*

32- Test tube number: 58
Provenance: K1 A-L 5
Identification: – 1 well preserved fruit stone of *Celtis integrifolia*
– 1 half fruit stone of *Celtis integrifolia*
– 5 damaged fragments of *Ziziphus spina-christi*
– 3 completely burned unidentifiable fruit stones

33- Test tube number: 59
Provenance: K1?
Identification: – 10 fragments of *Celtis integrifolia*

34- Test tube number: 60
Provenance: K1 A-G8
Identification: – 1 unidentifiable remain

35- Test tube number: 63
Provenance: K1 VSTR. 12
Identification: – 3 fruit stones of *Ziziphus spina-christi*
– 6 fragments of *Ziziphus spina-christi*
– 5 fragments of *Vigna unguiculata*
– 1 un identifiable fruit stone
– 1 *Grewia bicolor Juss*

36- Test tube number: 64
Provenance: K1 STR 8
Identification: – 1 fruit stone of *Vigna unguiculata*
– 10 fragments of *Vigna unguiculata*

37- Test tube number: 65
Provenance: K1 BSQB-C-G-H SU 38
Identification: – 52 fruit stones of *Ziziphus spina-christi*, two of them with impressions from rodent teeth
– 1 fragment of unidentifiable fruit stone
– 1 fragment of *Grewia bicolor Juss*.

38- Test tube number: 66
Provenance: K1 BSQB-C-G-H SU 38
Identification: – 34 *Grewia bicolor Juss* fruit stones, the bulk of them are charred and 1 of these is well preserved
– 1 fragment of *Ziziphus spina-christi*
– 1 unidentifiable fruit stone

39- Test tube number: 68
Provenance: K1 V STR 6
Identification: – 1 fragmentary fruit stone of *Ziziphus spina-christi*

40- Test tube number: 69
    Provenance: K1 VINTERFACE STR 10-12
    Identification: – 2 fragments of *Vigna
                        unguiculata*
                      – many fragments of charcoal

41- Test tube number: 70
    Provenance: K1 V STR. 10
    Identification: – fragments of charcoal

42- Test tube number: 71
    Provenance: K1 V
    Identification: – 1 fragment of *Vigna unguiculata*
                      – small charcoal fragments

43- Test tube number: 72
    Provenance: K1 E?
    Identification: – 3 fragments of unidentifiable fruit
                        stones
                      – charcoal fragments

44- Test tube number: 73
    Provenance: K1 V STR. 8
    Identification: – 1 fragment of charcoal

45- Test tube number: 74
    Provenance: K1 V STR. 14
    Identification: – 4 well preserved grains of *Vigna
                        unguiculata*
                      – 1 damaged grain of *Vigna
                        unguiculata*
                      – 15 small fragments of *Vigna
                        unguiculata*

46- Test tube number: 75
    Provenance: K1 V STR 8
    Identification: – 2 fragments of *Vigna unguiculata*
                      – many charcoal fragments

47- Test tube number: 76
    Provenance: K1 V INTERFACE STR 10-12
    Identification: – 2 fragments of *Ziziphus spina-
                        christi* fruit stones
                      – 3 charred grains of *Vigna
                        unguiculata*

48- Test tube number: 77
    Provenance: K1V ST R. 12
    Identification: – 4 fragments of grains of *Vigna
                        unguiculata*
                      – 1 unidentifiable grain

49- Test tube number: 78
    Provenance: K1 V STR 12
    Identification: – 2 fragments of *Vigna unguiculata*
                      – 1 big damaged grain of *Vigna
                        unguiculata*

50- Test tube number: 79
    Provenance: K1 V STR. 10
    Identification: – 1 fragment of *Vigna unguiculata*
                      – charcoal fragments

6.1 PHYTO-GEOGRAPHY AND CHARACTERISTICS OF THE GRAINS AND FRUIT STONES

Mahal Teglinos (K1) is the major site of the Gash Group culture. It has rendered cultural remains that range in period between Classic to Final Gash Group (Ca. 2000-1400 B.C.). In addition to the fruit stones and grains collections from Mahal Teglinos, an inventory of beads, fish bones, insect remains and petrified pieces was also conducted. Emphasis, however, is placed on the analysis of the fruit stones and the grains due to the specific scope of this research. The summary of the quantification of the above listed (identified) specimens is as follows:

1. *Celtis integrifolia*
   – Complete fruit stones- 75
   – Fragments- 133

2. *Ziziphus spina-christi*
   – Complete fruit stones- 79
   – Fragments- 103

3. *Grewia bicolor Juss.*
   – Total number of seeds- 36

4. *Vigna unguiculata*
   – Complete fruit stones- 14
   – Fragments- 55

5. Beads
   – Total number- 9

6. Petrified piece
   – Total number- 1

7. Fish bone
   – Total number- 1

8. Insect fragments
   – Total number- 3

9. Charcoal pieces
   – Total number- 82

10. Unidentifiable grains and fruit stones
    – Total number- 93

6.1.1 *Grewia bicolor Juss.*

Grewia bicolor Juss. is a shrub or a tree within the Tiliaceae family. There are many other species that belong to this family like *Grewia grisea N.E. Br., Grewia kwebensis N.E.Br., Grewia mossambicensis Burret, Grewia miniata Mast. Ex Hiern, Grewia salvifolia Heyne ex Roth.* The *bicolor Juss* variety can grow as tall as 9-14 meters. The bark is grey and sometimes yellow-brown. The leaves can range between 1 to 8 cm in length and have dark green upper side and white or grey blue, hairless lower side. At the time of extreme heat during the dry season the leaves tend to bend downwards. It

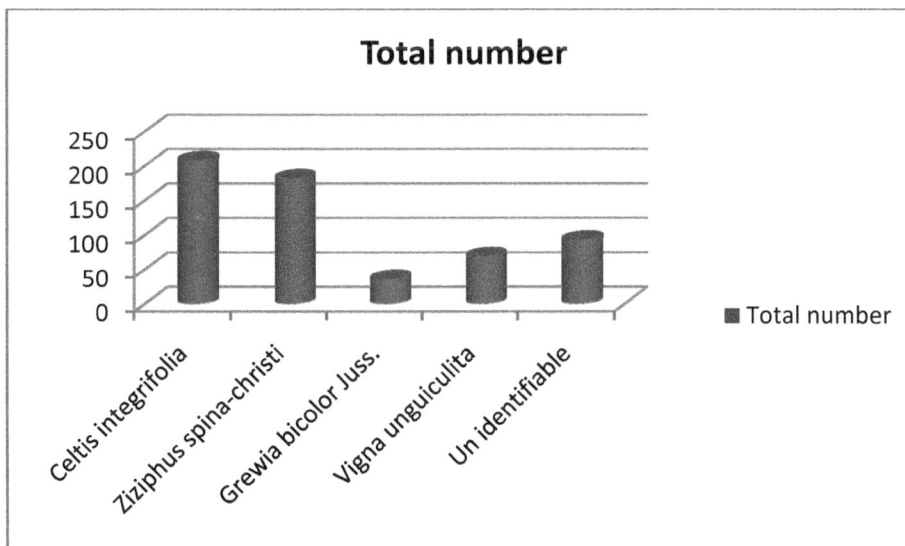

Figure 6.1 A graph showing the total number of the grains and fruit stones

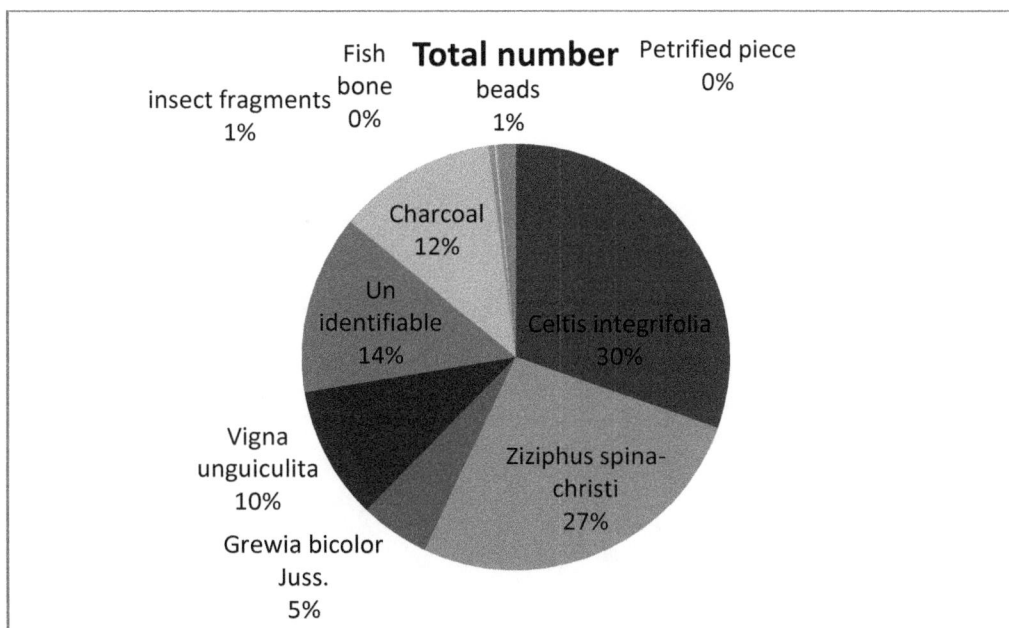

Figure 6.2 A pie chart showing the total number of all findings as a percentage

Figure 6.3 Grewia Bicolor Juss.
from Mahal Teglinos, Kassala, K1

produces small, yellow and shiney flowers which have 0.8 cm long sepals. The plant gives flowers and fruits during the rainy season. The fruits are about 5 mm in diameter. They are round and can have different colors: brown, yellow brown or purple-black (Maydell 1990: 291) (see the sample from Mahal Teglinos, Figure 6.3).

The geographical preference of *Grewia bicolor Juss.* are the Semiarid and sub humid tropical Africa and India. It has a particular preference for calcareous soils. It also grows along river banks with sandy soils and stony escarpments. It often grows in Sahelian bushlands. An average annual rainfall of 200-800 mm is sufficient for its complete life cycle (ibid).

The fruits of *Grewia bicolor Juss.* are edible. In West Africa, in Niger, it is used to prepare a local drink called '*madi*' in Hausa language. It is a good source of food for varieties of birds. The fruits and leaves are consumed by cattle. The nutritional value of the leaves is good. The woods is used as walking sticks, as bowls, tool handles and fire woods (ibid).

6.1.2 *Ziziphus spina-christi (L.) Desf.*

The name "spina-christi" derives from the legend that the crown of Jesus Christ was made from branches of this Ziziphus species.

Maydell 1990: 407

A discussion of the various family level varieties and the archaeobotanical history of *Ziziphus sp.* are provided under chapter V (section 5.6). Here a further detail is provided on its phyto-geography, plant biology and human utilization. *Ziziphus spina-christi (L.) Desf.* is a shrub within the Rhamnaceae family. It is also known by its alternative synonym *Ziziphus amphibian A. chev.* The phyto-geographical study of this plant demonstrated its wide distribution along the Sahara and Sahel in Africa, from Senegal all the way to the Sudan and Arabia. An average annual rainfall of 50-300 mm is sufficient for the growth of *Ziziphus spina-christi (L.) Desf.* It also grows well along river banks and seasonally inundated lands (Maydell 1990: 407).

The leaves of *Ziziphus spina-christi (L.) Desf.* can vary in length between 4-6 cm and are browsed by sheep and goats. Fruits can have a maximum of 1 cm length, red brown, fleshy and edible (El Amin 1990: 295) (see the sample from Mahal Teglinos, figure 6.4). Unlike the case of *Celtis integrifolia*, there are two seeds within the cover of *Ziziphus* varieties. The wood is used for posts, tool handles, furniture, and carpentry. It is an important source of fire wood and charcoal. Branches are used for fencing. Leaves and branches have medicinal importance for bandages to treat skin wounds and body part sprains.

Figure 6.4 Ziziphus sp. *fruit stone from Mahal Teglinos, Kassala, K1*

6.1.3 *Celtis integrifolia Lam.*

Celtis integrifolia Lam. is a large tree within the Ulmaceae family. This species can grow as high as 25 meters. It has a unique stem that could have a thickness of 1.5 metre. The roots have often a swollen shape. The bark of the tree has a smooth surface and is grey in color. Leaves are green in color and oval in shape. *Celtis* trees give flower from February to April. The fruits have single seed, fleshy, elliptical and about 1 cm long. The seeds are white in color (see the sample from Mahal Teglinos in figure 6.5) (Maydell 1990: 231).

This plant is common in tropical climatic setting, between 3 to 16 degrees north of the equator. It is widely available from Senegal to East Africa. Outside of Africa, it grows within the Arabian Peninsula. *Celtis* requires an annual rainfall of between 500 and 700 mm. It grows in plains and dune lands. It has a special preference for loam, clay and alluvial soils (ibid.).

The leaves can be used in soups. The younger leaves and the fresh fruits are eaten as a salad. The bark is used as a traditional medicine for rheumatism. The roots of *Celtis* can be used to treat mental disorders. Different parts of this species are used to cure headaches, sterility, oedema, asthenia, boils, for wound covering, to facilitate delivery and as a vermifuge (ibid.).

Figure 6.5 Non-carbonized Celtis *fruit stones from Mahal Teglinos, Kassala, K1*

6.1.4 Cowpea (*Vigna unguiculata*)

Cowpea is predominantly a savanna plant widely growing in the semi-arid and sub-humid areas of Africa and Asia. It is a leguminous plant that currently grows in most places of Central and West Africa. For most inhabitants of sub-Saharan Africa, cowpea is an important source of protein in their diet. The cotyledons alone possess about 22-27 per cent protein. The leaves of this plant are an important source of vitamin C. The plant is consumed by humans by roasting, boiling and after grinding into flour. Parts of the plant are also used for medicinal purposes and in the production of dyes. It is also used as a fodder for livestock (D'Andrea *et al.*, 2007: 690).

Cowpea can adapt well in marginal environments where it is not suitable for the growth of other plants. In West and Central Africa, cowpea is a reliable source of food in times of drought. It is often intercropped with pearl millet and sorghum. There is an assumption that humans first gathered wild cowpea to use it as an animal fodder (ibid: 691-692).

There is no clear understanding of the domestication history of cowpea. One precluding factor for the lack of understanding is the presence of huge varieties in the morphology of both the domesticated and the wild progenitor. The mix between the two forms (wild and domesticated) has also increased the variation. Based on the absence of the wild form outside of Africa, it is concluded that this plant was domesticated in Africa. The two probable areas for the domestication of cowpeas are Northeast Africa and tropical West Africa. More research is, however, required to locate a single area of origin within the continent (Coulibally *et al.*, 2002: 358-66).

In India, cowpea was recovered from an archaeological context which is dated back to 1700-1500 B.C. The date from West Africa is somewhat earlier 1830-1595 B.C. based on AMS dating. The closeness in time range may lead us to hypothesize an early dispersal to the Indian Sub-continent (D'Andrea *et al.*, 2007: 693).

6.2 SUMMARY

Four of the most commonly identified macrobotanical remains recovered by dry screening method from Mahal Teglinos, Kassala; *Grewia bicolor Juss., Ziziphus spina-christi, Celtis integrifolia and Vigna unguiculata* adapt basically to semi-arid and sub humid environmental conditions. On the average, these species require an annual rainfall of 200-700 mm. The Sahara and Sahelian zone, thus, seems to be a favorable setting within Africa. All of these plants can be consumed by human beings in one way or another, used as medicine and utilized as a source of fodder for livestock. Besides, some of these plants happen to be important raw materials for the making of household objects, furniture and construction of houses and fences.

Based on analogy from archaeobotanical and ethno-archaeological studies from west Africa, and on the basis of the fact that the grains and the fruit stones were recovered from cultural deposits, I argue that these plants could also be an additional source of subsistence for the prehistoric inhabitants of Northeast Africa in general and the Kassala area in particular.

Chapter VII
SURVEY AND TEST EXCAVATION AT KASSALA, NORTHEASTERN SUDAN

7.1 SURVEY

Members of the Antiquities Department from Khartoum National Museum and State of Kassala Ministry for Archaeology, Tourism and Wild Life conducted extensive survey of potential sites in Kassala and the nearby localities in June 2010. With the objective of recovering more archaeological and archaeobotanical data and with the idea of preparing an archaeological map of the area, some of the sites (UA 53, UA 17, 14, UA 129, and K1; see maps 7.1 for a general location of the study area and map 7.2 for drainage systems, geographical location and distribution of the sites) were re-visited by members of the Italian Archaeological Mission in Eastern Sudan of the University of Naples," L'Orientale" from November 2 to 19, 2010. In due course, sherds with vegetal remain impressions were also collected. Summary and laboratory analysis report of the sites is provided in the following sub-topic. A test excavation was also conducted at the site of Mahal Teglinos, the report of which will also be presented in this chapter.

7.1.1 Site code: UA 53

Culture: Gash Group and Jebel Mokram Group
Chronology: Late 3rd-early 1st millennium B.C. (see open archive of the University of Naples, "L'Orientale", http://opar.unior.it/460/1/AMReport_Eng.pdf: 11).
Function: Settlement\Cemetry
GPS: 36°12'44''.6770 E
       15°07'17''.4488 N

7.1.1.1 *Sample Code: S53-a*

A very crude baked clay similar to the samples from the excavation spot at Mahal Teglinos. It is very rich in plant temper. The temper material mainly belongs to chaff of Sorghum composed of empty glumes, grains and spikelets. On the external part, there is an attachment of clay and chaff on the original surface.

7.1.1.2 *Sample Code: S53-b*

In this sample, the presence of chaff of sorghum is not evident.

7.1.1.3 *Sample Code: S53-c*

This sample is similar to samples from the excavation spot at Mahal Teglinos. The temper material belongs to the chaff of sorghum. The quantity of sorghum chaff inclusion, however, is generally limited.

7.1.1.4 *Sample Code: S53-d*

A crude baked clay similar to the samples from the excavation spot. A high quantity of chaff of sorghum is used as temper material. Along the edge of the sample, a very clear mineralized grain of *Sorghum sp.* is identified.

7.1.1.5 *Sample Code: S53-e*

A crude fired clay with high quantity of chaff temper belonging to sorghum. It, however, exhibits little evidence of grain imprints. On the external part, there is an attachment of clay and chaff on the original surface.

7.1.1.6 *Sample Code: S53-f*

A crude fired clay with high quantity of chaff temper belonging to *Sorghum sp.* Grain imprints of sorghum are not evident.

7.1.2 Site code: UA 17

Culture: Two phases of occupation, the Butana Group and the Hagiz Group (http://opar.unior.it/460/1/AMReport_Eng.pdf:8)
Chronology: Early 3rd millennium B.C. and 500 B.C. to 500 A.D.
Function: Settlement\ Islamic Cemetry

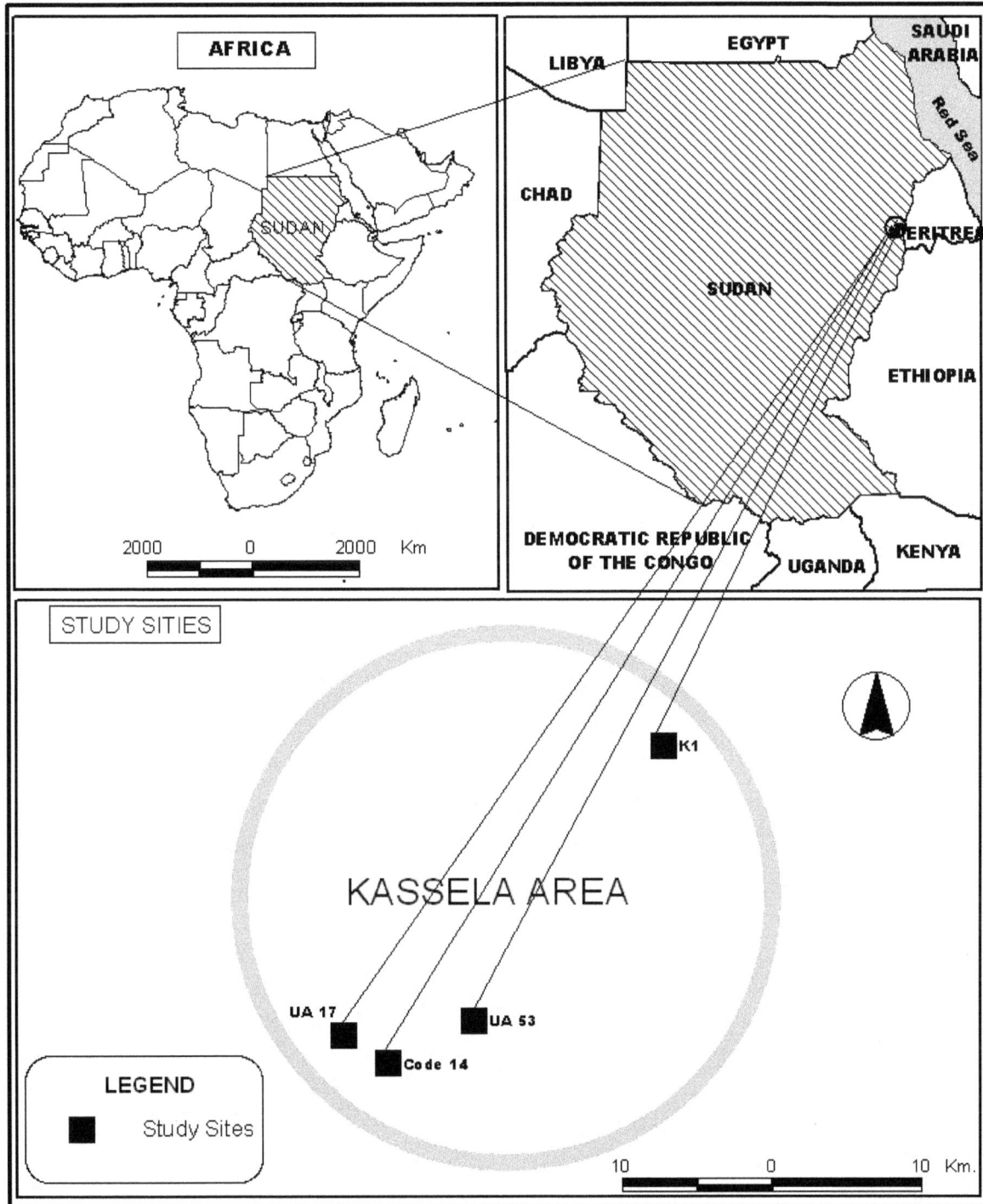

Figure 7.1 Map of Kassala and the surveyed areas

GPS: 36°03'32''.7719 E
  15°06'37''.2315 N

A piece of sherd is investigated under the site code UA 17. The sherd exhibits no grain impression. However, the presence of chaff belonging to Sorghum is evident.

7.1.3 Site code: 14

Culture: From the archaeological materials visible on the surface, it is categorized as belonging to the Butana

Group, the Gash Group and Jebel Mokram (http://opar.unior.it/460/1/AMReport_Eng.pdf:6)
Chronology: Early 3rd millennium B.C. to Early 1st millennium B.C.
Function: Settlement\Cemetry
GPS: 36°06'03''.9709 E
  15°04'40''.3365 N

7.1.3.1 *Sample Code: S14a*

The sample exhibits a rich quantity of chaff temper. The chaff belongs to sorghum. There are clear and

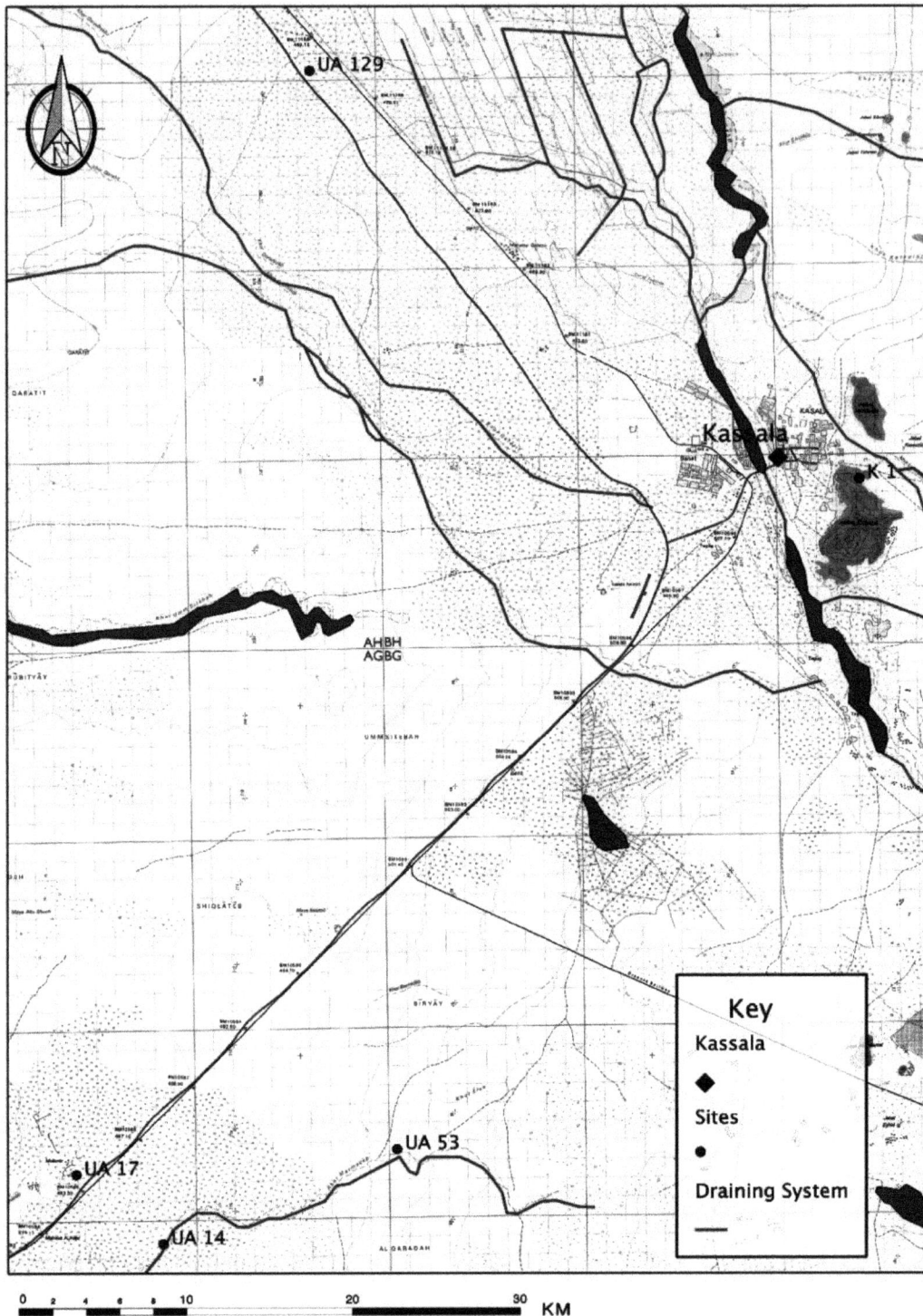

Figure 7.2 A map showing drainage systems, geographical location and distribution of the sites

identifiable impressions of *Sorghum sp.* on both surfaces. Analysis of this sample will continue by breaking the sample and looking for charred remains.

7.1.3.2 *Sample Code: S14b*

It is the lip (mouth) part of a crude pot. The quantity of chaff temper is limited in this fragment. *Sorghum bicolor* grain impressions are identified on both the internal and external surfaces. The crudeness of the sherd is similar to samples from the excavated spot at Mahal Teglinos, K1.

7.1.3.3 *Sample Code: S14c*

A crude baked clay. This sample exhibits a high percentage of chaff mainly of glumes of sorghum.

7.1.3.4 *Sample Code: S14d*

The only sample that demonstrated a different composition of plant material. The temper material in this sample belongs mainly to small seeded plants. Along the edge of the sample there are the whole mineralized grain of millet and an imprint of the same plant side by side visible under microscope. Based on the small, parallel, horizontal microscopic lines on the imprint, the plant is comparable to *Setaria sp.*

Figure 7.3 An imprint of Setaria *and its mineralized grain*

7.1.4 Site code: UA 129

Culture: Hagiz Group (http://opar.unior.it/460/1/ AMReport_Eng.pdf:15).
Chronology: 500 B.C. to 500 A.D.
Function: Settlement\Cemetery
GPS: 36°10'18''.1302 E
       15°38'09''.4625 N
Remarks: This site is located 30 kilometers to the Northwest of Kassala. It is a Beja land where the Hadendewiya group is currently residing. They inhabited the area from Kassala all the way to Port Sudan. They widely cultivate sorghum. According to local informants, the Beniamir Bejas are not present at this specific site.

7.1.4.1 *Sample Code: S129-a*

A relatively well-prepared and smoothened piece of sherd. There is a consistent presence of chaff of sorghum as temper material. There are grain impressions of sorghum on both the internal and external surfaces.

7.1.4.2 *Sample Code: S129-b*

Crude fired clay similar to the excavated samples. The presence of chaff of sorghum is consistent. Grain impressions of Sorghum were not identified.

7.1.5 Site code: K1

Culture: Jebel Mokram Group
Chronology: 2nd millennium B.C.
Function: Settlement
GPS: 36°25'57'' E
       15°26'57'' N
Remark: It is located in Mahal Teglinos very near to K1 V.

A single piece of fired clay from this site demonstrated wild and cultivated garin imprints of *Sorghum bicolor.*

7.2 EXCAVATION AT MAHAL TEGLINOS, K1 VI

The spot for excavation at Mahal Teglinos, Kassala, was chosen due to observation of large circular fired clay area very rich in vegetal remains while surveying the site. At first sight the exposure was thought to be a fire place/hearth. The surface of the excavated floor is also rich in lithic artifacts. Two by two meters trench was opened. Later the 2 x 2 m was reduced to 1 x 2 m with the intention of clearing the whole area of the fired circular clay. A maximum depth of 70 cm was excavated. The GPS co-ordinates of the excavation spot were 36°25'57'' E and 15°26'57'' N. The excavation spot is labeled as K₁VI, 2010.

7.2.1 Collections from the surface floor

The surface is characterized by fine grained grey sandy soil. On the Northeast part of the floor an exposed fired clay bulk is observable. From the surface of the excavated spot around 76 pottery fragments and 145 fragments of fired clay were collected. All of the fragments of the fired clay were very rich in vegetal remains.

A total number of thirty four (34) stone tools belonging to the LSA/microliths category were also collected from the surface floor. The raw materials used for the manufacturing of the stone tools include quartz, basalt and chert. The table below (table 7.1) summarizes the number of stone tools in terms of the raw material used. As can be seen from the data and the chart, quartz is the dominant raw material utilized for the manufacturing of the stone tools followed by basalt. Small sized fragments of bones of a bovid are also among the collections from the surface.

Table 7.1 Table showing a summary of raw materials and stone tools

No.	Raw material	Total Number
1	Quartz	21
2	Basalt	11
3	Chert	2

7.2.2 Stratigraphic layer-1 (SU-1)

The next layer has a brownish and greyish sandy soil. Stratigraphic layer-1 is measured about 20 cm below the surface and it goes down to ca. 45 cm. From this surface a total of 31 sherds were collected, 29 of which have vegetal remains.

7.2.3 Stratigraphic layer-2 (SU-2)

This layer has whitish and greyish sandy soil. Stratigraphic layer-2 is measured about 45 cm from the surface and the excavation was concentrated to the Southeast and Southwest section of the square. The layer

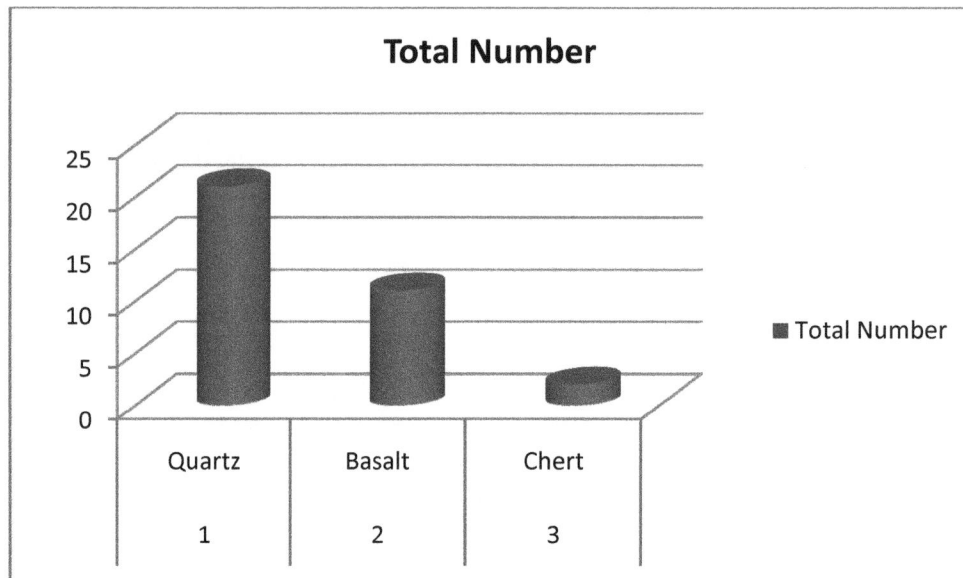

Figure 7.4 A graph showing the summary of raw materials and stone tools

Figure 7.5 A picture showing quartz and chert tools from surface floor (stratigraphic unit-0)

rendered 31 pot fragments which are all parts of a single pot. The pot is decorated with parallel incised lines. The spot in which fragments of a single pot was recovered were more likely a living floor since we were also able to uncover a lower grinding stone.

7.3 LABORATORY ANALYSIS OF THE EXCAVATED SHERDS

Microscopic examination of the baked clays from K1 VI, 2010 exhibited the details of the compositions of the samples. The clay soil has quite a proportion of sand particles. Other mineral grains including quartz are also observable. Chaff of Sorghum is used as temper material consistently and uniformly in all of the samples from the excavated site. An in-depth analysis of the grain and chaff impressions using different comparative sorghum species (wild and domesticated) enabled us to categorize

some of the imprints as belonging to an intermediate morphotype. In addition, a Leica Qwin soft ware is used to measure the difference in the dimensions between the wild and cultivated Sorghum bicolors. Length of the wild Sorghum bicolor grain imprint is 9.0 mm and its width 3.0 mm, whereas the cultivated variety has a length of 7.9 mm and a width of 2.6 mm (see figure 15, 16 and 17 for a comparison of the dimensions of wild, cultivated and modern variety of Sorghum). Small stems and leaves of straw were also used as temper materials. The internal surface of the baked clay fragments is coarse in general and has high porosity, whereas the external part is smoothened fairly using plant fabric and show low porousity.

By breaking the samples, it was possible to observe more burned plant parts such as spiklets and glumes of Sorghum, small seeded plants and other cereals. Below, a summary of plant impression analysis for some selected samples is presented.

7.3.1 Sample-3
Sample code-S3-1

A pinkish, red-brown fired clay with dark burned edges. The length and width of the sample are 105 and 60 mm. The thickness of the sherd is 24 mm. It is full of chaff belonging mainly to sorghum. There are three different types of imprints on this sample, Setaria sp., wild sorghum bicolor and Vigna unguiculata.

7.3.2 Sample-3
Sample code- S3-2

A red brown fired clay with 88 mm length and 74 mm width. The thickness of the sample is 30 mm. It is chaff tempered, most being sorghum. An imprint of cultivated sorghum bicolor was identified from this sample.

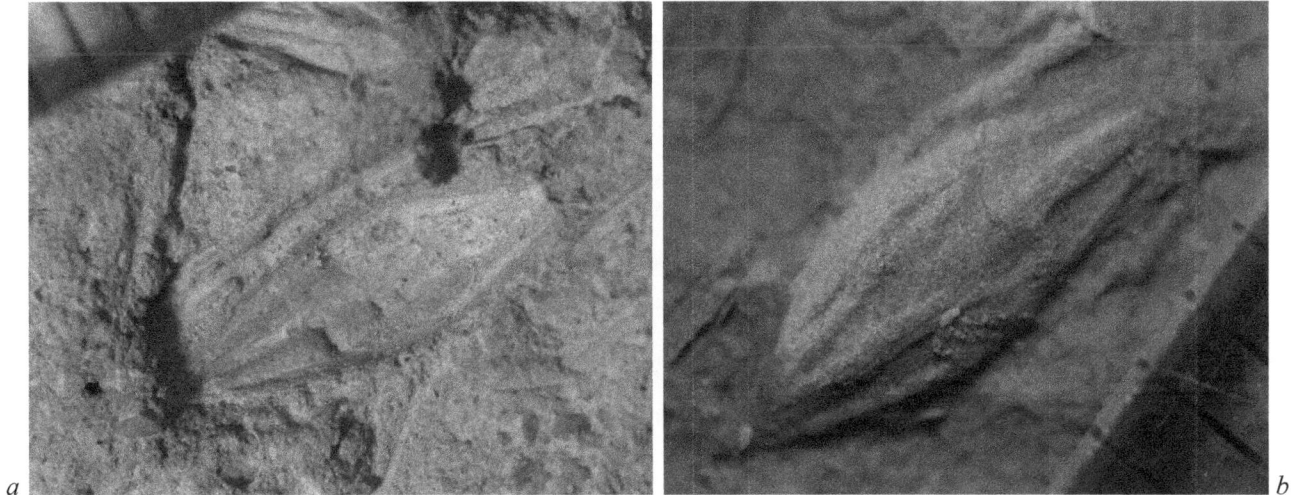

Figure 7.6 Wild Sorghum bicolor a. the imprint and b. the cast

Figure 7.7 An imprint of Vigna unguiculata

7.3.3 Sample-3
Sample code- S3-3

This piece of fired clay exhibited eleven identifiable plant impressions (see figures 7.8 and 7.9). The impressions belong to a fruit stone, spikletes of sorghum, and grains. The morphology of the grain impressions can be basically divided into two, a bit rounded and enlongated. Most of the rounded impressions can be compared with cultivated sorghum or intermediary morphotype i.e. not fully domesticated, whereas close observation of the morphotypes of the enlongated impressions demonstrated that they belong to the wild progenitor. This intermediary morphotype, probably, indicates one of the earliest evidence towards the domestication of the plant. By breaking the sample, it was possible to see chaff and spikelets of sorghum as an imprint, imprints of small stems and leaves of straw.

The fired clay has a pinkish, brownish and light grayish color. The exterior has a finished surface and the interior is rough and unfinished. The length and the width of the baked clay are 82 mm and 68 mm respectively. The thickness of the sherd is 22 mm.

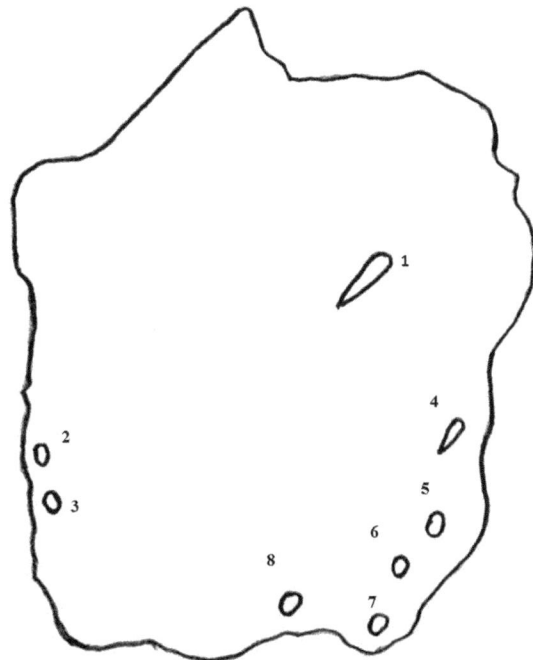

Figure 7.8 Positions of grain\fruit stone impressions on the external surface of the sherd, Sample code- S3-3
Keyfor the seed impressions:
1. *Imprint of the grain of Sorghum, Sorghum bicolor, wild.*
2. *Imprint of the grain of sorghum, Sorghum bicolor, wild.*
3. *Imprint of the grain of Sorghum, Sorghum bicolor, wild.*
4. *Imprint of the grain of Sorghum, Sorghum bicolor, cultivated*
5. *Imprint of the grain of Sorghum, Sorghum bicolor, cultivated*
6. *Imprint of the grain of Sorghum, Sorghum bicolor, cultivated*
7. *Imprint of the grain of Sorghum, Sorghum bicolour, cultivated*
8. *Imprint of the grain of Sorghum, Sorghum bicolor, cultivated*

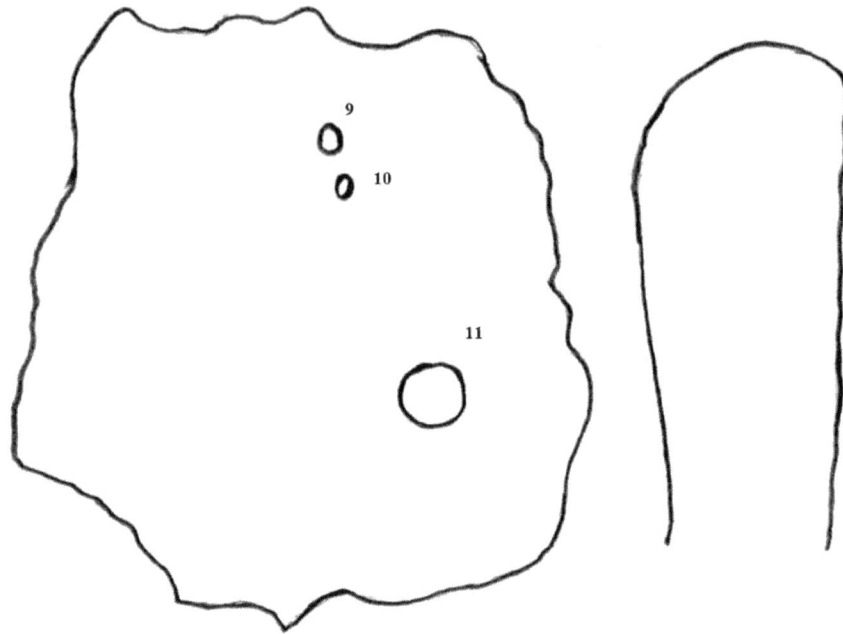

Figure 7.9 Positions of grain impressions on the internal surface of the sherd, Sample code- S3-3
Key for the impressions:

9. *A very refined impression of glume and spikelet base*
10. *A very refined impression of glume and spikelet base*
11. *Large impression of a fruit stone, unidentifiable*

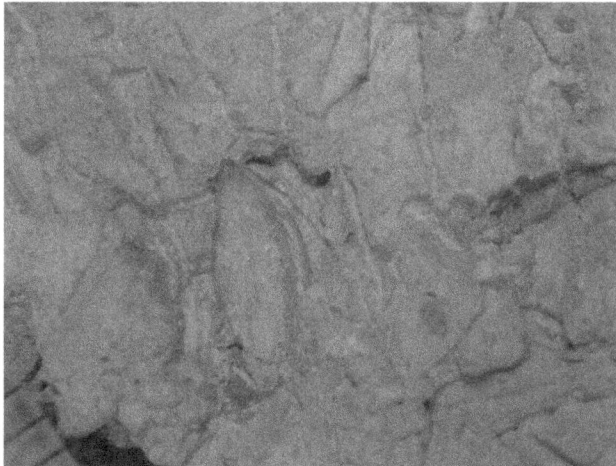

Figure 7.10 An imprint of wild sorghum,
Sorghum bicolor

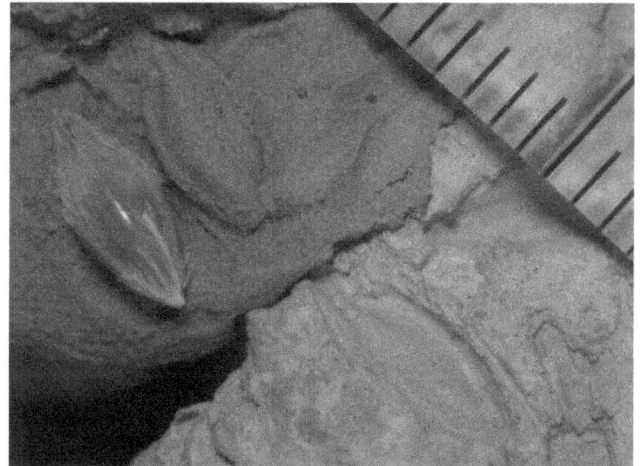

Figure 7.11 An imprint of cultivated Sorghum bicolor,
its cast and its comparative grain from collection

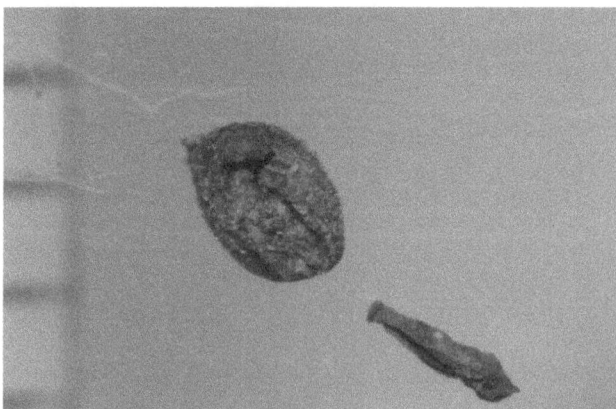

Figure 7.12 Charred grain of cultivated
Sorghum bicolor *from a broken fire clay*

Figure 7.13 Spikelet bases of Sorghum bicolor

7.3.4 Sample-3
Sample code- S4

Brown, pinkish and reddish chaff tempered baked clay. It exhibits stamped decoration made with a rolling stick. Length and width of the sherd is 68 mm and 65 mm respectively and its thickness is 33 mm. As in sample SU2-1, it has a plastered attachment on its external surface. On the external surface two very refined imprints of *Sorghum sp.* are documented among many. The imprints belong to the intermediate morphotype of *Sorghum bicolor*. Along the edge of the exterior surface, a sterile glume imprint of Sorghum is documented.

7.3.5 Sample-3
Sample Code-S5

A reddish brown sample with dark edges. The length and width of the smple are 63 mm and 58 mm respectively. The thickness of the sherd is 28 mm. On the interior and exterior imprints of wild and cultivated *Sorghum bicolor, Setaria sp.* and *Ziziphus spina-christi* were identified.

Figure 7.14 An imprint of Ziziphus spina-christi

7.3.6 Sample-3
Sample Code-S6

A redish brown fired clay with 56 mm length and 46 mm width. The thickness of the sample is 27 mm. It is chaff tempered belonging mainly to sorghum. Its grain imprints are compared with both wild and cultivated *Sorghum bicolor.*

7.3.7 Sample-3
Sample code-S7

This sample is the mouth of a crude fired clay vessel, red brown and chaff tempered. The length and width of the sample are 52 mm and 40 mm respectively. Thickness of the sample is 28 mm. From this sample both wild and cultivated grain imprints of *Sorghum bicolor* were identified.

7.3.8 Sample-3
Sample code-S8

A grayish and brownish fired clay. The length, width and thickness of the sample are 39 mm, 34 mm and 9 mm. This sample demonstrated very clear wild grain imprints of *Sorghum bicolor* on its inner surface.The amount of chaff used is very high. The external surface is roughly finished or smoothed, whereas the interior has a coarse surface.

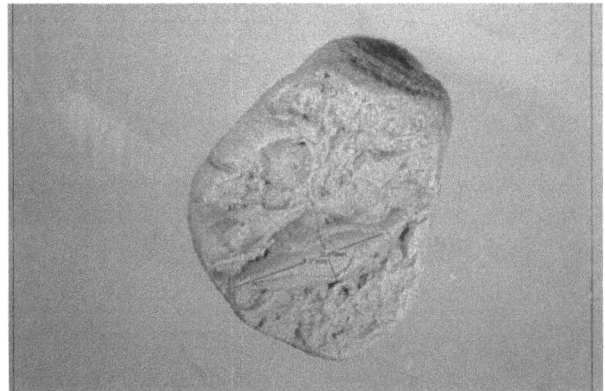

Figure 7.15 Calculated dimension of wild Sorghum bicolor *(9 mm x 3 mm) grain imprint*

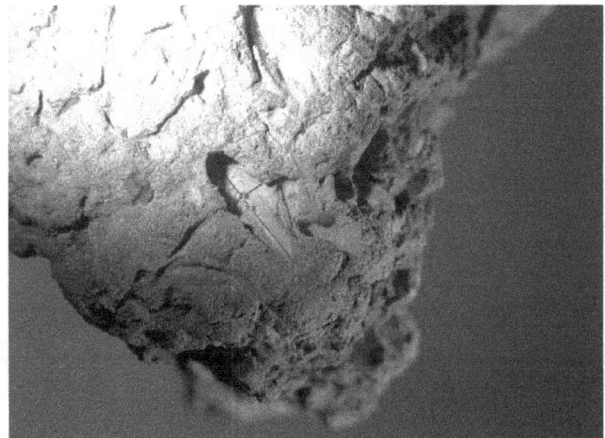

Figure 7.16 Estimated dimension of cultivated sorghum, Sorghum bicolor *(7.9 mm x 2.6 mm)*

Figure 7.17 Estimated dimension of modern variety of sorghum, durra (4.7 mm x 2.7 mm) after comparing the cavity with Sorghum durra comparative collection

7.3.9 Sample-3
Sample code-S9

A redish-brown sample with 38 mm length and 33 mm width. The thickness of the sherd is 8 mm. This sample exhibited imprints of wild and cultivated grains of *Sorghum bicolor*.

7.3.10 Sample-3
Sample code-S10

A relatively very small sample, reddish brown in color, with 25 mm length and 19 mm width. The thickness of the sample is 10 mm. From this sample imprints of wild and cultivated grains of *Sorghum bicolor* were identified. Along its edge impression of *Setaria sp.* is identified. The dimmension of the wild *Sorghum bicolor* identified is 8.93 mm length and 3.08 mm width. This piece of sherd is a very good example for the amount of chaff used within a small fragment (see figure 7.18).

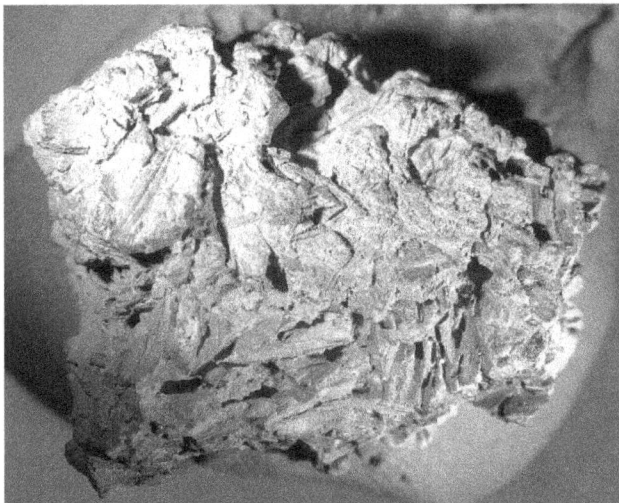

Figure 7.18 Microscopic image showing high percentage of chaff in a very small fragment (25 mm x 19 mm)

7.3.11 Sample-4
Sample code- SU2-1

Brown, reddish and pinkish baked clay. Like other fragments, it has many chaff inclusions. It is the mouth of a crude pot. On the exterior part of the original surface, there is a secondary attachment. The purpose of the attachment is not clear. It is probably a manifestation of re-use. The thickness of the sherd is 32 mm whereas length and width are 71 mm and 77 mm. On both surfaces of this fired clay, imprints of both wild and domesticated *Sorghum bicolor* were identified.

7.3.12 Sample 4
Sample code: SU2-2

Reddish-brown baked clay with a thickness of 27 mm. The length and width of the sherd is 78 mm and 77 mm. On the exterior surface, there are dorsal and ventral part impressions of sorghum. In this sample both wild and cultivated *sorghum bicolor* imprints were identified. By breaking the sample, glumes of sorghum were identified. It was also possible to see that it is not well fired. It is rather dried clay.

7.4 TAXONOMY OF *SORGHUM BICOLOR (LINN.) MOENCH*

Sorghum is a genus name under the Gramineae family. This grass has one of the most enormous and complex variations morphologically. The category *Sorghum bicolor (Linn.) Moench* includes both semiwild Sorgum plants that could often be seen as wild and cultivated Sorghums (De Wet and Huckabay 1967: 787-788). *Sorghum bicolor var. verticilliflorum* is the commonly available wild grass type for the drier parts of the African savanna. The following taxonomic classification demonstrates the line under which *Sorghum bicolor (L.) Moench* is found. The summary is based on De Wet and Harlan 1971: 129-135. (See table on the next page).

7.5 SUMMARY

The surveyed sites range in time between 500 B.C. to the 3rd millennium B.C. which culturally includes the Hagiz Group, the Jebel Mokram Group, the Gash Group and the Butana Group. The spot chosen for excavation rendered materials that had a very strong affinity with the Jebel Mokram Group, 2nd millennim B.C. The types of plant impressions on sherds from the survey and on the fragments of the baked clay from the excavation spot are similar: cultivated and wild *Sorghum bicolor* (L.) *Moench ssp.* The data from the survey and excavation highly coincides with the result of plant impression examination provided in this volume in chapter IV which in turn supports the result of Costantini *et al.*, 1982, published three decades ago. Furthermore, with the analysis of the baked clay from the excavated trench it is possible to distinguish one of the earliest evidence for cultivated sorghum morphotype (see the summary of samples and their identification in table 7.2).

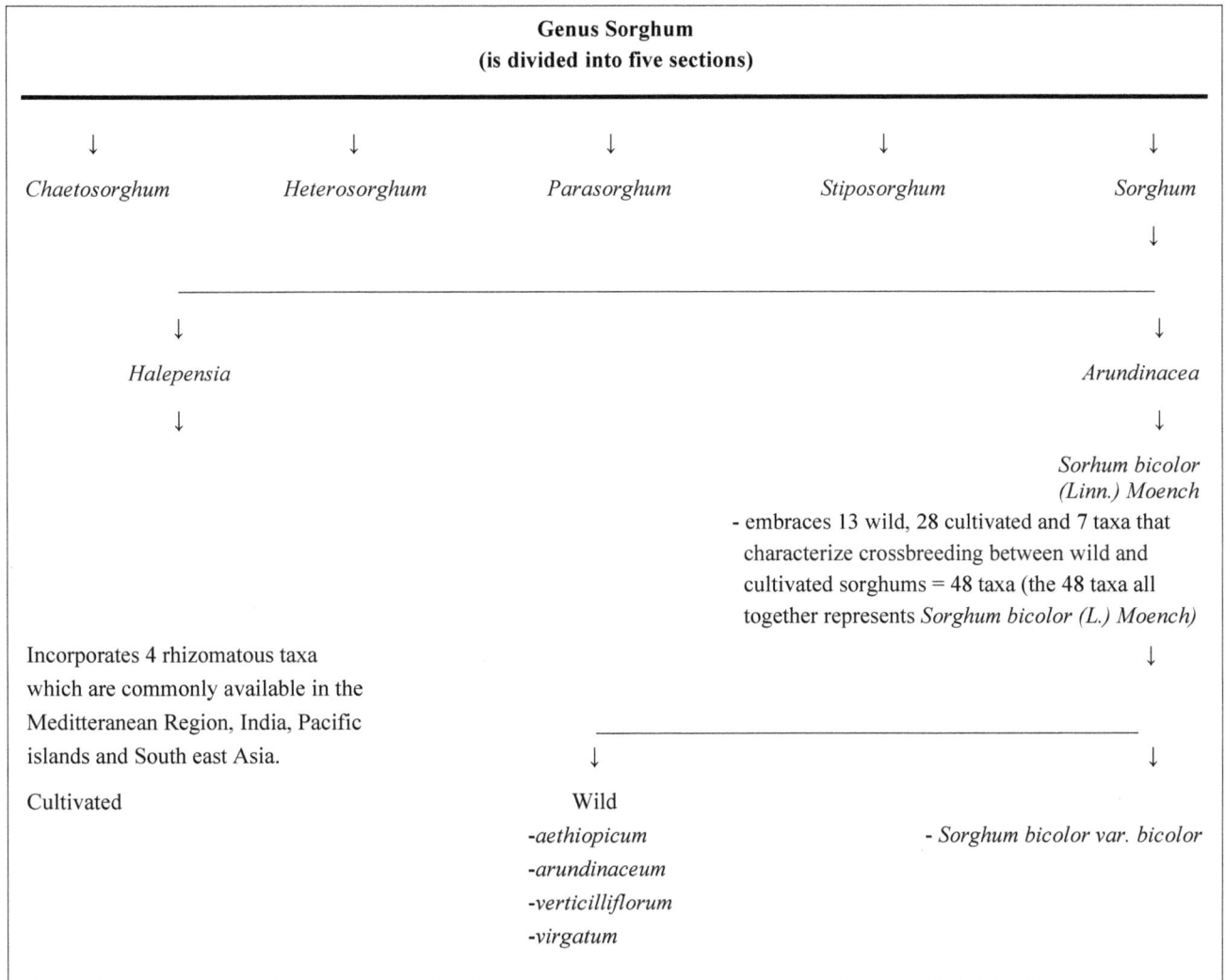

Table 7.2 Samples and their identification

No.	Sample Code	Type	Source (Excavation/Survey)	Identification (*Sorghum bicolor*, Wild and Cultivated)		Identification other than *Sorghum bicolor*
				Wild shape	Cultivated shape	
1	SU2-1	Fired clay	excavation	+	+	
2	SU2-2	»	»	+	+	
3	S3-1	»	»	+		Imprints of *Setaria sp.* and *Vigna unguiculata*
4	S3-2	»	»			
5	S3-3	»	»	+	+	
6	S4	»	»	+	+	
7	S5	»	»	+	+	Fruit stone of *Ziziphus spina-christi* and *Setaria sp.*
8	S6	»	»	+	+	
9	S7	»	»	+	+	
10	S8	»	»	+		
11	S9	»	»	+	+	
12	S10	»	»	+	+	Imprint of *Setaria sp.*
13	S129-a	Sherd	Survey	+		
14	S129-b		»	+		
15	S53-a	»	»	+	+	
16	S53-b	»	»	+		
17	S53-c	»	»	+		
18	S53-d	»	»	+	+	
19	S53-e	»	»	+		
20	S53-f	»	»	+	+	
21	S14-a	»	»	+	+	
22	S14-b	»	»	+	+	
23	S14-c	»	»	+		
24	S14-d	»		+		Imprints and mineralized grain of *Setaria sp.*
25	S14-e	»				Imprint and grain of *Setaria Sp.*

Chapter VIII
BOTANICAL DATA FROM SOIL SAMPLES, POT FRAGMENTS AND FIRED CLAYS: ANALYSIS OF COLLECTIONS FROM PREVIOUS FIELD SEASONS, 1980-1995

Ever since the beginning of archaeological survey and reconnaissance in Eastern Sudan in 1980, there have been attempts to reconstruct ancient food systems and the vegetation history of the region. This can be manifested by the amount of soil samples, fired clay, baked clay and pot sherds collected for plant impression analysis and seeds and fruit stones recovered from dry screening in almost every field season (Field Reports 1980, 1987). This objective is expressed as one of the five main aims of the mission in the 1984 field season report as follows;

The (investigation of) origin of food production in the area, with particular emphasis to the domestication of sorghum, by means of the systematic collection and analysis of the vegetal and animal evidence.
(1984 field season: 4 see also Fattovich 1993b:225)

With the exception of the 1982 and 1983 field seasons, the result of which in the field of archaeobotany were analyzed and published partially in the form of a report (Costantini *et al.*, 1982, 83), most of the samples collected were not investigated. From field work conducted in 1980, 1984 and 1987, a total of one thousand twenty three (n=1023) fired clay, baked clay and pot sherd fragments, 6 kilos of soil samples and forty two (42) seeds and fruit stones were kept in the store room of the Bio-archaeological laboratory of the Oriental Art Museum, Rome. The samples were kept in six boxes which in total contain sixty nine (69) sample bags and two (2) test tubes. The investigation of these samples was conducted as part of my data compilation process for this volume. Seeds and fruit stone samples were studied in particular, the result of which is presented in chapter VI. This is because all of these samples were from the same excavation spot at Mahal Teglinos with similar cultural affinity and chronology.

While screening the soil samples for a possible identifycation of macro and micro plant body residues, five

different meshes were used (2800 mm, 2000 mm, 1000 mm, 500 mm and 250 mm). For the analysis of the plant impression identification and seeds and fruit stones, the same methodology described in chapter I is employed.

The identification of the seeds and fruit stones provided *Celtis integrifolia* (Complete (n=6), fragments (n=20), burned (n=3)), *Ziziphus spina-christi* (fragments (n=4)), and charcoal pieces (n=11). Among the collection there are one half complete bead and lithic materials (n=48). The raw materials for the manufacturing of the stone tools include chert, quartz and schist.

The objective of studying the samples emanates from the need to present a complete history of the identification of plant species from the various field seasons and to provide initial data for researchers interested in resuming work in this field of study and the region under consideration. Although it is difficult to process the identification of all the data to the desired levels, species level, an attempt is made to lay a frame work for the edible and non-edible plants of the study area. This chapter summarizes cultural affiliations, chronology, description and identification of the samples.

1. Information from Sample box: Sudan, Mahal Teglinos, bag no. 21 and 23
    Inventory number: K1, 1987, BSKP, 16.
    Culture: 2300-1850 B.C. i.e. belonging to Middle Gash Group. K1/1987 BSKP charcoal samples (n=4) were also dated by the *Labotatoire du Radiocarbon, Gin-sur-Yvette,* France, which provided dates caliberated to a maximum of 3350 B.C. and a minimum of 1870 B.C. (Fattovich 1993b. 245-246).
    Description: reddish fired clay
    Total number: 43
    Identification: Very loosely consolidated fired clay. Clay, sand, quartz and other mineral inclusions

are used in the manufacturing process. Vegetal inclusions are generally limited and the few available belong to the Gramineae family.

2. Information from Sample box: Sudan, Mahal Tegli-nos, bag no. 21 and 23
   Inventory number: K1, 1987, BSKP, 15.
   Culture: 2300-1850 B.C. (Middle Gash Group).
   Description: reddish baked clay
   Total number: 24
   Identification: Limited chaff temper in general. Clay, sand, quartz and other mineral inclusions are used in the manufacturing process. In one of the larger fragments two different seed imprints of *Vigna unguiculata* were identified on the internal surface.

3. Information from Sample box: Sudan F., Kassala, bag no. 14.
   Inventory number: K1, AC 11 (soil sample).
   Culture: 2500-1000 B.C. This broad dating belonging to the Gash Group is suggested by Fattovich (1989:493).
   Description: White ash collected from a fire place
   Total number: 1 bag (ca. 600 gm)
   Identification: White consolidated ash/mineralized soil collected from a fire place. It has 14 bigger pieces apart from the loose soil samples. The soil sample was sieved using different mesh sizes. From 2.8 mm mesh size, fragments of fish bones, pot sherds, charcoals, baked clay, animal bones and a fruit stone like rounded soil (insects make this rounded shelter to protect themselves from external bodies and these can often be confused with fruit stones, see figure 8.1) were recovered. From 2.0 mm mesh size two grains of a cereal (wheat/barley), two fragments of charcoal, fish bones and bone harpoons (fish teeth see figure 8.2) were identified. The availability of fish bones and bone harpoons in such cultural context can be an example of possible acquatic resources utilization as an additional means of subsistence. Two charred grains of *Setaria sp.* (a grain and a grain together with the glume) (figures 8.3 and 8.4), two charred grain of wheat/barley, one charred fruit stone and one charred legume were collected from 1.0 mm mesh size.

4. Information from Sample box: Mahal Teglinos, bag no. 25 and 27.
   Inventory number: K1, 1987, BSKP, 24.
   Culture: 2700-2300 B.C. (Early Gash Group).
   Description: reddish, brown and black baked clay
   Total number: 51
   Identification: Very loosely consolidated fired clay. Clay, sand, quartz and other mineral inclusions are used in the manufacturing process. Vegetal inclusions are generally limited and the few available belong to the Gramineae family.

5. Information from Sample box: Sudan, Mahal Tegli-nos, bag no. 21 and 23

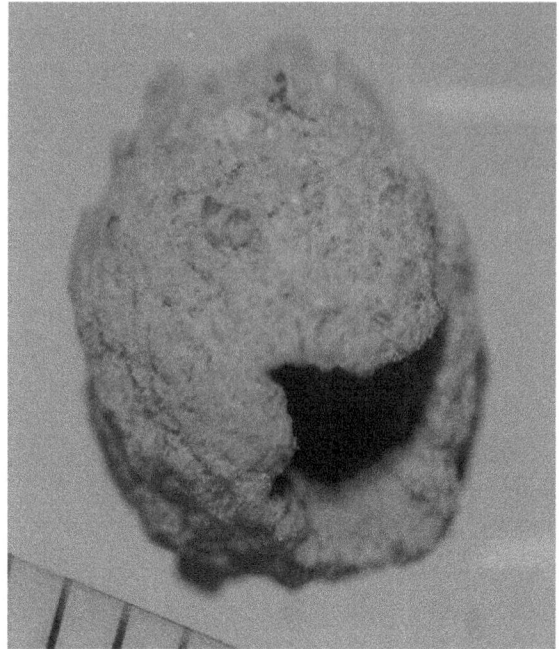

Figure 8.1 Insect made fruit stone

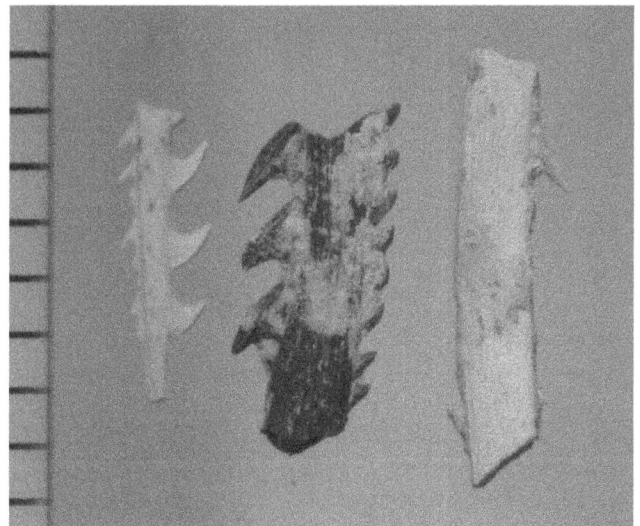

Figure 8.2 Bone harpoons

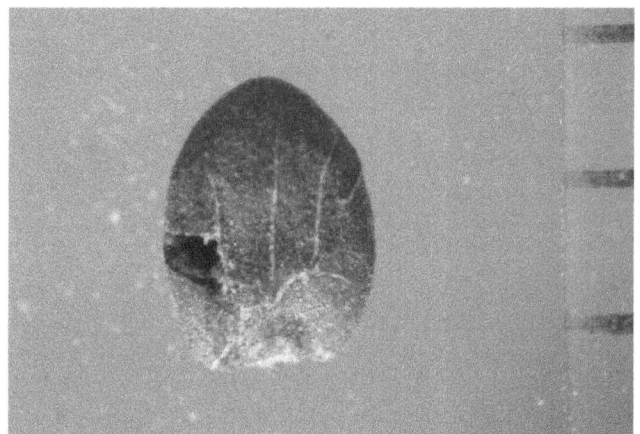

Figure 8.3 Charred grain of Setaria sp.
from 1 mm mesh size

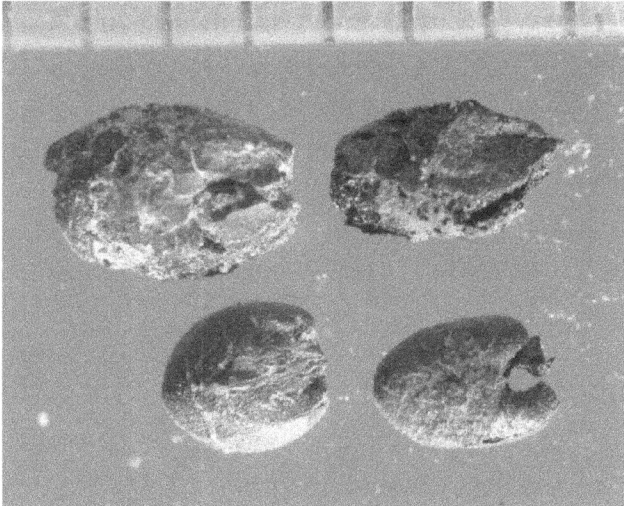

Figure 8.4 Charred grains of Setaria sp. with their glumes (above) and charred grains of Setaria sp. without glumes (below)

Inventory number: K1, 1987, BSKP, 26.
Culture: 2700-2300 B.C. (Early Gash Group).
Description: grey and black burned clay
Total number: 70
Identification: The composition of the sherds is clay, mineral grains, chalk/gypsum and a lot of chaff temper belonging to the small seeded millets. On one of the sherds a fruit stone impression (unidentifiable) is documented.

6. Information from Sample box: Sudan, Mahal Teglinos, bag no. from 21 to 45.
Inventory number: K1, BSKP, 25.
Culture: 2700-2300 B.C. (Early Gash Group).
Description: reddish, brownish and dark grayish fragments of sherd.
Total number: 20
Identification: The composition of the sherds is clay, mineral grains, chalk/gypsum and a lot of chaff temper belonging to the small seeded millets. An imprint of *Setaria sp.* is identified in one of the sherds.

7. Information from Sample box: Sudan, Mahal Teglinos, bag no. from 21 to 45.
Inventory number: K1, BSKP, 28.
Culture: 3000-2700 B.C. (Proto Gash Group).
Description: dark grey and reddish fragments of fired clay.
Total number: 3
Identification: Very loosely consolidated fired clay. Clay, sand, quartz and other mineral inclusions are used in the manufacturing process. Vegetal inclusions are generally limited and the few available belong to the Gramineae family.

8. Information from Sample box: Sudan, Mahal Teglinos, bag no. from 21 to 45.
Inventory number: K1, BSKP, 19.
Culture: 2700-2300 B.C. (Early Gash Group).

Description: brown and reddish fragments of sherd.
Total number: 13
Identification: There are seven pieces under the sample number of BSKP 19. The sherds are composed of clay, gypsum/chalk, and occasional presence of sand particles and chaff of *Millet sp.* The pot sherds are made in two layers; the original body is grayish in color, whereas the secondary attachment is reddish. In both the internal and external surfaces of one of the sherds there are mineralized/silicified imprints of *Millet sp.* (figure 8.5). In each cell of the graminea, there are two parts; the organic part and silica and it is the silica that survives most of the time. On the internal surface of the same sherd there is an imprint of a fragment of a leaf (figure 8.6).

Figure 8.5 Mineralized/silicified remain of millet grain

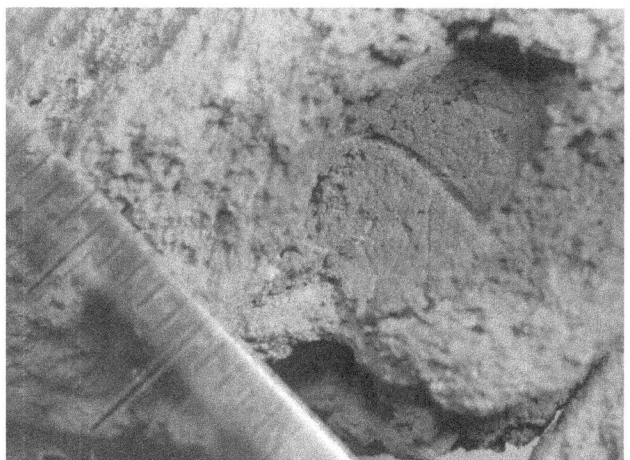

Figure 8.6 Imprint of fragment of a leaf

9. Information from Sample box: Sudan, Mahal Teglinos, bag no. from 21 to 45.
Inventory number: K1, 1987, BSKQ 17.
Culture: 2300-1850 B.C. (Middle Gash Group)
Description: reddish fragments of fired clay.

Total number: 33

Identification: There are thirty three pieces under the sample number of BSKQ 17. The sherds are composed of clay, gypsum/chalk, and occasional presence of sand particles and chaff of *Millet sp.* The pot sherds are made in two layers; the original body is grayish in color, whereas the secondary attachment is reddish. An imprint of the spikelet of barley grain, imprint of fruit stone, two imprints of *Millet sp.*, stalk of a cereal, and a spikelet of emmer wheat (see figures 8.7 and 8.8) are among the identified plant remains.

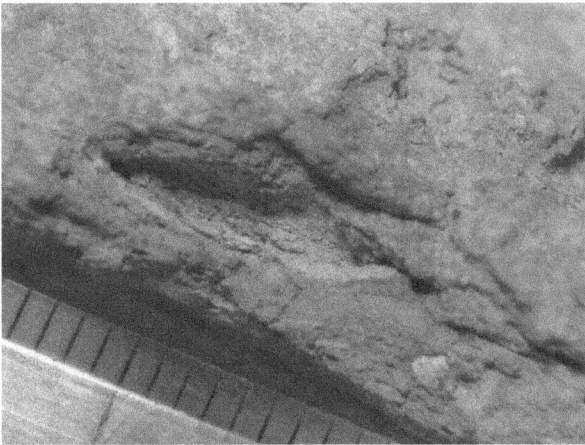

Figure 8.7 Imprint of a spikelet of Hordeum sp. *grain*

Figure 8.8 Spikelet imprint that could be comparable with emmer wheat

10. Information from Sample box: Sudan, Mahal Teglinos, bag no. from 21 to 45.

    Inventory number: K1, BSKQ 20.

    Culture: 2700-2300 B.C. (Early Gash Group).

    Description: reddish fragments of fired clay.

    Total number: 10

    Identification: The composition of the sherds is clay, mineral grains, chalk/gypsum and a lot of chaff temper belonging to the small seeded millets. A grain imprint with corrugated surface (belonging to leguminasea) is identified on one of the sherds.

11. Information from Sample box: Sudan, Mahal Teglinos, bag no. from 21 to 45.

    Inventory number: K1, 1987, BSKP, 18.

    Culture: 2300-1850 B.C. (Middle Gash Group).

    Description: reddish and brownish fragments of fired clay.

    Total number: 23

    Identification: The composition of the sherds is clay, mineral grains, chalk/gypsum and a lot of chaff temper belonging to the small seeded millets. A glume of *Sorghum sp.* is identified in one of the sherds.

12. Information from Sample box: Sudan, Mahal Teglinos, bag no. from 21 to 45.

    Inventory number: Various (not specified)

    Culture: from the inventory numbers on the pieces of the fragments it is possible to see that most of the collections belong to 2700-2300 B.C. (Early Gash Group).

    Description: reddish and brownish fragments of fired clay.

    Total number: 15

    Identification: In this sample bag, there are burned clays and ceramics. For all of the pieces an inventory number is given (K1 BBSKQ 6, BSKP 11, BSKQ 12, BSKP 13, BSKP 17, BSKP 19, BSKP 20, BSKP 21, and BSKP 30). It is difficult to read the inventory number on the remaining six. The compositions in these collections are clay, sand, chaff of abundant small millets and chaff of barley (small amount). In one of the pieces (without inventory number), two glume impressions of barley are identified. The same piece provided an impression which resembles the glume of *Sorghum durra* (figure 8.9). By breaking a sample (BSKP 30), a mineralized grain of leguminasea and its imprints are also identified. Another broken sample (BSKQ?) demonstrated a mineralized grain similar to *Sorghum bicolor durra* and its cast (figure 8.10).

Figure 8.9 Imprint of Sorghum sp. *grain with its comparative plant specimen*

Figure 8.10 A mineralized grain similar to Sorghum bicolor durra *with its comparative plant specimen*

13. Information from Sample box: Sudan, Mahal Teglinos, bag no. from 21 to 45.
    Inventory number: BSKP 9
    Culture: 1850-1700 B.C. (Classic Gash Group).
    Description: reddish and brownish fragments of fired clay.
    Total number: 3
    Identification: The composition of the sherds is clay, mineral grains, chalk/gypsum and a lot of chaff temper belonging to the small seeded millets. In one of the sherds a wild grain imprint is identified that can be compared with astragalus?

14. Information from Sample box: Sudan, Mahal Teglinos, bag no. from 21 to 45.
    Inventory number: BSKP 19
    Culture: 2700-2300 B.C. (Early Gash Group).
    Description: reddish and brownish fragments of fired clay.
    Total number: 14
    Identification: The composition of the sherds is clay, mineral grains, chalk/gypsum and a lot of chaff temper belonging to the small seeded millets. Among these collections, an imprint of barley, *Hordeum sp.*, two unidentifiable charred grains and a fruit stone (unidentifiable) were documented.

15. Information from Sample box: Sudan, Mahal Teglinos, bag no. from 21 to 45.
    Inventory number: BSKP 6
    Culture: 1700-1500 B.C. (Late Gash Group).
    Description: reddish and brownish fragments of burned clay.
    Total number: 10
    Identification: These are crude sherds which might have been parts of a big jar/storage facility. They are heavily tempered with chaff belonging to smashed millets and straw. The composition consists of clay, mineral grains and chaff. The great portion of the chaff is completely burned.

The original storage was probably kept near a fire place as can be deduced from burned surfaces.

16. Information from Sample box: Sudan, Mahal Teglinos, bag no. from 21 to 45.
    Inventory number: BSKQ 22
    Culture: 2700-2300 B.C. (Early Gash Group).
    Description: reddish and brownish fragments of fired clay.
    Total number: 8
    Identification: The composition of the sherds is clay, mineral grains, chalk/gypsum and a lot of chaff temper belonging to the small seeded millets. Plant impressions are generally very low in number.

17. Information from Sample box: Sudan, Mahal Teglinos, bag no. from 21 to 45.
    Inventory number: BSKQ 28
    Culture: 2700-2300 B.C. (Early Gash Group).
    Description: dark grayish and reddish fragments of fired clay.
    Total number: 6
    Identification: The composition of the sherds is clay, mineral grains, chalk/gypsum and a lot of chaff temper belonging to the small seeded millets. No plant impressions are identified among these collections.

18. Information from Sample box: Sudan, Mahal Teglinos, bag no. from 21 to 45.
    Inventory number: BSKP 26
    Culture: 2700-2300 B.C. (Early Gash Group).
    Description: dark brown fragments of fired clay.
    Total number: 12
    Identification: The composition of the sherds is clay, mineral grains, chalk/gypsum and a lot of chaff temper belonging to the small seeded millets. On one of the collections (not a pot sherd, better classified as an artifact), there are four finger impressions.

19. Information from Sample box: Sudan, Mahal Teglinos, bag no. from 21 to 45.
    Inventory number: BSKQ 24
    Culture: 2700-2300 B.C. (Early Gash Group).
    Description: grayish and brownish fragments of fired clay.
    Total number: 9
    Identification: The composition of the sherds is clay, mineral grains, chalk/gypsum and a lot of chaff temper belonging to the small seeded millets. On one of the sherds an imprint of *Vigna unguiculata* is identified?

20. Information from Sample box: Sudan, Mahal Teglinos, bag no. from 21 to 45.
    Inventory number: BSKQ 26
    Culture: 2700-2300 B.C. (Early Gash Group).
    Description: grayish and brownish fragments of fired clay.
    Total number: 4

Identification: Very loosely consolidated fired clay. Clay, sand, quartz and other mineral inclusions are used in the manufacturing process. Vegetal inclusions are generally limited and the few available belong to the Gramineae family.

21. Information from Sample box: Sudan, Mahal Tegli-nos, bag no. from 21 to 45.
Inventory number: BSKP 27
Culture: 2700-2300 B.C. (Early Gash Group).
Description: greyish and brownish fragments of fired clay.
Total number: 12
Identification: The composition of the sherds is clay, abundant mineral grains, chalk/gypsum and a little chaff temper belonging to the small seeded millets. There are four unidentifiable fruit stone impressions (a kind of fruit epidermic) on one of the sherds.

22. Information from Sample box: Sudan, Mahal Tegli-nos, bag no. from 21 to 45.
Inventory number: BSKP 17
Culture: 2300-1850 B.C. (Middle Gash Group).
Description: reddish fragments of fired clay.
Total number: 25
Identification: There are fourteen pieces under the sample number of BSKP 17. The sherds are composed of clay, gypsum/chalk, with the occasional presence of sand particles and chaff of *Millet sp.* The pot sherds are made in two layers; the original body is grayish in color, whereas the secondary attachment is reddish. Only one of the fourteen shrds has exhibits an impression, a grain of barley on the external surface.

23. Information from Sample box: Sudan, Mahal Tegli-nos, bag no. from 21 to 45.
Inventory number: BSKQ 16, 24
Culture: Between Early Gash Group (2700-2300 B.C.) and Middle Gash Group (2300-1850 B.C.).
Description: reddish fragments of fired clay.
Total number: 22
Identification: There are twenty two pieces under the sample number of BSKQ 16. The sherds are composed of clay, gypsum/chalk, with the occasional presence of sand particles and chaff of *Millet sp.* The pot sherds are made in two layers; the original body is grayish in color, whereas the secondary attachment is reddish. In one of the pieces a grain imprint of *Vigna unguiculata* is identified.

24. Information from Sample box: Sudan, Mahal Tegli-nos, bag no. from 21 to 45.
Inventory number: BSKP 22
Culture: 2700-2300 B.C. (Early Gash Group).
Description: reddish fragments of fired clay.
Total number: 12
Identification: There are nine pieces under the sample number of BSKP 22. The sherds are composed of clay, gypsum/chalk, with the

occasional presence of sand particles and chaff of *Millet sp.* The pot sherds are made in two layers; the original body is grayish in color, whereas the secondary attachment is reddish.

25. Information from Sample box: Sudan, Mahal Tegli-nos, bag no. from 21 to 45.
Inventory number: BSKQ 23
Culture: 2700-2300 B.C. (Early Gash Group).
Description: dark brown fragments of fired clay.
Total number: 5
Identification: These are crude sherds which might have been parts of a big storage facility. They are heavily tempered with chaff belonging to smashed millets and straw. The composition is consists of clay, mineral grains and chaff. The great portion of the chaff is completely burned. The original storage was probably kept near a fire place like BSKP 6.

26. Information from Sample box: Sudan, Mahal Tegli-nos, bag no. from 21 to 45.
Inventory number: BSKP 14
Culture: 2300-1850 B.C. (Middle Gash Group).
Description: reddish fragments of fired clay.
Total number: 26
Identification: Very loosely consolidated fired clay. Clay, sand, quartz and other mineral inclusions are used in the manufacturing process. Vegetal inclusions are generally limited and the few available belong to the Gramineae family.

27. Information from Sample box: Kassala bag numbers 1 to 79
Inventory number: Kassala 1984 SEG 38
Culture: latter half of 1st millennium B.C. (Late Jebel Mokram/Hagiz Group).
Description: lithics made of cherts and quartz
Total number: 47
Identification: Plant impressions are generally low and unidentifiable.

28. Information from Sample box: Kassala bag numbers 1 to 79
Inventory number: K1 AF 10, 40
Culture: 2500-1000 B.C. This broad dating, belonging to the Gash Group, is suggested by Fattovich (1989:493).
Description: fruit stones and charcoal pieces kept in a test tube.
Total number: 24
Identification: Eleven fragments of *Celtis integrifolia*, two complete fruit stones of *Celtis integrifolia*, and eleven charcoal pieces.

29. Information from Sample box: Kassala bag numbers 1 to 79
Inventory number: K2 A-H2
Culture: Belongs to both Jebel Mokram (2nd-1st millennium B.C.) and Hagiz Group (500 B.C.-200/300 A.D.) according to Fattovich (1989:494-497).

Description: grayish fragments of sherd

Total number: 1

Identification: Very low concentration of vegetal materials. Plant impressions are not identifiable.

30. Information from Sample box: Kassala bag numbers 1 to 79

Inventory number: K1 A-A 4-5

Culture: 2500-1000 B.C. belonging mainly to the Gash Group.

Description: dark grayish fragments of sherd

Total number: 7

Identification: Plant impressions are generally low and unidentifiable.

31. Information from Sample box: Kassala bag numbers 1 to 79

Inventory number: K1 A-A2

Culture: 2500-1000 B.C. belonging mainly to the Gash Group.

Description: reddish fragment of sherd

Total number: 1

Identification: This sample exhibits a low concentration of vegetal materials. Plant impressions are not identifiable

32. Information from Sample box: Kassala bag numbers 1 to 79

Inventory number: K10

Culture: 1500-500 B.C. belonging to the Jebel Mokram Group.

Description: reddish fragment of sherd

Total number: 1

Identification: Baked clay with impressions of plant body parts on both interior and exterior surface of the sample. The impressions are not identifiable.

33. Information from Sample box: Kassala bag numbers 1 to 79

Inventory number: K1 A-A1

Culture: 2500-1000 B.C. belonging mainly to the Gash Group.

Description: reddish fragment of sherd

Total number: 4

Identification: High concentration of quartz, sand particles and low concentration of chaff belonging to *Millet sp.* constitute the inclusions in this sample. In one of the sherds two imprints of the grains of *Millet sp.* are identified.

34. Information from Sample box: Kassala bag numbers 1 to 79

Inventory number: K1 A-AG1

Culture: 2500-1000 B.C. belonging mainly to the Gash Group.

Description: reddish fragments of sherd

Total number: 3

Identification: No plant impressions are identified in this sample.

35. Information from Sample box: Kassala bag numbers 1 to 79

Inventory number: K1 5

Culture: ca. 1500-1400 B.C. (Final Gash Group).

Description: brownish and reddish fragments of sherd

Total number: 5

Identification: Four out of the five fragments demonstrate concentration of materials. One sample (K1 I 3) is a burned clay very rich in vegetal inclusions. The plant imprints in this sample, however, are not identifiable.

36. Information from Sample box: Kassala bag numbers 1 to 79

Inventory number: K1 AA3

Culture: 2500-1000 B.C. belonging mainly to the Gash Group.

Description: brownish and reddish fragments of sherd

Total number: 2

Identification: In the internal part of one of the two sherds, a very refined imprint of a grain of *Setaria sp.* is identified. Plant material inclusions on both of the sherds are generally few.

37. Information from Sample box: Kassala bag numbers 1 to 79

Inventory number: K1 A-B2

Culture: 2500-1000 B.C. belonging mainly to the Gash Group.

Description: grayish and brownish fragments of sherd

Total number: 1

Identification: Very low concentrations of plant materials are observable in this sample. Plant impressions are not identifiable.

38. Information from Sample box: Kassala bag numbers 1 to 79

Inventory number: K1 A-H1

Culture: 2500-1000 B.C. belonging mainly to the Gash Group.

Description: reddish fragment of sherd

Total number: 1

Identification: Very low concentration of vegetal materials. The plant impressions are not identifiable.

39. Information from Sample box: Kassala bag numbers 1 to 79

Inventory number: K1 67 (65?)

Culture: ca. 1500-1400 B.C. (Final Gash Group).

Description: reddish fragments of sherd.

Total number: 7

Identification: This sample comprises six sherds and one lithic piece made of chert. Plant materials belonging to *Graminea sp.* are used as inclusions.

40. Information from Sample box: Kassala bag numbers 1 to 79

Inventory number: ES1 1980

Culture: 2500-1000 B.C. belonging to the Gash Group.

Description: brownish and reddish fragments of sherd

Total number: 16

Identification: High concentration of quartz inclusions. Vegetal imprints are generally few. However, it is possible to observe that smoothening of the sherds was done using plant material (ES1/269 shows a good example of such a smoothing process). ES1/276 exhibits more than 12 imprints of *Millet sp.* on its internal surface (figures 8.11 and 8.12). Most of the impressions are compared with *Setaria sp.* A spikelet of *Setaria sp.* is also identified on the same surface (figure 8.13). By breaking the sample, it was not possible to see grain impressions. Chaff is only present on the internal surface. The external surface exhibits no presence of chaff. The internal surface is reddish in color and the external one is dark and burned. Most of the chaff is compared with chaff of *Setaria sp.* Limited plant materials (Millet sp.), quartz and sand particles constitute the inclusions in all of the sherds under ES1 1980.

Figure 8.11 A picture showing the concentration of Setaria sp. *imprints on the internal surface of ES1/276 1980*

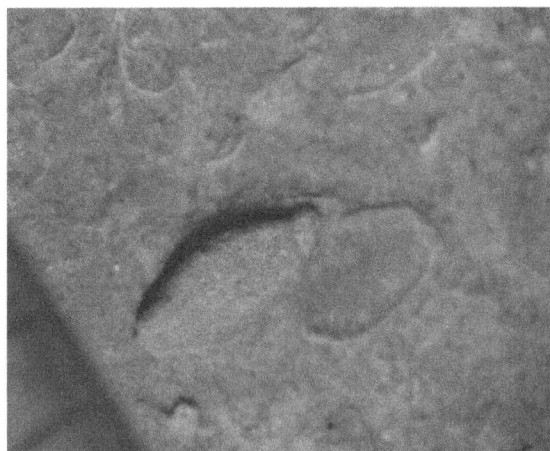

Figure 8.12 An imprint of Setaria sp. *from sample ES1/276 1980*

Figure 8.13 Spikelet imprint of Setaria sp. *from sample ES1/276 1980*

41. Information from Sample box: Kassala bag numbers 1 to 79

    Inventory number: K1 A-K5

    Culture: 2500-1000 B.C. belonging mainly to the Gash Group.

    Description: grayish and brownish fragment of sherd

    Total number: 1

    Identification: Low concentration of plant materials. The plant impressions in this sample are not identifiable.

42. Information from Sample box: Kassala bag numbers 1 to 79

    Inventory number: ES2 1980

    Culture: 6th-4th millennium B.C, based on comparison with Early Khartoum and Pre-Saroba Malawiya sites (Fattovich 1989: 484-486).

    Description: brownish and reddish fragments of sherd

    Total number: 26

    Identification: All of the sherds exhibit a high concentration of sand particles and quartz as inclusions. Eleven of the twenty six sherds are decorated in various techniques. The following table describes the decoration techniques and patterns employed in each sample and gives information on vegetal impressions.

43. Information from Sample box: Kassala bag numbers 1 to 79

    Inventory number: K1 II 1

    Culture: ca. 2000-1500 B.C. (Middle to Late Gash Group).

    Description: reddish and brownish fragments of sherd

    Total number: 17

    Identification: Smoothing of most of the sherds in this sample was done using plant materials as can be seen on both interior and exterior surfaces. In one of the sherds (K1 II 1 43) a grain imprint of *Millet sp.* is identified.

Table 8.1 Decoration patterns/techniques and vegetal impressions for ES2 1980

No.	Inventory No.	Decoration pattern/technique	Remark on vegetal impressions
1	ES2/8	Bone/wood impressed	No imprints
2	ES2/9	Bone/wood impressed	Not identifiable
3	ES2/10	Bone/wood impressed	Not identifiable
4	ES2/12	Combed	No imprints
5	ES2/13	Bone/wood impressed	Burned plant materials along the edge of the fragment
6	ES2/14	Two parallel line incisions	Not identifiable
7	ES2/15	Bone/wood impressions along the exterior surface of the sherd	Not identifiable
8	ES2/16	Lip internal part is impressed	A grain of *Millet sp.*
9	ES2/18	Lip is impressed using finger nails	No vegetal imprints
10	ES2/19	No decoration	Not identifiable
11	ES2/20	No decoration	Not identifiable
12	ES2/21	No decoration	Not identifiable
13	ES2/22	No decoration	Not identifiable
14	ES2/23	No decoration	Not identifiable
15	ES2/24	No decoration	No imprints
16	ES2/25	No decoration	Not identifiable
17	ES2/26	No decoration	Not identifiable
18	ES2/27	No decoration	Not identifiable
19	ES2/28	No decoration	Plant inclusions mostly belonging to the Gramineae are observable
20	ES2/29	No decoration	No identifiable
21	ES2/30	No decoration	Some signs of smoothing using plant materials on both surfaces
22	ES2/31	No decoration	Many plant inclusions belonging to the Gramineas genera
23	ES2/32	No decoration	Grain impressions belonging to the *Millet sp.*
24	ES2/33	Nail impressed along the lip on the exterior part	Not identifiable
25	ES2/M1	No decoration	No imprints
26	ES2	Bone/wood impressed	No imprints

44. Information from Sample box: Kassala bag numbers 1 to 79
Inventory number: K1 A-H4
Culture: 2500-1000 B.C. belonging mainly to the Gash Group.
Description: dark grayish fired clay
Total number: 54
Identification: Very little chaff temper in general. Clay, sand, quartz and other mineral inclusions are used in the manufacturing process. The few plant inclusions observable belong to the Gramineae family.

45. Information from Sample box: Kassala bag numbers 1 to 79
Inventory number: K1 A-H9
Culture: 2500-1000 B.C. belonging mainly to the Gash Group.
Description: dark grayish fired clay
Total number: 39
Identification: Very little chaff temper in general. Clay, sand, quartz and other mineral inclusions are used in the manufacturing process. The few plant inclusions observable belong to the Gramineae family.

46. Information from Sample box: Kassala bag numbers 1 to 79
Inventory number: K1 A-A2
Culture: 2500-1000 B.C. belonging mainly to the Gash Group.
Description: reddish fragment of sherd
Total number: 1
Identification: Plant impressions are generally few and unidentifiable.

47. Information from Sample box: Kassala bag numbers 1 to 79
Inventory number: K1 AG9 39
Culture: 2500-1000 B.C. belonging mainly to the Gash Group.
Description: Complete and fragments of fruit stones and a bead
Total number: 17

Identification: Four complete fruit stones of *Celtis integrifolia*, nine fragments of *Celtis integrifolia*, three burned fragments of *Celtis integrifolia* and one half complete bead.

48. Information from Sample box: Mahal Teglinos, bag numbers from 1 to 20.
Inventory number: K1 14
Culture: ca. 1500-1400 B.C. (Final Gash Group).
Description: reddish and brownish fragments of sherd
Total number: 3
Identification: Very little chaff temper in general. Clay, sand, quartz and other mineral inclusions are used in the manufacturing process. The few plant inclusions observable belong to the Gramineae family.

49. Information from Sample box: Mahal Teglinos, bag numbers from 1 to 20.
Inventory number: K1 1984 AB
Culture: 2500-1000 B.C. belonging mainly to the Gash Group.
Description: brownish baked clay
Total number: 14
Identification: Very little chaff temper in general. Clay, sand, quartz and other mineral inclusions are used in the manufacturing process. The few plant inclusions observable belong to the Gramineae family.

50. Information from Sample box: Mahal Teglinos, bag numbers from 1 to 20.
Inventory number: K1 A-B 11
Culture: 2500-1000 B.C. belonging mainly to the Gash Group.
Description: brownish fired clay
Total number: 12
Identification: Very little chaff temper in general. Clay, sand, quartz and other mineral inclusions are used in the manufacturing process. The few plant inclusions observable belong to the Gramineae family.

51. Information from Sample box: Mahal Teglinos, bag numbers from 1 to 20.
Inventory number: K1 1984 AG 8
Culture: 2500-1000 B.C. belonging mainly to the Gash Group.
Description: dark grey fired clay
Total number: 65
Identification: Very little chaff temper in general. Clay, sand, quartz and other mineral inclusions are used in the manufacturing process. The few plant inclusions observable belong to the Gramineae family.

52. Information from Sample box: Mahal Teglinos, bag numbers from 1 to 20.
Inventory number: K1 A C-B 17
Culture: 2500-1000 B.C. belonging mainly to the Gash Group.

Description: greyish fired clay
Total number: 18
Identification: Very little chaff temper in general. Clay, sand, quartz and other mineral inclusions are used in the manufacturing process. The few plant inclusions observable belong to the Gramineae family.

53. Information from Sample box: Mahal Teglinos, bag numbers from 1 to 20.
Inventory number: K1 1984 AF 5
Culture: 2500-1000 B.C. belonging mainly to the Gash Group.
Description: dark clay fired clay
Total number: 30
Identification: Very little chaff temper in general. Clay, sand, quartz and other mineral inclusions are used in the manufacturing process. The few plant inclusions observable belong to the Gramineae family.

54. Information from Sample box: Mahal Teglinos, bag numbers from 1 to 20.
Inventory number: JM3 1980
Culture: ca. 1500-1000 B.C. (Early Jebel Mokram).
Description: reddish baked clay
Total number: 3
Identification: There are three larger fragments of sherds within the bag of this inventory number. All of them are full of plant materials (heavily chaff tempered). One of the three sherds (JM3-1) exhibited six glume imprints of *Sorghum sp.* on its external surface and five grain imprints of *Sorghum bicolor bicolor* on its internal surface. By breaking the second sample (JM3-2), it was possible to see abundant mineralized grains of *Sorghum sp.*, and its glumes and spikelets, and the imprint of *Ziziphus sp.* with fragments of mineralized grains of the same fruit stone inside it (see figures 8.14 and 8.15 below).

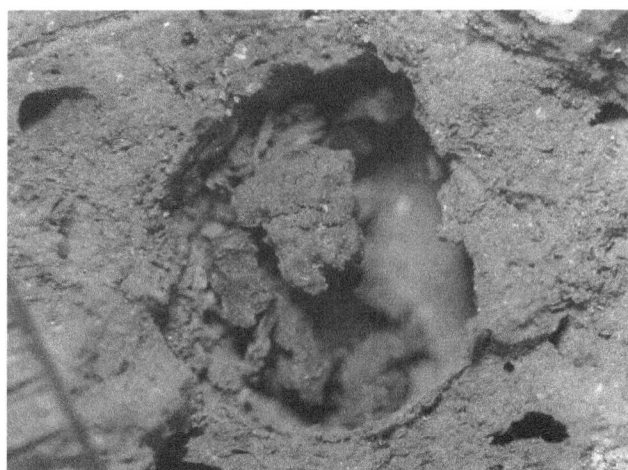

Figure 8.14 Imprint of Ziziphus sp. *with its charred fragments inside it*

76

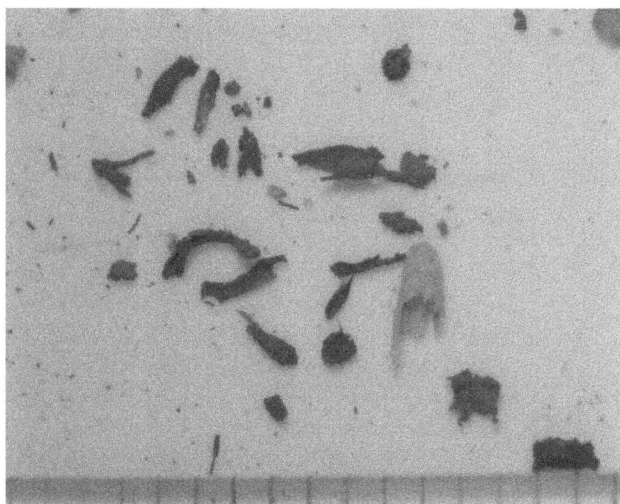

Figure 8.15 Mineralized and charred chaff remains of Sorghum sp. *from the broken sample of (JM3-2)*

55. Information from Sample box: Mahal Teglinos, bag numbers from 1 to 20.
Inventory number: K1 A e-B (1-3) 21
Culture: 2500-1000 B.C. belonging mainly to the Gash Group.
Description: dark grayish baked clay
Total number: 19
Identification: Very little chaff temper in general. Clay, sand, quartz and other mineral inclusions are used in the manufacturing process. The few plant inclusions observable belong to the Gramineae family.

56. Information from Sample box: Mahal Teglinos, bag numbers from 1 to 20.
Inventory number: K1 1984 AA 4-5
Culture: 2500-1000 B.C. belonging mainly to the Gash Group.
Description: dark brown baked clay
Total number: 12
Identification: A high concentration of quartz inclusions is observable under a high power stereo microscope. Vegetal imprints are generally few. However, there is rounded a grain imprint of *Sorghum sp.*, on the exterior surface.

57. Information from Sample box: Mahal Teglinos, bag numbers from 1 to 20.
Inventory number: K1 1984 AG4
Culture: 2500-1000 B.C. belonging mainly to the Gash Group.
Description: brown and dark baked clay
Total number: 14
Identification: Very little chaff temper in general. Clay, sand, quartz and other mineral inclusions are used in the manufacturing process. The few plant inclusions observable belong to the Gramineae family.

58. Information from Sample box: Mahal Teglinos, bag numbers from 1 to 20.

Inventory number: K1 1984 AG
Culture: 2500-1000 B.C. belonging mainly to the Gash Group.
Description: dark grayish baked clay
Total number: 28+
Identification: Very little chaff temper in general. Clay, sand, quartz and other mineral inclusions are used in the manufacturing process. The few plant inclusions observable belong to the Gramineae family.

59. Information from Sample box: Mahal Teglinos, bag numbers from 1 to 20.
Inventory number: K1 1984 AC-B 15
Culture: 2500-1000 B.C. belonging mainly to the Gash Group.
Description: red- brown baked clay
Total number: 12
Identification: Very little chaff temper in general. Clay, sand, quartz and other mineral inclusions are used in the manufacturing process. The few plant inclusions observable belong to the Gramineae family.

60. Information from Sample box: Mahal Teglinos, bag numbers from 1 to 20.
Inventory number: K1 A e-B (1 x 3) 23
Culture: 2500-1000 B.C. belonging mainly to the Gash Group.
Description: dark grayish baked clay
Total number: 14
Identification: Very little chaff temper in general. Clay, sand, quartz and other mineral inclusions are used in the manufacturing process. The few plant inclusions observable belong to the Gramineae family.

61. Information from Sample box: Mahal Teglinos, bag numbers from 1 to 20.
Inventory number: K1 1984 AG 8
Culture: 2500-1000 B.C. belonging mainly to the Gash Group.
Description: a pebble of schist
Total number: 1

62. Information from Sample box: Mahal Teglinos, bag numbers from 1 to 20.
Inventory number: K1 A B-e 14
Culture: 2500-1000 B.C. belonging mainly to the Gash Group.
Description: dark grayish baked clay
Total number: 11
Identification: Plant impressions are generally few and unidentifiable.

63. Information from Sample box: Mahal Teglinos, bag numbers from 1 to 20.
Inventory number: K1 III 82
Culture: 1500-500 B.C. (Jebel Mokram Group).
Description: black, grayish and reddish fragments of sherd
Total number: 19

Identification: All of the sherds ex abundant chaff inclusions belonging to *Sorghum sp.* Glume imprints of sorghum are observable in most of the sherds. Burnishing/smoothening of the original pottery was done using by plant material as can be deduced from the impressions on both surfaces. One of the sherds (III 1 a), in particular, is heavily chaff tempered belonging to *Sorghum sp.* A few refined grain impressions of *Sorghum bicolor bicolor* are identified from sample K1 III 1 b and on the exterior surface of sample K1 III 1 c there is a grain impression of *Setaria sp.* (see figure 8.16).

Figure 8.16 Grain impression of Setaria sp. *from sample K1 III 1 C*

64. Information from Sample box: Mahal Teglinos, bag numbers from 1 to 20.
Inventory number: K1 1984 AG 2
Culture: 2500-1000 B.C. belonging mainly to the Gash Group.
Description: dark grayish and brownish baked clay
Total number: 14
Identification: Plant impressions are generally few and unidentifiable.

65. Information from Sample box: Mahal Teglinos, bag numbers from 1 to 20.
Inventory number: K1 1984 AJ 7
Culture: 2500-1000 B.C. belonging mainly to the Gash Group.
Description: dark grayish baked clay
Total number: 21
Identification: Plant impressions are generally few and unidentifiable.

66. Information from Sample box: Mahal Teglinos, bag numbers from 1 to 20.
Inventory number: K1 15
Culture: ca. 1500-1400 B.C. (Final Gash Group).
Description: soil sample
Total number: 1.5 kg.
Identification: A very low concentration of vegetal materials belonging to the Gramineae is observed in mesh size 2.0 mm and 1.0 mm.

67. Information from Sample box: Mahal Teglinos, bag numbers from 1 to 20.
Inventory number: K1 A-H 8
Culture: 2500-1000 B.C. belonging mainly to the Gash Group.
Description: dark grayish baked clay and soil samples (2 kgs). The soil samples were composed of fired clay, smaller sized stones, small clay fragments and many plant remains
Total number: 35 (for the baked clay)
Identification: Dry sieving was used to screen more artifact and ecofact remains using various mesh sizes. Using the 2.8 mm mesh size it was possible to screen the coarse fragment of sherds. Almost all of these coarse fragments have red exterior and black interior parts. The black surface on the interior part is a result of the burning of organic substances, an additional evidence for the inclusion of plant materials as temper. In one of these sherds, a mineralized grain impression of *Setaria sp.* was identified (see figure 8.17 below). From the 2 mm mesh, a charred grain comparable with *Setaria sp.*, fragments of *Ziziphus sp.*, (n=7), carbonized fragments of *Ziziphus sp.* (n=6), fragments of fish bones (n=3), smaller animal bones (n=3), the neck part of insect remains (n=4) were recovered (see figures 8.18, 8.19 and 8.20). A charred grain of *Setaria sp.* was identified from a 1 mm mesh. Two grains of *Millet sp.* were also recovered among the fine grained sediments collected from the 0.5 mm mesh size.

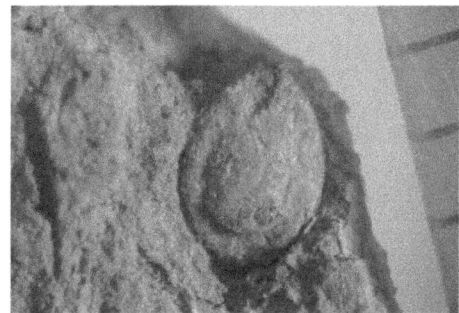

Figure 8.17 A mineralized grain of Setaria sp.

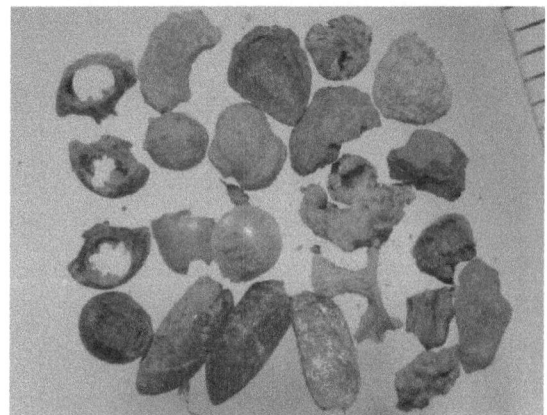

Figure 8.18 Fragments of fruit stones, mineralized grains, insect remains and smaller animal bones recovered from 1 mm mesh size

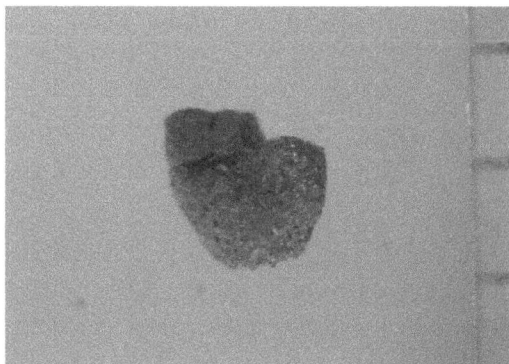

Figure 8.19 Charred grain of Setaria sp. *recovered from 1 mm mesh size*

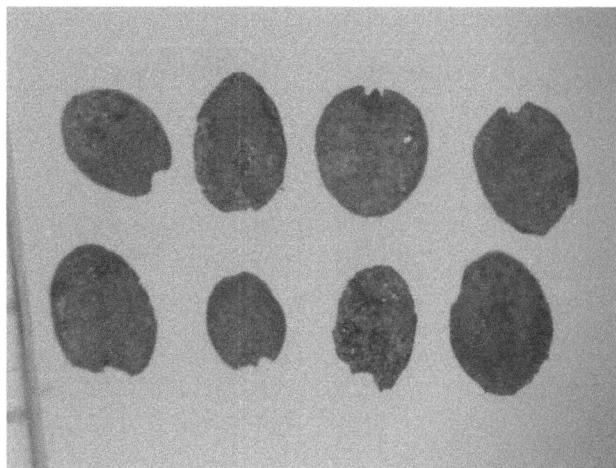

Figure 8.21 Setaria virdis *charred grains*

Figure 8.20 A small charred fruit stone of Ziziphus sp.

68. Information from Sample box: Mahal Teglinos, bag numbers from 1 to 20.
    Inventory number: Kassala C3 JE2 1 14
    Culture:
    Description: Soil sample (300 gm)
    Total number: 1 bag
    Identification: This soil sample was not directly collected from surface. It is rather a residue of crude pot fragments. The sample was sieved using 2.0 mm, 1.0 mm, 0.5 mm and 0.25 mm mesh sizes. It provided abundant charred grains, fruit stones, fish bones, castes of seeds and charcoal fragments (n=92). Some of the charred grains of *Setaria sp.* are even identifiable to the lowest level possible (see the samples of *Setaria virdis* in figure 8.21).

8.1 SUMMARY

This chapter has presented the archaeobotanical study of soil samples, pottery fragments and fired clay from cultural contexts ranging in time between ca. 6000 B.C. and 200/300 A.D. In such a broad spectrum of time, Cultural Groups such as the Amm Adam Group, the Gash Group, the Jebel Mokram Group, and the Hagiz Group are represented. From the soil samples charred grains of *Setaria sp.*, cereals (wheat and barley), fruit stones of *Ziziphus sp.*, leguminasea (mainly *Vigna unguiculata*), sterile glumes, spikelets and charred grains of *Sorghum sp.* Have been identified, quite in consistence with the plant imprints identified from the same sites and cultural contexts. The plant impression analysis suggests that small seeded millets were under cultivation since the 6th millennium B.C. Uncharred fruit stones of *Ziziphus sp.* and *Celtis intergrifolia* are also among the identified fruit stones from soil samples. These fruit stones were abundantly recovered from sieves of the 1991 excavation (K1 V) as presented in chapter VI.

With the intention of providing a complete picture of the subsistence base of the various cultural Groups which occupied parts of Northeastern Africa, table 8.2 summarizes the chronology and means of economic livelihood. The data presented in this table has been extracted from chapters I, IV and VIII.

Table 8.2 The subsistence bases of the various Cultural Groups that have occupied parts of Northeast Africa

No.	Cultural Groups	Chronology	Subsistence bases
1	Amm Adam	ca. 6,000-4,000 B.C.	– Small seeded grasses, *Millet sp.*
2	Butana	Ca. 4,000-2,700 B.C.	– *Hordeum sp.* – *Triticum monoccocum/dicoccum* – *Panicum sp.*
3	Gash Group	Ca. 2,7000-1,500 B.C.	– *Sorghum verticilliflorum* – *Sorghum bicolor bicolor* – *Millet spp. (Setaria sp. Eleusine sp., Panicum sp., Phallaris sp.)* – *Hordeum sp.* – *Triticum sp.* – *Zizipus sp.* (mainly *Z. spina christi)* – *Celtis integrifolia* – Leguminasea (mainly *vigna unguiculata*) – Fish (aquatic adaptation)
4	Agordat	Ca. 2,500-1,500 B.C.	– *Sorghum verticilliflorum* – *Millet sp.*
5	Jebel Mokram	Ca. 1,500 B.C.-500 B.C.	– *Sorghum bicolor bicolor* – *Panicum sp.* – *Ziziphus sp.*
6	Hagiz	Ca. 500 B.C.-200/300 A.D.	– *Sorghum bicolor bicolor* – *Panicum sp.* – *Pennisetum sp.* – *Eleusine sp.*

Chapter IX
RECONSTRUCTING SUBSISTENCE AND
THE ENVIRONMENTAL CONTEXT:
A SYNTHESIS OF THE DATA

The understandings of the beginning of agriculture and reconstruction of food systems have been important subjects in the study of African prehistory. Various approaches were used by different researchers to address these problems. Theories were also drafted to be tested on the ground. Attempts to explain the beginning of agriculture within the framework of a set of theories like as diffusionism and authochtonous development happen to be grand ideas for discussion for decades. Indirect evidences like the presence of grinding stones, microlithic tools, pottery and rock art have been taken as indicators of the beginning of food production since the late 1960s. Recent studies show that the above stated cultural remains that were considered as indicators for the onset of food production could not give us a direct clue about the type of plant cultivation and their domestication history (Macdonalds 2000:9, Neumann 2005:255). There is still a lack of detail and direct data at a continent level. More data on plants utilized are, thus, being sought on the basis of identification of plant impressions, palynology, and phytolith analysis from archaeological sites.

With the objective of addressing the same subject of discussion, this volume summarizes the results of plant impression analysis from sites near *Kashim el-Girba*, Kassala, Jebel Mokram and *Shurab el Gash* and analysis of grains and fruit stones from K1, Mahal Teglinos, Kassala, in the Eritrean-Sudanese lowlands. The interpretation given and the result of the findings are expected to manifest to a limited degree the subsistence base of the pre-historic inhabitants of the lowland areas of Northeast Africa between ca. 6000 B.C. and 200/300 A.D.

9.1 THE SUBSISTENCE BASE: WHICH CROPS WERE CONSUMED?

Ethnographic and ethno-archaeological case studies indicate that plant impressions on pottery are, most often,

created at the time of production. This is because there are more chances of adding plant materials while collecting the clay soil and during manufacturing before the clay is baked. Depending on the stage of production the plant bodies that are included could be intentional or unintentional. As it is explained in detail in chapter II of this volume, wetness of the clay increases the chance of getting impressions. There is, therefore, a direct temporal and spatial association between pottery production and plant impression formation. It is with the background of this premise that the subsistence base of the prehistoric inhabitants of the Gash Delta is approached. Due to the difficult morphological features of some of the imprints, species level identification for some Gramineae is not yet provided. In order to acquire supplementary data for the plant impressions, grains, seeds and fruit stones were also recovered from soil samples. The data presented here is an analysis of almost sixteen years of field work and data accumulation; 1980-1995 in the first round and the 2010 field season in the second round.

In most of the sites, small seeded grasses, millets, and sorghum happen to be the preferred crops for consumption. What is commonly available across the sites is Panicum. Panicum seems to be available as a food crop from Kassala, a low lying site, along the Gash Delta, near the Eritrean boarder all the way to *Kashim el-Girba*, on the western part of the Atbara River. The millet varieties are predominantly identified from the site of Kassala (like *Eleusine, Panicum, Setaria* and *phalaris*) in addition to grains of sorghum and the Middle Eastern domesticate barley, *Hordeum Vulgare*. Analysis of grains and fruit stones from Mahal Teglinos, Kassala, has demonstrated the occurrence of other edible plants like cowpea (*Vigna unguiculata*), *Ziziphus spina-christi, Celtis integrifolia Lam.*, and *Grewia bicolor Juss.* At the cave site of Shaqadud, situated within the Butana area, *Ziziphus sp.* and *Grewia sp.* were gathered as food plants (Majid 1989:463).

The plant impressions on pot sherds identified from *Kashim el-Girba* provided wheat, barley, and *Panicum sp. Lolium*, a weed of cultivated cereals (mainly wheat and barley) was also recovered. From the sites of the *Shurab el Gash* area most of the millet grains (*Pennisetum, Eleusine* and *Panicum*) were identified. The same sites have also rendered grains of sorghum as imprints. From the sites of the Jebel Mokram area *panicum sp.* and other small seeded millets were identified.

Formerly Costantini *et al.* (1982:23) identified barley *Hordeum sp.* from the excavation units of Kassala I and II. This recovery was debatable as the savannah area of Eastern Sudan is not a natural habitat for the growth of barley and wheat. Magid (1989:464-465) has commented "until more information is provided, the presence of barley in this area at ca. 2000 B.C. will remain questionable". Magid based his argument on the fact that this area was a typical savannah land by ca. 2000 B.C. and still is at the present time. He, thus, stated that it is difficult to expect barley to be growing in the savannah area with summer rains and warm winters.

The adequate data that Magid (1989) has demanded seems to be available from two sites in Eastern Sudan: Kassala with evidence of barley imprints and from sites belonging to *Kashim el Girba* with evidence of wheat and barley imprints (*Hordeum sp. and Triticum sp.\Triticum monococcum\dicoccum*). In addition, from 2.0 mm and 1.0 mm mesh soil samples (Sample code K1 AC 11) four charred remains of cereals (wheat/barley) were recovered as discussed in chapter VIII of this volume. Fuller (in press) argues that barley and emmer wheat were present ever since the A-Group, around the 4th millennium B.C. According to him cultivation of these winter crops is possible because the original Nubian agriculture 'focused on winter cultivation based on receding Nile floods'.

The data shows that there is evidence for wheat and barley in Neolithic and late-Neolithic contexts in sites like Kassala, *Kashim el-Girba*, Afyen, Toshka west, Buhen, Ukma and Sai. The same crops were recovered in Napatan and Meroitic periods from Qasr Ibrim, Qustul/Ballanna, Kawa and Meroe (Fuller in press). The question that should be posed at the moment is only the third question that Magid had put forward in his (Magid 1989: 464) publication which is 'if we assume that barley was imported, then where could it have come from? Again if it was imported, one would also expect to find the evidence of other imported material culture that might indicate its origin(s). Is there any such evidence?'

To the north of Eastern Sudan barley grows naturally in Egypt and among the first evidence for domesticated barley, ca. 4,000 B.C., has come from the same area (Magid 1989:464). To the east and southeast, a few hundred kilometers away, the highlands of Ethiopia experience a typical temperate climate in which the growing of wheat and barley is possible. Although barley is a Middle Eastern crop, the diversity is huge in Ethiopia. Today out of the more than 180 agricultural

varieties of barley in the world 170 of them are reported from Ethiopia (Asfaw 2007: 86). The likelihood of acquiring these crops from the North and from East and Southeast is great for two reasons;

1- Fattovich (Fattovich *et al.*, 1984; Fattovich, 1993) argues that there was a large scale cultural contact and 'circuit of exchange' that stretched from Egypt to South Arabia. In this cultural interaction the prehistoric inhabitants of the highlands of Ethiopia and Eritrea and the Gash Group people were involved. Mahal Teglinos, a major site of the Gash Group culture at Kassala, probably played an intermediary role between the highlands of Ethiopia and Egypt. The evidence for the occurrence of contact is the presence of potsherds with similar decoration techniques and patterns at Agordat (Western Eritrea), Mahal Teglinos, Erkowit (near the Red Sea, with abundant lithic artifacts) and at Subr, near Aden in Southern Arabia. In all of these sites, obsidian tools of an Ethiopian origin were discovered.

2- The prehistoric inhabitants of Eastern Sudan had an economic subsistence based on the cultivation of crops and animal husbandry as the evidence shows for the Gash Group and the Jebel Mokram Group (Fattovich *et al.*, 1984). According to Sadr (1987:288) most of the area south of Egypt and the Eastern part of the Sudan was controlled by militant pastoralists by ca 3700\ 3820-3500\3550 BP. The Pan-grave cultural group of Upper Egypt and Lower Nubia and the Jebel Mokram Group of the southern Atbai were both pastoralists who were expanding their frontiers in different directions. At the time Agordat, western Eritrea, was occupied by people who practiced specialized pastoralism and cultivation of crops like sorghum and millet (Beldados 2006: 64). The Beni Amir and the Beja, the present day pastoral communities in western Eritrea, seasonally cross to the Eastern part of the Sudan. With the idea of pastoralism, exchange items and material cultures could pass from one territory to another.

Mahal Teglinos, in Eastern Sudan has also provided rich data on sorghum cultivation. The evidence from the same site has also pushed forward the domestication history of the crop. On the basis of assessment of the archaeobotanical studies in Northern Nubia, Fuller (in press) states 'Despite the evidence for morphologically wild sorghum and several other wild savanna millet grasses (*Panicum, Paspalum, Setaria, Pennisetum*) from impressions of temper in Neolithic ceramics from the Central Sudan, there is no evidence that these were cultivated'. He further elaborates his idea and concludes the same paragraph stating 'if cultivation of sorghum had begun we would expect some evidence for shifts towards domesticated morphotypes'. Although evidence for cultivated millet grasses is not provided here to demon-strate an ongoing domestication process, morphological change of sorghum in the form of an intermediary between wild and domesticated, i.e. not fully domesticated, is provided in this work from the analysis of fired clay from the excavation at Mahal Teglinos (K1 VI, 2010) as presented in chapter VII. Such an intermediary morphotype for sorghum belongs to the early phase of the Mokram group culturally, (ca. 1500-1000 B.C.)

9.2 CAN RESOURCE AVAILABILITY BE DEDUCED?

Would it not be much more consistent to assume that Africa's way is unique, because of its rich environmental resources, especially in the savannas, and the particular role of mobile pastoralism as two factors postponing agriculture for several millennia?

Neumann 2005:266.

While discussing the plant impression study from the sites belonging to the *Kashim el-Girba* area under chapter IV, there was an attempt to decipher resource availability through the analysis of the character of imprints. The *Kashim el-Girba* sherds demonstrated dorsal and ventral surfaces of glumes together with their grains. The great quantity of the charred grains in relation to chaff has intrigued so as raise the question why did they use the edible grains directly instead of utilizing the chaff, the waste\by-products? The probable explanation for this question has to do with resource availability. It seems that the inhabitants at *Kashim el-Girba* (ca. 3500-2500 B.C.) had a rich source of millet (like *Setaria sp., Panicum sp.* and *Eleusine sp.*). The fact that they exploited their edible grain resources for uses other than consumption could show that shortage of these grains was not their immediate problem. If there were scarcity of consumable resources, the pre-historic inhabitants of *Kashim el-Girba* would have been forced to use only the chaff as inclusions.

At Kassala (ca. 2500-1400 B.C.), unlike the case of *Kashim el-Girba*, they used chaff, as components in the composition of their pottery not grains. This probably indicates that resources were not in excess at this particular site. The same is true for the site of *Shurab el-Gash* where the impressions are of a mix of glumes of *Pennisetum sp.* and *Eleusine sp.*

Archaeobotanical, ethno-archaeological and ethno botanic researches have shown that wild plant resources were\are abundant in Africa and play an important role in the subsistence economy. The exploitation of wild resources has been crucial in the economy of Africa throughout the Holocene and continues to be so up to the present time (Neumann 2005: 265, Hildebrand 2003:242). Neumann argues that the rich environmental resource of the savanna, in particular, is a discouraging factor for the early beginning of agriculture in Africa where the theory of the 'middle ground economies' could be best manifested.

9.3 TRADITIONAL TREATMENTS INFERRED: PLANTS WITH MEDICINAL VALUE

Based on ethnographic analogies of present day use of plants for their medicinal value, the possible pre-historic

application of some of the identified plants was also inferred. From Mahal Teglinos, Kassala the fruit stones of *Ziziphus spina-christi (L.)* were recovered as an imprint in a sherd and about 200 complete and damaged fruit stones from soil samples. Ethnographic studies have shown that the leaves and branches of this species have medicinal significance for bandages to treat skin wounds and body part sprains (El Amin 1990: 295).

The other plant variety which has medicinal advantages is *Celtis integrifolia Lam.* About 220 complete and damaged fruit stones of this species were recovered from soil samples from the same site, Mahal Teglinos, Kassala. According to ethnographic observations, different parts of this plant can be used for treatments. Traditionally, the bark of *Celtis integrifolia Lam.* is used to cure rheumatism. The roots of the same plant can be used as a medicine for mental disorders. Other illnesses and disorders that can be cured by using different parts of *Celtis* include headaches, sterility, oedema, asthenia and boils. Parts of the same species could also be utilized for wound covering, to facilitate delivery and as a vermifuge (El Amin 1990: 295).

9.4 PLANTS AS RAW MATERIALS

To reconstruct ancient human-plant interactions in various ways, an attempt is also made to reconstruct the uses of plants as raw materials for different purposes. Inference is based on ethnographic and ethnobotanic observations from sites within the same climatic zone, the Saharan and sahelian zone. Here the possible application is for Kassala, since most of the larger trees were recovered from this site through the study of fruit stones sieved from soil samples.

Ethnographic studies in arid and semi-arid areas of Northwestern Ethiopia demonstrated that *Ziziphus Spina-christi* (*Ziziphus sp.* in general) has a range of uses. The wood of this plant is utilized in carpentry for the making of furniture and is a good source of fire wood and charcoal. The wood is also used as pillars or wall supports while houses are built. Branches are used for the fencing of residential quarters and farming plots.

The wood of *Grewia bicolor Juss.* can be used for the making of bowls, tool handles and walking sticks and as firewood.

9.5 WHAT DO THE PLANTS TELL US ABOUT THE PALEOENVIRONMENT?

Plants do have a special preference for certain environmental conditions depending on their biological characteristics. The amount of rainfall or local hydrology, sunlight and soil types are the main factors that dictate plant growth. The degree of the availability of these resources differs from region to region and from one climatic zone to the other. There is, therefore, a direct relation between plant growth and environmental setting. On the basis of this very fact, an attempt is made to comment on the late Holocene palaeoenvironment of the lowland areas of Northeast Africa between Ca. 4000 B.C. and early 1st millennium A.D. The table below (table 9.1) presents the type of plants identified as pottery imprints and from soil samples in terms of their ecological preference.

According to the table on plant preference for a certain ecological condition, the dominant type of setting is the arid and semi-arid zones of tropical Africa with the exception of *Triticum sp.* and *Hordeum sp.* Currently, the lowlands of Northeastern Africa are part of the Saharan and sahelian zone. This is no different from what the evidence tell us about the mid to late Holocene climatic condition. The situation was a bit different for the Early Holocene. Based on the analysis of botanical material from southern Atbai, Wickens (1982:23-51) has suggested that during the early Holocene (ca. 10,000-5000 B.C.) the environment of the area was more of a deciduous savanna woodland.

Table 9.1 Ecological preference of the major plants in this study

No.	Plant types	Ecological preference
1	*Celtis integrifolia Lam.*	Common in a tropical climate
2	*Echinocloa sp.*	Tropical, sub-tropical and temperate zones
3	*Eleusine sp.*	Arid and semi arid conditions
4	*Grewia bicolor Juss.*	Semiarid and sub humid tropical Africa and India
5	*Hordeum sp.*	Temperate climate with winter rain
6	*Lolium sp.*	Forest and forest margins
7	*Panicum sp.*	Arid environments
8	*Pennisetum sp.*	Commonly cultivated in the Sahel zone close to the Sahara in tropical Africa and the Sudan
9	*Setaria sp.*	Arid and semi arid conditions, within the tropics
10	*Sorghum cf. bicolor*	Arid and semi arid conditions
11	*Triticum sp.*	Temperate climate with winter rain
12	*Vigna unguiculata*	Marginal environments unsuitable for the growth of other plants
13	*Ziziphus spina-christi (Ziziphus sp.)*	Sahara and Sahel in Africa, from Senegal all the way to the Sudan and Arabia

BIBLIOGRAPHY

ABAWA, G. (2009) – Cultivation of Teff in Gojam, an ethnoarchaeological Approach on understanding the Origin of Agriculture in Ethiopia, unpublished M. Phil. thesis, Department of Archaeology, University of Bergen, Norway.

ABBAS, S.A. MUHAMMED and JAEGER, SUSAN E. (1989) – The early ceramic of the Eastern Butana (Sudan). In *Late Prehistory of the Nile Basin and the Sahara, Poznan,* Lech Krzyzaniak and Michal Kobusiewicz (eds.), 473-480.

ABBO, SHAHAL; LEV-YADUN, SIMICHA and GOPHER, Avi (2010) – Agricultural Origins: Centers and noncenters; A Near Eastern Reappraisal, *Critical Review in Plant Sciences,* 29:317-328.

ARKELL, A.J. (1949) – *Early Khartoum.* Oxford: University Press.

ARKELL, A.J. (1953) – *Shaheinab.* London: Oxford University Press.

ASFAW, Z. (2000) – 'The Barleys of Ethiopia' breeders' in *Genes in the Field, On-Farm Conservation of Crop Diversity,* Brush B. Stephen (ed.), 77-107.

BARAKAT, H. and FAHMY, A. GAMAL EL-DIN (1999) – Wild Grass as Neolithic Food Resources in the Eastern Shara: A Review of Evidence from Egypt, in *The Exploitation of Plant Resources in Ancient Africa,* Van der Veen M. (ed.). Kluwer Academics\Plenum Publishers, New York, 63-72.

BELDADOS, A. (2004) – The impact of environment on the evolution of food Producing societies in mid-Holocene and after in Ethiopia. M.A. thesis, Addis Ababa University, Department of History, Archaeology Unit.

BELDADOS, A. (2006) – The Agordat Material, Eritrea and its Implication for Early Food Production and Regional Contact. M.A. thesis. University of Bergen. Norway.

BELDADOS, A. (2007) – New Perspectives on the Agordat Material: A Re-examination of the collection in Khartoum National Museum, Kartoum, *Nyame Akuma,* 67: 4-10.

BRANDT, S.A. (1984) – New Perspectives on the Origins of Food Production in Ethiopia. In Clark, J.D and Brandt, S.A (eds.): *From Hunters to Farmers: The causes and Consequences of Food Production in Africa.* University of California Press, Berkeley, 173-190.

BARD, K.A., and FATTVICH, R. (1995) – The IUO and UB Excavation at Bieta Giorgis, Aksum, an Interim Report. Nyame Akuma 45: 25-27.

BARD, K.A.; DI BLASI, M.C.; FATTOVICH, R.; MANZO, A.; PERLINGIERI, C. and CRECSENZI, L. (1996) – The B.U.\I.O.U Excavation at Bieta Giorgis, (Aksum: Ethiopia) a preliminary report on the 1996 field season. *Nyame Akuma,* 46:21-24.

BARD, K.A.; COLTORTI, M.; DI BLASI, M.C.; DRAMIS, FATTOVICH, R. (2000) – The environmental history of Tigray (northern Ethiopia) in the Middle and Late Holocene: A preliminary outline. *African Archaeological Review* 17 (2), 65-86.

BEDIGIAN, D. (2003) – Evolution of sesame revisited: domestication, diversity and prospects. *Genetic Resources and Crop Evolution* 50: 779-787.

BENVENUTI, M.; CARNICELLI, S.; BELLUOMINI, G.; DAINELLI, N.; DI GRAZIA, S. FERRARI, G.A.; IASIO, C.; SAGRI, M.; VENTRA, D.; BALEMWAL, ATNAFU; SEIFU, KEBEDE (2002) – The Ziway Shala Lake Basin (MER, Ethiopia): a Revision to Basin Evolution with special reference to the Late Quaternary. *Journal of African Earth Sciences,* 35:247-269.

BOARDMAN, S. (2000) – Archaeobotany in Phillipson, D.W. (Ed.), *Archaeology in Aksum, Ethiopia, 1993-7.* Vols. I and II. The British Institute in Eastern Africa and the Society of Antiquaries, London, 363-368.

BONEFILLE, R. and MOHAMMED, U. (1994) – Pollen-Inferred climatic fluctuations in Ethiopia during the last 3000 years. *Paleogeography, paleoclimatology, paleoecology,* 109: 331-343.

BUTLER, A.; STEMLER, L.; HARLAN, J. (1977) – Evolutionary history of Cultivated Sorghums (Sorghum bicolor (Linn.) Moench) of Ethiopia,

Bulletin of the Torrey Botanical Club, Vol. 102, No. 6, 325-333.

BUTLER, A. (2003) – The Ethiopian Pea: Seeking the evidence for separate Domestication, In *Food Fuel and Fields, Progress in African Archaeobotany*, Heinrich-Barth-Institut, Koln, Germany.

BUTZER, K. (1975) – Patterns of Environmental Change in the Near East During Late Pleistocene and Early Holocene Times, in F. Wendorf and A.E. Marks, eds., *Problems in Prehistory: North Africa and the Levant*. Dallas: Southern Methodist University Press, 389-404.

BUTZER, K. (1981) – Rise and Fall of Aksum, Ethiopia: A Geoarchaeological Interpretation. *American Antiquity*, 46(3): 471-495.

BUTZER, K. (1982) – Empires, Capitals and Landscapes of Ancient Ethiopia. *Archaeology*, 35(5): 30-37.

BUURMAN, J. (1994) – "Progress in Old World Palaeoethnobotany: A Restrospective View on the Occasion of 20 Years of the International Work Group for Palaeoethnobotany". *Antiquity*, June 1994.

CAPPERS, R.T.J.; BEKKER, R.M. and JANS, J.E.A. (2006) – *Digital Seed Atlas of the Netherlands*. Barkhuis Publishing, Netherlands, Vol. 4.

CECCARELLI, S. and GRANDO, S. (2000) – 'Barley landraces from the Fertile Crescent: a lesson for plant breeders' in *Genes in the Field, On-Farm Conservation of Crop Diversity*, Brush B. Stephen (ed.), 51-71.

CIFERRI, R. (1939) – Frumenti e Granicoltura Indigena in Etiopia, *L'Agricoltura Coloniale* n. 6, pp. 337-349.

CIFERRI, R. (1942a) – Il Neuch o Guizotia dell'Africa Orientale Italiana, *Rassegna Economica dell' Africa Italiana* vol. 30, n. 1, pp. 110-121.

CIFERRI, R. (1942b) – I Sorghi o "Durre" dell'Africa Orientale Italiana, *Rassegna Economica dell' Africa Italiana* vol. 30, n. 4, pp. 164-176.

CIFERRI, R. (1942c) – La cerealicoltura in Africa Orientale: VIII – Generalità botanico-agraria sui sorghi *L'Italia Agricola* vol. 78, n. 2, 1941, pp. 79-86.

CIFERRI, R. (1942d) – La cerealicoltura in Africa Orientale: IX – Le durre *L'Italia Agricola* vol. 79, pp. 294-304.

CIFERRI, R. (1942e) – I Cereali a Cariossidi Minute dell'Africa Orientale Italiana, *Rassegna Economica dell' Africa Italiana* vol. 30, n. 7, pp. 346-351.

CIFERRI, R. (1943) – L'Istituzione del "Triticum abyssinicum" per i Frumenti Indigeni d'Etiopia *Rassegna Economica dell'Africa Italiana* vol. 30, n. 5, pp. 274-281.

CLARK, J.D. (1977) – The Origins of Domestication in Ethiopia. In Leaky, R.E. and Ogot, A.B. (eds.) *proceedings of the Eigth pan-African Congress of Pre history and Quaternary Studies*, Nairobi, 268-270.

COSTANTINI, L.; FATTOVICH, R.; PARDINI, E.; PIPERNO, M. (1982) – Preliminary Report of Archaeological Investigation at the Site of Teglinos (Kassala). *Nyame Akuma* 21: 30-33.

COSTANTINI, L.; FATTOVICH, L.; PIPERNO, M. and SADR, K. (1983) – Gash Delta Archaeological Project: 1982 field seaon, *Nyame Akuma: A Newsletter of African Archaeology*, Vol. 23, 17-19.

COSTANTINI, L. (1984) – Plant Impressions in Bronze Age Pottery from Yemen Arab Republic. In *East to East, IsMEO*, Vol. 34-Nos. 1-3.

COSTANTINI, L. (1990) – Ecology and Farming of the Proto-historic communities in the Central Yemeni Highlands. *The Bronze Age Culture of Hawlan at Tiyal and Al-Hada (Republic of Yemen). A first General Report*. 187-204.

COSTANTINI, L. and AUDISIO, P. (2001) – Plant and Insect Remains from the Bronze Age Site of RAS AL-Jinz (RJ-2), Sultanate of Oman. *Paleorient*, Vol. 26: 143-156.

COULIBALY, S.; PASQUET, R.S.; PAPA, R. and GEPTS, P. (2002) – AFLP Analysis of the Phenetic Organization and Genetic Diversity of *Vigna unguiculata* L. Walp. Revels Extensive Gene Flow Between Wild and Domesticated Types. *Theoretical and Applied Genetics* 104: 147-173.

D'ANDREA, C. and TSUBAKISAKA, Y. (1990) – Plant Remains Preserved in Kassala Phase Ceramics, Eastern Sudan, *Nyame Akuma*, N.33: 16.

D'ANDREA, A.C. (1997) – Archaeobotanical remains from Bieta Giyorgis excavations, Aksum, 1996-1997: preliminary report, Unpublished MS.

D'ANDREA, A.C.; MITIKU, HAILE; BUTLER, E.A.; LYONS, D.E. (1997) – Ethnoarchaeological research in the Ethiopian Highlands, *Nyame Akuma*, 47, 19-26.

D'ANDREA, A.C.; MITIKU, HAILE; BUTLER, E.A.; (1999) – Ethnoarchaeological Approach to the Study of Prehistoric Agriculture in the Ethiopian Highlands, In *Exploitation of Plant resources in Ancient Africa*, (Van der Veen, editor) Kluwer Academic: Plenum Publishers, New York, 101-122.

D'ANDREA, C.A.; KAHLHEBER, L.A.; LOGAN, L.A.; WATSON, J.D. (2007) – Early domesticated cowpea (*Vigna unguiculata*) from Central Ghana. *Antiquity* 81: 686-698.

D'ANDREA, C.; SCHMIDT, P. and CURTIS, C.M. (2008a) – Paleobotanical Analysis and Agricultural Economy at Early 1st millennium BCE sites around Asmara. In *The Archaeology of Ancient Eritrea* (Eds. Shmidt, R.P., Curtis, C.M and Teka, Z.)

D'ANDREA, C. (2008b) – T'ef (Eragrostis tef) in *Ancient Agricultural Systems of Highland Ethiopia Economic Botany*, The New York Botanical Garden Press, Bronx, NY 62 (4) pp. 547-566.

D'ANDREA, C.; RICHARDS, P.; PAVLISH, A.L.; BEUKENS, R.; WOOD, S.; MANZO, A. and WOLDE KIROS, H.S. (2011) – Stable isotopic analysis of human and animal diets from two pre-Aksumite/Proto-Aksumite archaeological sites in northern Ethiopia, *Journal of Archaeological Science* 38 (2011) 367-74.

DANIEL, H. (2004) – *Noog* (Guizotia abyssinica (L.f.) Cass., Compositae) Agriculture in Ethiopia: An Ethnoarchaeological Study, unpublished M.A. thesis, Addis Ababa University, Department of History, Archaeology Unit.

DE CANDOLLE, A. (1985) – *Origin of Cultivated plants.* D Appleton and Company, New York.

DELORIT. R.J. (1970) – *An Illustrated Taxonomy Manual of Weed Seeds*, Agronomy Publications, River Falls, Wisconsin.

DE WET, J.M.J. and HUCKABAY, P.J. (1967) – The Origin of Sorghum bicolor. II. Distribution and Domestication. *Evolution* 21: 787-802.

DE WET, J.M.J. and HARLAN, J.R. (1971) – The Origin and Domestication of Sorghum bicolor, *Economic Botany*, Vol. 25, N.2: 129-135.

DIMBELBY, G.W. (1969) – Pollen Analysis, in *Science in Archaeology*, A survey of Progress and Research, Revised and enlarged Edition, Brothwell D. and Higgs E, eds. Thames and Hudson, Great Britain, 167-173.

DINCAUZE, F.D. (2000) – *Environmental Archaeology, Principles and Practice*, Published.

DJ ACLAND (1971) – *East African Crops*, Published by arrangement with the Food and Agriculture Organization of the United Nations, Longman Group Limited, 17-18.

EHRET, C. (1979) – On the Antiquity of Agriculture in Ethiopia. *Journal of African History* 20: 161-177.

EL AMIN, H. MOHAMMED (1990) – *Trees and Shrubs of the Sudan*, Biddles Ltd Guildford and King's Lynn, England.

ELFFERS, J.; GRAHAM, R.A. and DEWOLF, G.P. (1964) – *Flora of Tropical East Africa*, Vol.

EVANS, G.J. (1978) – *An Introduction to Environmental Archaeology.* Unwin Brothers Limited. The Gresham Press, Old Working, Surrey, Great Britain.

FAHMY, A.G. (1995) – A Historical Flora of Egypt. Ph.D. thesis. University of Cairo.

FATTOVICH, R. and PIPPERNO, M. (1982) – Archaeological Researches in the Gash Delta, Kassala Province (1980-1981 Field Seasons). Paper presented at the Vth International Conference on Nubian Studies, Heidelberg (Spet. 1982).

FATTOVICH, R.; MARKS, E.A. and ALI, M.A. (1984) – The Archaeology of the Eastern Sahel, Sudan: Preliminary results. In *The African Archaeological Review*, 2: 173-188.

FATTOVICH, R. and M. PIPPERNO (1986) – Archaeological Researches in the Gash Delta, Kassala Province (1980-81 Field Seasons). In: Krause, M. (ed.), *Nubische Studien, Proceedings of the symposium of the International Society of Nubian Studies*, Heidelberg 1982: 47-53. Mainz.

FATTOVICH, R. (1989) – The Later Prehistory of the Gash Delta (Eastern Sudan). In *Late Prehistory of the Nile Basin and the Sahara, Poznan,* Lech Krzyzaniak and Michal Kobusiewicz (eds.) 481-498.

FATTOVICH, R. (1993a) – The Gash group of the Eastern Sudan: an outline. *Environmental Change and Human Culture in the Nile basin and Northern Africa until the Second Millennium B.C. Poznan,* 439-448.

FATTOVICH, R. (1993b) – Excavation at Mahal Teglinos (Kassala), 1984-1988; a Preliminary Report, *Kush,* Journal of the Sudan National Board for Antiquities and Museums, V. XVI, 225-285.

FATTOVICH, R. (1994) – The Contribution of the Recent Field Work at Kassala (Eastern Sudan) to Ethiopian Archaeology, *Etudes ethiopiennes*, V.1, (Claude Lepage, editor), de la Societe francaise pour les etudes ethiopiennes publication, Paris, 43-51.

FATTOVICH, R. (1995) – Archaeological Excavations at Biete Giyorgis (Aksum, Tigrai): a preliminary report on the 1994 field season, *Nyame Akuma* 43, 34-37.

FELDMAN, M. (1976) – Triticum spp. In *Evolution of Crop plants*, Simmonds, N.W. (ed.), J.W. Arrowsmith Ltd., Bristol, Graet Britain, 120-128.

FINNERAN, N. (2001) – A new Perspective on the Stone Age of the Northern Ethiopia Highlands: Excavation at Anqqer Baahti, Aksum, Ethiopia 1996. *Nyame Akuma* 45: 35-42.

FULLER, D.Q. (2009) – Advances in archaeobotanical method and theory: charting trajectories to domestication, lost crops, and the organization of agricultural labour in *New Approaches to Prehistoric Agriculture,* edited by Sung-Mo Ahn and June-Jeong Lee, Seoul: Sahoi Pyoungnon.

FULLER, D.Q., In Press – The Economic basis of the Qustul Splinter State: Cash Crops, Subsistence Shifts, and Labour Demands in the Post-Meroitic transition, an article submitted to the Proceedings of the Meroitic Studies conference, Vienna 2008 in a special number of Beitrage zur Sudanforschung, edited by Michel Zach.

GASSE, F. (1977) – Evolution of Lake Abhe (Ethiopia and TFAI) from 70,000 BP. *Nature*, 265:42-45.

GASSE, F. and STREET, F.A. (1978) – Late Quaternary lake –level fluctuations and Environments of the Northern Rift Valley and Afar Region (Ethiopia and Djibouti). *Paleogeography, Paleoclimatology, and Paleoecology*, 24:279-325.

GASSE, F. and STREET, F.A. (1978) – Late Quaternary lake – level fluctuations and Environments of the Northern Rift Valley and Afar Region (Ethiopia and Djibouti). *Paleogeography, Paleoclimatology, and Paleoecology,* 24:279-325.

GASSE, F.; ROGNON, P. and STREET, F.A. (1980) – Quaternary History of the Afar and Ethiopian Rift Lakes. In M.A.J. Williams and H. Faure (eds.). *The Sahara and the Nile*. Rotterdam: Balkema, pp. 361-400.

GASSE, F. and ROBERTS, N.C. (2005) – Late Quaternary Hydrologic Changes in the Arid and Semi Arid Belt of Northern Africa, H.F. Diaz and R.S. Bradley (eds.),

The Hadley Circulation: Present, Past and Future, Kluwer Academic Publishers, Netherlands; 313-345.

HAALAND, R. (1981) – Migratory Herdsmen and Cultivating Women; The Structure of Neolithic Seasonal Adaptation in the Khartoum Nile Environment, PhD dissertation, University of Bergen.

HAALAND, R. (1992) – Fish, pots and grains: Early and Mid Holocene adaptations in the central Sudan. *African Archaeological Review*, 22: 153-73.

HAALAND, R. and MAGID. A. (1995) – *Aqualithic sites along the rivers Nile and Atbara, Sudan.* Bergen: Alma Mater.

HAALAND, R. (1999) – The Puzzle of the late emergence of domesticated Sorghum in the Nile Valley. In The *Prehistory of food*, Gosden, C. and Hather, J. (Eds.), 397-418.

HARLAN, J.R. (1969) – Ethiopia: a center of diversity. *Economic Botany* 23: 309-314.

HARLAN, J.R. (1971) – Agricultural Origins: Centers and non-Centers, *Science* 174:468-474.

HARLAN, J.R. and STEMLER, A. (1976) – Plant Domestication and Indigenous African Agriculture. In *Origins of African Plant Domestication*, Jack R. Harlan, Jan M.J. De wet and Ann B.L. Stemler (eds.), Mouton Publishers, The Hague, Paris; 3-19.

HEDBERG, I. and EDWARDS, S. (1995) – *Poaceae (Gramineae), Flora of Ethiopia and Eritrea*, Addis Ababa, Ethiopia and Sweden Uppsala Vol. 7.

HELBAEK, H. (1969) – Palaeoethnobotany in *Science in Archaeology*, A survey of Progress and Research, Revised and enlarged Edition, Brothwell D. and Higgs E, eds. Thames and Hudson, Great Britain, 206-212.

HILDEBRAND, E. (2003) – Enset, Yams and Honey: Ethnoarchaeological Aproaches to the Origin of Horticulture in South West Ethiopia. Ph.D. dissertation, Washington University, Saint Louis, Missouri.

HILDEBRAND, E. and BRANDT, S. (2010) – An Archaeological Survey of the Tropical Highlands of Keffa, Southwestern Ethiopia, *Journal of African Archaeology* vol. 8(1), 2010, 43-63.

HILDEBRAND, E.; BRANDT, S. and GEBREMARIAM, J. (2010) – The Holocene Archaeology of Southwest Ethiopia: New Insight from the Kaffa Archaeological Project, *African Archaeological Review* (2010): 27: 255-289.

HOELZMANN, P.; GASS, F.; DUPONT, M.L.; SALZMANN, U.; STAUBWASSER, M.; LEUSCHNER, C.D. and SIROCKO, F. (2004) – Palaeoenvironmental changes in the arid and sub arid belt (Sahara-Sahel-Arabian Peninsula), 150 KYR to present, R.W. Battarbee *et al.* (eds.) *Past Climate Variability through Europe and Africa*. Springer, Dordrecht, the Netherlands; 220-48.

JONSELL, B. (1983) – Brassicaceae: Oil plants in Ethiopia, their taxonomy and agricultural Significance. *Agricultural Research Report*, 921:45-87.

KELECHA, W. (1977) – A Glossary of Ethiopian Plant names, (second edition), unpublished material, Addis Ababa, Ethiopia.

KRYSTYNA, W. and DAHLBERG, J. (1999) – Sorghum in the Economy of the Early Neolithic Nomadic Tribes at Nabta Playa, Southern Egypt, in *The Exploitation of Plant Resources in Ancient Africa*, Van der Veen, M. (ed.). Kluwer Academics\Plenum Publishers, New York, 12-31.

KRZYZANIAK, L. (1978) – New Light on Early Food Production in Central Sudan. *Journal of African History* 19: 159-172.

L'AFRICA ITALIANA AL PARLIAMENTO NAZIONALE, 1882-1905, Roma, Tipographia Dell' Unione Cooperativa editrice, a manuscript obtained from the archives of the Universita degli Studi di Napoli, L' Orientale, 1907.

LAMB, A.G.; LENG, M.; LAMB, H. and MOHAMMED, U. (2000) – A 9,000- year oxygen and Carbon Isotope Record of Hydrological change in a small Ethiopian Crater Lake. *The Holocene*, 10(2): 167-177.

LIVINGSTONE, D.A. (1980) – Environmental Changes in Nile Head waters, in M.A.J. Williams and H. Faure, eds., *The Sahara and the Nile*. Rotterdam: AA Balkema, 339-359.

LYONS, D. and D'ANDREA, C.A. (2003) – Griddles, Ovens, and Agricultural Origins: An Ethnoarchaeological study of Bread Baking in Highland Ethiopia. *American Anthropologist*, 105, 515-530.

MACDONALD, K. (2000) – The Origin of African Livestock, Indigeneous or Imported? In *The Origins and Development of African Livestock: Archaeology, Genetics, Linguistics and Ethnography*. Roger M. Blench and Kevin C. MacDonalds, eds. London: University College, London Press: 2-17.

MAGID, A. (1982) – The Khartoum Neolithic in the Light of Archaeobotany: A case study from the Nofolab and the Islang sites, unpublished M.A. thesis, University of Khartoum.

MAGID, A. (1984) – Acrobotanical Remains from Shaqadud: Interim Note. *Nyama Akuma* 24: 25-27.

MAGID, A. (1989a) – Exploitation of plants in the Eastern Sahel (Sudan), 5,000-2,000 B.C. In *Late Prehistory of the Nile Basin and the Sahara, Poznan,* Lech Krzyzaniak and Michal Kobusiewicz (eds.), 459-468.

MAGID, A. (1989b) – *Plant Domestication in the Middle Nile Basin. An Archaeobotanical Case study*. BAR: Oxford: Cambridge Monographs in African Archaeology 35.

MAGID, A. (2003) – Exploition of food-plants in the Early and middle Holocene Blue Nile areas, Sudan and neighbouring areas. *Complutum*, 14:345-372.

MAGID, A. (2004) – The study of Archaeobotanical Remains: Vitalizing a debate on Changing Conceptions and Possibilities, *Arqueo Web* 6(1)-May 2004:1-14.

MANUAL FOR TESTING AGRICULTURAL AND VEGETABLE SEEDS, United States Department of Agriculture, Production and Marketing Adminstration in coope-ration with the Bureau of Plant Industry, soils and Agricultural Engineering, Washington, No. 30, 1952.

MARKS, E.A. (1989) – The Later Prehistory of the Central Nile Valley: a View from its Eastern Hinterlands, *Late Prehistory of the Nile Basin and the Sahara, Poznan*, 443-450.

MARKS, E.A. and RODOLFO. F. (1989) – The Later Prehistory of the Eastern Sudan. In *Late Prehistory of the Nile Basin and the Sahara, Poznan*, Lech Krzyzaniak and Michal Kobusiewicz (eds.) 451-458.

MARKS, E.A. (1993) – Climatic and cultural changes in the Southern Atbai, Sudan, from the fifth through the third millennium B.C. *Environmental change and Human culture in Nile basin and Northern Africa until the second millennium B.C Poznan*, 3:431-438.

MARSHAL, F. and HILDEBRAND, L. (2002) – Cattle Before Crops: The Beginning of Food Production in Africa. In *Journal of World Prehistory* 16:100-135.

MAYDELL, V. HANS-JURGEN (1990) – *Trees and Shrubs of the Sahel: Their Characteristics and Uses*, Typo-druck-Rossdorf gmbh, D-6101 Robodorf, Germany.

MOHAMMED, U. and BONNEFILLE, R. (1998) – A late Glacial/Late Holocene pollen record from a highland peat at Tamsaa, Bale Mountains, south Ethiopia. In *Global and Planetary Change* 16-17:121-129.

MOHAMMED, U.M.; BONNEFILLE, R. and JOHNSON, T. (1996) – Pollen and Isotopic records of late Holocene sediments from Lake Turkana, N. Kenya. In *Paleogeography, paleoclimatology, paleoecology* 119(3-4): 371-383.

MURDOCK, G.P. (1959) – *Africa: Its people & their culture History*. New York: Mc Graw Hill.

MUNRO-HAY, C.S. (1984) – *The Coinage of Aksum*. Manohar publications, Daryaganj, New Delhi, India and R.C. Senior Ltd, Butleigh Court Tower, England.

NESBITT, M. (2001) – Evolution of Wheat: integrating archaeological and biological evidence, in *Wheat Taxonomy: the legacy of John Percival*, Caligary, P.D.S and Brandham, P.E. (eds.). The Linnean, Special Issue no. 3. Linnean Society of London.

NEUMANN, K. (2005) – The Romance of Farming: Plant Cultivation and Domestication in Africa. In *African Archaeology, A Critical Introduction*, Stahl A.B. (ed.), Blackwell Publishing; 249-275.

PHLLIPSON, W.D. (1977) – The excavations of Gobedra Rock-shelter, Axum: an Early occurrence of cultivated Finger millet, in Northern Ethiopia. *Azania*, 12-53-82.

PHLLIPSON, W.D. (1994) – The B.I.E.A Aksum Excavations, 1993; *Nyame Akuma*, 41, 15-25.

PHLLIPSON, W.D. (1995) – The B.I.E.A Aksum Excavations, 1994; *Nyame Akuma*, 44, 28-34.

PHLLIPSON, W.D. (1996) – The B.I.E.A Aksum Excavations, 1995; *Nyame Akuma*, 46, 24-33.

PURSEGLOVE, J.W. (1976) – Eleusine coracana, Pennisetum americanum (Gramineae), In *Evolution of Crop plants*, Simmonds N.W. (ed.), J.W. Arrowsmith Ltd., Bristol, Graet Britain, 91-93.

RENFREW, J.M. (1973) – *Palaeoethnobotany. The Prehistoric Food Plants of the near East and Europe.* Methuen and Co. Ltd.

RENFREW, C. and BAHN, P. (1996) – *Archaeology Theories, Methods and Practice*, USA by Donnelley and Sons Company.

SADR, K. (1987) – The Territorial Expanse of the Pan-Grave Culture. *Archeologie du Nil Moyen*, 2: 265-291.

SADR, K. (1988) – The Development of Nomadism: The View from Ancient North East Africa, Unpublished PhD dissertation, Southern Methodist University.

SADR, K. (1990) – The Medjay in Southern Atbai, *Archeology du Nil Moyen*, 4:63-84.

SADR, K. (1991) – *The Development of Nomadism in Ancient Northeast Africa*. University of Pennsylvania press. Philadelphia.

SHINNER, J.L. (1971) – *The Prehistory and Geology of Northern Sudan*. Dallas: Report to the National Science Foundation Grant GS 1192.

SIMMONDS, N.W. (1976) – *The Evolution of Crop Plants*, J.W. Arowsmith Ltd. Bristol, Britain.

SIMOONS, F.S. (1965) – Some Questions on the Economic Prehistory of Ethiopia, *Journal of African History* 6: 1-13

STEMLER, A.B.L; HARLAN, J.R. and DE WET, J.M.J. (1977) – The Sorghum of Ethiopia, *Economic Botany* 31: 446.

STREET, F.A. and GROVE, A.T. (1976) – Environmental and climatic implications of late Quaternary lake-level fluctuations in Africa. *Nature* 261:385-90.

STREET, F.A. (1980) – The Relative Importance of Climate and local Hydrological Factors in Influencing Lake Level Changes, in M. Sarnthein, E. Seibold, and P. Rognon, eds., *Sahara and Surrounding Seas*. 137-158.

VAVILOV, N.I. (1951) – *The Origin Variation, Immunity and Breeding of Cultivated Crops*. New York.

VAVILOV, N.I. (1957) – Mirovye resursy sortov khlebnykh zlakov, zernovykh bobovykh, l'na I ikh ispol'zovanie v selektsii. Opyt agroekologicheskogo obozreniya vashneishikh polevykh kul'tur. Moscow (translated by M. Paenson and Z.S. Cole 1960, World resources of cereals, Leguminous seed crops and Flax, and their Utilization in Plant Breeding, Jerusalem).

VOGT, B. and BUFFA, Vittoria (2005) – Cultural Interactions with the Horn of Africa. In *Akten der Ersten Internationalen Litteman-Konferenz*, (Heraus-gegeben von Walter Raunig und Steffen Wenig Eds.). Harrassowitz Verlag. Wiesbaden, 437-456.

WARREN, A. (1970) – Dune Trends and their Implications in the Central Sudan, *Zeitschrift Geomorphologie*, NF, Supplement 10: 154-180.

WASYLIKOWA, K. and MARTENS KUBIAK, L. (1995) – Wild sorghum from the early Neolithic site Nabta Playa, S. Egypt. In (H. Kroll and R. Pasternak, eds.) *Res Archaeobotanicae*, 9th Symposium of the IWGP. Kiel: oetker Voges Verlag, pp. 345-358.

WELDEMICHAEL, K. (1977) – *A Glossary of Ethiopian Plant Names* (Second edition), unpublished archival material.

WENDROF, F.; SAID, R. and SCHILD, R. (1970) – Egyptian Prehistory: Some New Concepts, *Science* 169 (3951): 1161-1171.

WENDORF, F. and SCHILD, R. (eds.) (1980) – *Prehistory of the Eastern Sahara*, New York, Academic Press.

WESTERN, C.A. (1969) – Wood and Charcoal in Archaeology in *Science in Archaeology, A survey of Progress and Research,* Revised and enlarged Edition, Brothwell, D. and Higgs, E, eds. Thames and Hudson, Great Britain, 178-182.

WICKENS, G.E. (1975) – Changes in the Climate and Vegetation of the Sudan since 20,000, *Boissiera* 24: 43- 65.

WICKENS, G.E. (1982) – "Palaeobotanical Speculations and Quaternary Environments in the Sudan," in M.A.J. Williams and D.A. Adamson, eds., *A land Between Two Niles: Quaternary Geology and Biology of the Central Sudan.* Rotterdam: A.A. Balkema, 23- 51.

WILLIAMS, M.A.J. and ADAMSON, D.A. (1973) – The Physiography of the Central Sudan, *Geographical Journal* (London) 139: 498-508.

WILLIAMS, M.A.J., WILLIAMS, F.M. and BISHOPS, P.M. (1982) – Late Quaternary Study of Lake Beseka, Ethiopia, *Paleoecology of Africa*, 13: 93- 104.

WILLIS, J.C. (1973) – *A dictionary of flowering plants,* eighth edition, Royal Botanical Gardens, Cambridge at the University Press.

Field Reports

– Italian Archaeological Mission in Sudan (Kassala), Archaeological Survey of the Gash Delta, Kassala Province, Report of activity 1980, submitted to the Sudan Antiquities Service, Khartoum.

– Gash Delta Archaeological Project: 1980-1984 Field Seasons, Interim Report of activities submitted to the Sudan Antiquities Service, Khartoum, September 1984.

– Gash Delta Archaeological Project: 1987 Field Season, submitted to the Sudan Antiquities Service, Khartoum.

– Fernandez. V. 1999-2002. Spanish Archaeological Project in Benishangul, Ethiopia, 2002, Field Season Preliminary Report.

Internet Sources

– Diatoms,   http://www-marine.stanford.edu/profiles/diatoms.htm

– http\\wikepedia Encyclopedia

– *http://en.wikipedia.org/wiki/Salvia_merjamie*

MANZO Andrea with contribution by A. COPPA, Alemseged BELDADOS ALEHO and V. ZOPPI

2011. Italian Archaeological Expedition to the Sudan of the University of Naples

"L'Orientale" 2010 Field Season. Open Archive of the University of Naples

"L'Orientale" http://opar.unior.it/460/1/AMReport_Eng.pdf,pp 1-41.

VAVILOV, I.N. (1931) – http://www.tagari.com\PermInst\BillsArticles_IndividualPages\PreCursPerm_2_Vav

Informants

No.	Name	Age	Locality	Profession	Remarks
1	W\ro Roman Hailesilasse	44	Akatin, Salaklaka	Pot maker	Trainer for most upcoming pot makers
2	W\ro Workalem Biruh	32	Akatin, Salaklaka	Pot maker	
3	W\ro Hiwot Gebre Mariam	41	Grathitsa, Salaklaka	Pot maker	
4	W\ro Nigisti Haftishyimer	42	Adrar, Indabaguna	Pot maker	
5	W\ro Atsede Hafitishyimer	25	Kushet Adrar, Indabaguna	Pot maker	
6	W\ro Letecheal Haftishyimer	28	Kushet Adrar, Indabaguna	Pot maker	
7	Ato Gabresilasse Abraha	54	Shire	Farmer	

www.ingramcontent.com/pod-product-compliance
Lightning Source LLC
Chambersburg PA
CBHW061009030426
42334CB00033B/3424